MANN at SEA

*This magnificent view was taken by my Great Grandfather, Robert Applegarth Hendry 1st (1855-1921).of the **PS Empress Queen** of 1897 soon after she entered service. Arguably the finest cross channel paddle steamer ever built, she was used by the Isle of Man Steam Packet Company from her delivery in 1897 to 1914 when she was requisitioned for war service, but stranded off the Isle of Wight in 1916 and was a total loss. With smoke billowing up into the sky from her twin stacks and the wake boiling away from her paddle wheels It is an evocative portrait of a world that our Victorian ancestors were familiar with. It is also a world that my parents were just old enough to recall, as they were born of Manx families in 1906 and 1912. Both had a lifelong love for the Island and its shipping, and many vivid memories of those far off times. This book, which explores the intimate connection between our Island and the sea over the past quarter of a Millennium, draws heavily on their memories and the stories handed down to them, but has entailed more than forty years of research by myself. It has been a wonderful journey for me, and I hope you enjoy it too.*

"Let Storm Winds Rejoice and Lift up their Voice". The words of the Manx National Anthem are fitting for a small island, its coasts lashed by the gales of winter, as this portrait of Ramsey promenade taken in the early 1900s testifies. The iron railings that once graced the promenade have gone, replaced by a concrete wall after the war. The buildings that sprang up piecemeal in the nineteenth century, as Ramsey evolved from a fishing village into a select seaside resort, lacked the continuity of Douglas, and fell into disfavour in the eyes of the Ramsey Commissioners by the start of the 1960s, and foolishly, they were swept away, destroying the character of the town. I am glad I knew them, for their twentieth century replacements present a far more disjointed appearance. Only the eternal storms and the Queens Pier, itself under threat for more than quarter of a century, endure today.   (T H MIdwood)

MANN
at SEA

Robert Hendry

DEDICATION

About the time I started work on this book, I heard of the death of two very good friends of mine within a few weeks of one another. Harold Kelly of Castletown came from an old Manx family, and was a dedicated campaigner on public issues, such as saving the lovely Scarlett area from the hands of the developer. When, in 1985, the Isle of Man Steam Packet Company proposed to surrender a 30% stake in the company to non-Manx interests, Harold felt it was wrong that this proud Manx institution that had been formed by Manx people for Manx people should be allowed to pass out of Manx control. He stood up and said so. He was joined by Richard Leventhorpe, who had visited the Island and found himself so "at home" that he made it his home. Harold and Richard started a campaign to keep the Steam Packet in Manx hands. My late father and I read of their efforts, contacted them and worked with them. History records that we lost, and that is something I regret. That we fought is something I have no regrets over, and I recall with pride that we came within 2½% of success. Never before or since have ordinary shareholders accomplished so much in combat against a corporate takeover. Under the guidance of Sir John Bolton, an accountant, who is the architect of the Island's current financial strength, the IOM Government had acquired shares to guard against such a possibility. Although Sir John and I often crossed swords over conserving the Island's historic transport, this was a sound decision. Sadly, the Island government did not use the shares as he intended to protect Manx control, but voted for the take over. Had they voted as John Bolton had intended for continued independence, or done nothing, the Manx people would have won. Harold, a Manxman from generations back, Richard, a "Comeover", and my father, Dr Robert Preston Hendry, whose Manx ancestry I can trace back hundreds of years, served the Island they loved better than the Island's own government. This book is dedicated with affection and respect to all three. They led the fight, but numerous Packet employees, although unable to do anything in public, were anguished at this betrayal of past generations, and provided the ammunition that we could use, at the risk of their careers. I add their names with gratitude, though they must remain anonymous. From the dawn of the Steam Packet, I will add the names of John Wood, the brilliant Scots shipbuilder who gave the Island so much when he constructed the **Mona's Isle** in 1830, and Isabella Kerr Kayll, the Manx girl he fell in love with and tragically lost.

It was a close run thing whether my last book for "Manx Experience", or our first daughter, Anastasia Elaine, would appear first, but Anastasia was five weeks early, so won comfortably, and I was pleased to include a dedication to her in *100 Years of Mann*. This volume is for our second daughter Alexandra Amy, who was "launched" on 26 April 2009. Her first name, Alexandra, comes from my wife's side of the family. Her second name comes from a girl called Amy Stevenson (1683-1750) who enters these pages. Some of stories she recounted were handed down through her descendants to my mother and then to me, more than two centuries after Amy had departed this life. They were the starting point for my fascination with Manx history. My initial assumption that they would be riddled with errors was replaced with growing admiration as facts emerged that confirmed what she had bequeathed to us. For Amy's words to survive with such uncanny accuracy suggests she must have had a remarkable way with words. I hope she would approve of what I have written here, and that Alexandra Amy will in due course enjoy reading a little about her great x 7 grandmother.

Printed in the Isle of Man by
Mannin Media Group
Media House : Cronkbourne : Douglas : Isle of Man : IM4 4SB

Facing Page: *Probably taken from the inbound "Nine o'Clock boat" from Douglas to Liverpool, this portrait of the **SS Snaefell** off Formby heading for Douglas recalls the glory days of the Steam Packet when a fleet of ships in double figures served the Island, and made it one of the most successful tourist resorts in the British Isles for generations. Sadly those days are long gone, but it is as well that we remember the ships, the men who crewed them, and those who guided the affairs of the Steam Packet, which was lead with conspicuous ability from the 1830s to the 1960s. Shipping books are usually strong on ships, but weak on other aspects of the story, and its great managers, such as Edward Moore or William Mathias Corkill, were truly outstanding leaders, but along with able chairmen, such as Dalrymple Maitland and Alexander Robertson, are largely forgotten today, but in the pages that follow, we will meet these outstanding Manxmen and learn of what we owe to them.*

CONTENTS

Published by
The Manx Experience
Media House : Cronkbourne
Douglas : Isle of Man : IM4 4SB

Copyright © Robert Hendry 2009

ISBN No 1 873120 66 4

All rights reserved.
No part of this publication may be
reproduced, stored in a retrieval system,
or transmitted in any form or by any
means, electronic, mechanical,
photocopying, recording or otherwise,
without the written permission of
the publishers

Matthias Curghey was an old man. He had been born in 1669, when King Charles II was still on the throne, and as a child would have heard of the invasion of the Island by Parliamentary troops during the English Civil War. His father, Ewan Curghey, of Ballakillinghan, was married to Margaret Christian of Milntown, and had been a member of the House of Keys. Indeed he had been one of the deputation that had accompanied Illiam Dhone to discuss the surrender of the island's forces at the time of the invasion. Matthias became Vicar of Lezayre, moving to Patrick by 1703, and to German from 1710. In November 1729, at an age when many people would be thinking of retirement in our day, he travelled north to become Rector of Bride. More than twenty years later, he was still there. In 1749, at the age of eighty, he had buried his wife of many years, Dorothea, but he continued to minister to the parish. In that same year, the great Bishop Wilson took pity on Matthias, ordering that "whereas the Revd Mr Matthias Curghey, Rector of Kirk Bride, by reason of his great age and defect of his sight is rendered incapable of performing the whole service of the church in person, . . . We . . . do accordingly appoint the Parish Clerk and Schoolmaster, William Kewin . . . to assist the said rector". There were some rectors on the Island who took their duties so lightly that an entry in the parish register to mark a christening, marriage or death was more a matter of luck than anything else, but old Matthias was conscientious, and with the aid of school master Kewin, the records were well kept. It is probable that it was Will Kewin rather than Matthias who picked up a quill pen and began to record a sad episode, "Jon Xtian Ballakey & Danl his son, Wm Xtian, Patrick Xtian, and Thos Mylevory perished at sea on the Coast of England on or about 19th August 1751". It was common on the Island for families to be known by their farmsteads, and in Bride with its endless supply of Christians and Cowles, it was a necessity. Ballakey, or Ballakeigh, for the spelling has varied down the ages, had taken its' name from the McKie family who had been there as far back as 1515, their name attesting to their Scottish origin. However, the absence of a male heir meant that a McKie heiress married a Daniel Christian before 1600, and the farm was to be occupied by the family for the next 400 years, William or Daniel being the common names throughout that long period.

Old Matthias would have known young Daniel for most of his life, and had presided on the happy day when Daniel had married Isabel Kelly or Kelvy of Ramsey on 25 April 1746. In the few happy years that were allotted to the young couple before Daniel was lost at sea, they started a family, including William and Issable, and Issable was barely a year old as those sad words were entered in the parish register, and young William had not yet been christened. As the father and

The last five lines of this extract from the Bride parish register for 1751 have a deep poignancy, as they recall five Manxmen who paid the price that the restless sea claimed a quarter of a millennium ago. We will never know how many of our Island's sons and daughters have shared that fate, but they will not be alone. In the customary way of the time, "Christian" is recorded as "xtian". An element of uncertainty about the date is given by a posthumous will (which was then allowed in Manx law) that states the same fate, but gives the date as 17 September 1751. The two previous burials in the register are on 31 August and 22 September, so this entry must have taken place after 22 September. Because the original registers are so fragile, only an official copy on microfilm is available for public consultation, and I am indebted to Roger Sims for copying the actual register.

(Bride Parish Register reproduced by courtesy of Manx National Heritage)

son had both been lost at sea, there was no burial, so there was no strict requirement to record the event, but Matthias and the schoolmaster felt that important events in the life of his parish should be recorded. Seen in the wider context, Jon "Ballakey" and his companions were five Manxmen, out of countless legions, who have lost their lives in the restless seas that surround our Island. Until recently, I had not heard of them, so why have I opened the book with their story, or the fragment of it that survives, for we shall never know the precise details of that tragic voyage? What did Daniel think of, as the waves closed over his head? Were his last anguished thoughts of the children he would never see grow up? As with any maritime disaster, such as the better known and documented loss of the **SS Ellan Vannin**, it epitomises the relationship between "The Island" and the sea that surrounds it. A shield, to be sure, protecting and comforting, and giving the Island its special character, yet at the same time, a sword, ready to strike down without pity. More than a quarter of a millennium has passed since those events, yet the words strike a cord that we can still feel. In the media blizzard of today, we read of the plight of the dependents of those lost in tragedies across the globe. What of those who were left behind in 1751? Jon's widow, Joney, lost her husband and son, but had to summon up the strength to help her daughter-in-law, Isabel, to bring up the children who lost a father when Daniel went down to the sea, never to return. What of old Matthias, himself? 1752 and 1753 passed, and Matthias was laid to rest on 31 January 1754.

It was one tragedy amongst numberless tragedies since the human race first set foot on the shores of Mann, but for me, it had a special poignancy. Until the last morning of a visit to the Island in September 2008, when I was researching in the library of the Manx Museum, I had not heard of Jon "Ballakey" or his son Daniel. I knew about young William, and had found his resting place in the family plot in Bride churchyard, but I had not unravelled the jigsaw of William's parents. Then I found out about the sad day when his father and grandfather went down to the sea and out of his life forever, and realised the cruel fate that befell MY great-great-great-great-great-grandfather and his son. Until that day, tragedy at sea had been a distant event that happened to OTHER

people's families, not my own, but now I knew that the sea had claimed two generations of my own forbears on the same black day. I dedicated this book to two good friends, Harold and Richard, and to my father, but I will add Jon "Ballakey" and Daniel, to that dedication, for they are mine, and they represent all from our Island who went down to the sea in ships, never to return to their native shores.

The bounds of an Island are not defined by artificial man-made frontiers, but by the sea. That isolation from other lands is a blessing and a curse. As we have seen, it makes travel to other countries slower, harder and more perilous. It separates peoples from one another and that can breed suspicion and hatred. On the other hand, those twin curses also confer a benefit. Had England not been separated from France by 22 miles of sea, Napoleon's victorious armies would have swept into England with the same ease that they had conquered Europe. The flower of liberty would have been extinguished under the despotism of Napoleon Bonaparte. It was not a highly trained professional army that deterred Napoleon from invasion, for until Wellington's exploits in Portugal and Spain from 1809, the British army had been regularly defeated. Instead, it was the storm tossed ships of the Royal Navy that kept our shores inviolate. The same thing happened in 1914-1918, and again in 1940, when Hitler was master of Europe. The 22 miles of sea that protected civilisation from the triumph of barbarism, were the most important 22 miles in the world. With a slight difference in geography, the history of the world would have been altered, and the new Dark Age that Winston Churchill spoke of would have extinguished civilisation.

A similar distance separates the Isle of Man from St Bee's Head in Cumbria, and from Galloway. Had the geological events that created a ridge of high ground in the basin that was to become the Irish Sea occurred some 20 miles to the north, or to the east of where they actually happened, the Isle of Man would not have been an Island, but would have been a part of England or Scotland. Its history would have been totally different, and the "Island" would have been another County of England or Scotland, or more likely a small part of a larger County. Instead of a Manx nation, a Manx parliament and a Manx culture,

there might have been a Mann County Council, or a Mann District Council. Like Dingwall, in the Highlands of Scotland, there might be distant legends of a Norse meeting place, for Dingwall and Tynwald owe their name to the same Norse devotion to open air assembly places of the people. As with Dingwall, Tynwald would have decayed as Viking power ebbed after 1066. Whilst the liberties that local people have enjoyed would not have been markedly different, as would have been the case had the English Channel not protected civilisation from Napoleon or Hitler, life would have been very different. Mann might have become a tourist resort similar to Morecambe or Blackpool, but lacking a separate political entity, it would not have become a tax haven or an international player in the finance world, and more recently in the world of film. As I have commented, the 22 miles that are covered by water between Dover and Calais are the most important part of England, and the same can be said for the comparable stretches of water that separate the Island from Cumbria or Galloway. One paradox of this is that should you visit the Point of Ayre, you are closer to the Mull of Galloway than to Douglas. Even with the congested state of the Manx roads, you can be in Douglas within an hour, but to make the shorter trip to Galloway would take you to Douglas, then to Heysham or Liverpool, and a long car journey up the motorway network to Carlisle and across Dumfries and Galloway. Twelve hours later and you would not have completed the shorter journey because of the narrow stretch of water that separates Mann and Scotland. A few months before I started work on this book, my wife, Elena, and I visited the Mull of Galloway for the first time, and it was fascinating to see the opposite view to the one I had enjoyed so often from the Point of Ayre.

With binoculars, it is possible on a clear day to see steam plumes from the nuclear plant at Sellafield, the hills of Galloway, or the Mountains of Mourne in Ireland, but thousands of years ago, and long before Sellafield or binoculars, and before the first human being set foot on Mann, the inhabitants of Cumbria or Galloway, and of Ireland, which were all settled before Mann, could have seen across that short stretch of sea and wondered about the land on the skyline. A Mesolithic Irish people are regarded

I opened this book with the story of Jon Christian Ballakey and his son, two Manxmen who paid the price demanded from time to time by the sea that surrounds our Isle. Through the researches of Sue Pedersen, I found that another ancestor, John Joughin of Andreas, had perished at sea in August 1709. His great great grandson, another John Joughin, was born in Peel in 1804 and owned a fishing lugger, the **Hope**. *He died in 1868, almost forty years before his great granddaughter Elaine was born in 1906. She is the little girl with long curls in the centre of this picture. Many of the stories of the people involved with Manx shipping that have brought our maritime past alive in this book had been told to her around the time this view was taken. The boat was called* **Elaine** *after her, and was owned by her father. She had happy memories of excursions with friends and family, and of how she would look with pleasure at the name, which was painted in yellow letters on the varnished wooden backrest of the seat to the right. In the background, we can see the red cliffs in the vicinity of Cranstal, and the ground declining towards the Point of Ayre. Her family were friends with neighbours, the Swales, of Ramsey and it is possible that the other children are George Swales, later town Clark of Ramsey, and Bernard Swales, manager of the Ramsey Steam Ship Co in later years.*

as the earliest settlers in Mann. Setting out in primitive boats, not much different from the coracle that carried Saint Maughold to the headland that bears his name, some survived the crossing to establish communities around Castletown, Port St Mary, Peel, Michael and Ramsey. The perils of early sea crossings were not to be faced lightly, and many would have met the same cruel fate as Jon "Ballakey", so it is likely that there was little regular flow of people between Ireland and Mann. These small Mesolithic people were succeeded by Neolithic hunter-farmers who probably crossed from England. Bronze Age people followed, but all were subdued in the Celtic invasions that came later, and which gave the island its underlying character. Then came the Vikings. In many ways, a military elite, much as the Normans were in England, they were the conquerors, but like the Normans, were eventually absorbed by the native majority, so that the Island retained its Celtic nature, overlaid with Viking elements. As a result, it evolved differently to the communities on the adjoining coasts, close though they were.

When I was researching my Manx family roots, I realised that the majority of people who lived on the Island two hundred years ago, were born, grew up, married, raised a family and died in the same parish. My own mother, who was born in 1906, came from an affluent family who could afford to travel first class by train, but she did not venture off the island until she was in her late teens, and then only to visit her brother who was working in Liverpool. To someone who worked all their life on the land in Marown or Malew, the sea might seem an irrelevance, but the visitors who brought prosperity to the Island came by sea, as did many of the goods they used. Today we are more used to travel, but with the growth of air travel for domestic and international flights, there are many people who have never set foot on a ship in their lives. I suspect there will be well-travelled Islanders whose journeys to or from the Island have always been by air, and to whom the sea may seem as irrelevant as it did to some of our

ancestors, but a glance at the lorries that roll off the ferries bringing televisions, washing machines, computers and cans of beans reveals how much the sea influences our lives.

There have been many books on Manx shipping ever since A W Moore's excellent account of the Isle of Man Steam Packet appeared in 1904, and one might question the need for yet another book, but as I started researching, I realised how much there was that I did not know, despite repeated readings of the excellent books that had appeared in the past. If that seems unbelievable, it is sobering to realise that this book will appear almost exactly one hundred and eighty years after the meeting that took place in Douglas at which a provisional committee was set up to create the IOMSPCo. That is a long time, and over those years, around eighty vessels have been owned by, or chartered by the company. Telling the tale of those eighty vessels is a formidable undertaking, and that is the role that the majority of authors have concentrated upon. This is a perfectly valid approach, for even then there is so much to be said, that selection is inevitable. Sadly, by sticking to that simple remit, we risk losing sight of the wider connection between the Island and the sea. In this book, I have explored the bittersweet romance between the Island and the waters that surround it, and how they have been wooed, though not conquered over the centuries. Writers sometimes speak of the conquest of the oceans or of space, but this is foolish, as the sea reminds us at times. If we are too complacent and believe that we have conquered it, we will be reminded in a terrible way, as those on board the **RMS Titanic** discovered a century ago.

It was because there was so much that was unsaid, that I started gathering material for this book more than forty-two years ago. I realised that if I was to cover the whole subject, and not just the ships of the IOMSPCo, that I had to make a fundamental choice. It is one that countless authors have faced before. A book must be kept within manageable confines, so there is a finite amount of data that can be contained within it. I could tell the story of Manx shipping over the past couple of hundred years, and have widened the scope to cover the companies and vessels that have been largely ignored in the past, but it would be in outline only.

*When my mother was a little girl, the family would sometimes visit Douglas. She spoke of the pier being "black with people" and this Edwardian portrait of the Victoria Pier recalls what she had in mind. I have spent hours studying it. I commented about the direct services between Douglas and Blackpool that my mother spoke of, but this view epitomises it. On the left is the **PS Greyhound** which came from J & G Thompson's Clydebank yard in 1895 for the North Pier Steamship Co (Blackpool) Ltd, she was 230' x 27' and drew 10'. Her principal duties were from Blackpool to Douglas or Llandudno. She was taken over by the Blackpool Passenger Steamboat Co Ltd in 1905. After minesweeping duties in the Great War, she returned to these routes until 1923 when she was sold for service on Belfast Lough, being resold to Turkey in 1925. Behind her on the north face of the Victoria Pier is the IOMSPCo **Empress Queen** of 1897, her name commemorating the Diamond Jubilee. Her 372' length meant that she was one foot longer than the **Lady of Mann** of 1930, and her compound diagonal engines, working at 140 psi developed 10,000 i.h.p, and could drive her at 21.5 knots. She had one 68" diameter high pressure cylinder and two 92" low pressure cylinders, with an 84" piston stroke. She was requisitioned during the Great War, but wrecked off Bembridge Ledge in the Isle of Wight in February 1916. On the South side of the Victoria pier is one of the Fairfield twins of 1887, the **Queen Victoria** and the **Prince of Wales**. Due to the way the canvas is arranged on the railings, I believe it is the latter. One of the Douglas Head ferries, **Rose**, **Shamrock** or **Thistle** is loading at the berth at the landward end of the "South Victoria". Entering the harbour is the **PS Queen of the North**, which came from Laird of Birkenhead in 1895 for the Blackpool Passenger Steamboat Co Ltd. She was 221' 6" x 26' and drew just over 11' of water. She was 590 grt. Instead of the common diagonal compound engines, she was driven by four oscillating cylinders and developed 323 Nominal Horsepower. Apart from pleasure cruises along the Fylde coast, she provided a regular summer service to Douglas. Out of the four paddle steamers in this view, two have arrived from Blackpool, a route that is now completely forgotten. Judging by the angle of the sun, and with the majority of people coming off the pier, I think it is about 2.00pm, and that the **Empress Queen** has just arrived on the 10.30 sailing from Liverpool, there being a Liverpool sign by the boat. In the foreground, a little girl in a straw hat shows signs of wanting to break away from her mama or nursemaid and further on, a slightly older girl, in a knee length coat and a floral hat scans the crowd, perhaps waiting for a much loved family member. My own mother would be about her age at this time, and had an outfit like that, so who knows! Just to the left of the lamp post two ladies, one probably in her twenties with shoulder length hair, walk towards the pier. They are probably going to catch the ferry to Douglas Head and maybe take the double deck tramcar as far as Port Soderick. Many a fine romance began on the trams as passengers sat in enforced closeness to one another. I wonder if she met someone special ?*

Alternatively, I could create a much more detailed canvas, but at the cost of selectivity. The data that I had discovered, some of it at the eleventh hour, when it might otherwise have been consigned to the rubbish heap, was so compelling, that I decided that a selective approach was preferable. As with any difficult choice, there are plus and minus factors. The plus side

is that it permits an intimate glance at our past, and that can offer a fresh insight into what happened and why it happened. The minus side is that whole chunks of history must then be set aside. When I started work on this book, there was a list of thirty or so topics, each of which merited cover. That has been steadily whittled down until a round dozen remained. The

others are not unimportant; far from it, but a choice had to be made. Do I include this, or do I include that ? The idealist would demand BOTH, but that was not feasible. In reading this book, you may ask, "why is this subject ignored?" The answer is simple, space. To have included it, one of the themes that is explored would have had to be discarded. A different

*My mother was not amused. Conscious that I had no head for heights as a child, and unlike her, that I had even less affinities with a mountain goat, she was not in favour of my scrabbling around the steep cliffs on the seaward side of Douglas Head lighthouse, but if I was to compose the photo I wanted of the **SS Manxman** sailing from Douglas with the lighthouse in the foreground and Onchan Head in the background, in her last year of service in 1982, there was no other option. That I am still here to write these words indicates that I returned from the mission in one piece, but as a parent myself, I can now appreciate her anxieties.*

author would have made a different selection, but I hope you find my choice stimulating.

In a book on shipping, it is natural that ships take centre stage, but people matter more than things, and the true lifeblood of history is the interplay between people. I realised that with the exception of William Gill, the first Commodore of the Steam Packet fleet, the amount of information that I had read on the people who created the Steam Packet, and who ran it, could be encapsulated on the back of the proverbial postage stamp. Who were these people and what did they do? What were they like, and what impact did they have on events? If the story of the Steam Packet people could have been written on a postage stamp, the story of the people involved with less well documented companies would scarcely need a pinhead. As I researched I found I wanted to know something about them. By selecting a few topics, I could do that, and the story was a rich one, with triumph and tragedy, moments that must have brought

pride and moments that must have brought anguish to those involved.

I have spoken of a romance between the Island and the sea, but I have opened the book with a real romance that took place against the background of a naval war. It concerned a young naval officer and a pretty Manx girl, and how they met was a result of the influence of the sea. That they were not rent asunder was due to their own resourcefulness and the predominating influence of the sea. Their love affair, with its maritime background, sets the theme for much that follows. When the couple met, there was no regular passenger service to and from the Island, and even the Governor himself, an engaging character called Basil Cochrane, had to make ad hoc arrangements whenever a boat happened to have a cargo that justified a trip "across". That was all about to change, and English frustration with the "tax haven" situation that predated the Revestment of 1765 was the reason why regular passenger services were set up. **Chapter 2** opens as long ago as

1759, with a quote from Governor Cochrane on the state of sea communications, and the hazards of privateers and the weather. It examines how the first sailing packet service was established in 1767, and what happened between then and the birth of the Steam Packet in 1830. Popular belief has it that the Island seethed with indignation at the deplorable standard of services from the day steamer operations began in 1819 to the day the *Mona's Isle* first set sail in 1830. The truth was very different, as we find out in Chapter 2, for there was satisfaction at first, and the efforts of the pioneers, who included David Napier and G & J Burns were commendable, and have never been given their just recognition. However, that was all to change in 1828-29, and to set the scene for the birth of the Steam Packet.

In **Chapter 3**, we look at the birth of the Packet. it is a subject that has been worked over many times since A W Moore first described it in 1904, but once again, by homing in on specific aspects, we can cover material that will be fresh to the majority of readers. Rather than repeat the general description that has appeared in the past, I have concentrated on the people who made it happen. We meet a wealthy landowner turned banker, a master brewer, and a surgeon. Then, there is the ship builder who was born in Ulverston on the Cumbrian coast, but who worked in Liverpool and Douglas, and was responsible for the only Manx-built ship for the Packet. Not least there was the Manx girl who met and fell in love with a Scots ship builder. The success or failure of the Steam Packet depended on the wisdom of those who guided it at its inception, but also on the technical qualities of the *Mona's Isle* of 1830. No original plans seem to have survived for this or many other contemporary early steam ships, but William Sleigh, a distinguished research engineer, used decades of professional experience in managing complex engineering problems to create general arrangement drawings based on known dimensions and practice, and I have been privileged to include drawings and photographs of the model he created to remedy that deficiency. The chapter concludes with what will probably be as much of a bombshell to most readers as it was to me, when we discover what the St George company wanted to do after *St George's* lance was splintered on the fangs of Conister rock a few months after the *Mona's Isle* entered service.

The other shipping lines that have served the Island since 1830 have been largely ignored in previous books, and many readers might conclude that except for a few brief and inglorious challenges, the story of Manx shipping since 1830 was the story of the Packet. This is understandable, but wrong. In this volume, the coverage is roughly 50:50, with half the sections on the IOMSPCo and the balance looking at other lines.

In **Chapter 4** "Fairies at Sea", I have recalled an obscure company whose vessels sailed from Douglas to Laxey, the Dhoon Glen, and Ramsey. Paradoxically it was the discovery of a small oblong piece of pasteboard in 1967 that first drew my attention to the existence of the Mona Steamship Co, and was the catalyst to the creation of this book. To my surprise, the story takes us to India and to Australia. One of the characters we meet bore, as his middle name, the title of a river in Russia. Another was a newspaper proprietor, which explained the excel-

lent coverage that the company always received from one of the Island papers. We encounter a popular Manx auctioneer who lost a fortune in the Dumbell's bank crash. One director was father to a senior officer on the railway that brought the shipping company to its knees, and allegations of insider trading marred its last days. To my astonishment, I found that I had even known one of the characters when I was a toddler.

Chapter 5 takes us to sea with "The Diamond King". I suspect that few readers will know that he was a Manxman. In the 1880s and 1890s, Joe Mylchreest was a legend on the Island on account of his adventurous life and liberality in supporting good causes. One venture he backed was a shipping line from Peel to Northern Ireland. The service ran for just a few months and was offered to the Packet who ran it until the Great War. The brief lifespan of the Peel & North of Ireland Steamship Co and the passage of more than a century have effaced most traces, but the discovery of some papers and the convenient chance that my mother was related to another of the characters was a starting point. A handful of papers from 1911, when the route was operated by the Steam Packet, provided an intimate glimpse of the last years of this route. When Professor D B McNeill wrote his two volume account of Irish Passenger Steamship Services in the 1960s, I wrote to him about the Peel service, and he shared my delight that some of this data existed, though sadly it had been discovered too late for inclusion in his book. Forty years later it has seen the light of day.

Chapters 4 and 5 look at Manx based shipping companies that appeared and then vanished into oblivion. Man creates frontiers, but the sea has no such artificial barriers, and ships cross the barriers of nature and those created by man. Since time began, ships from afar have visited Manx waters, and **Chapter 6** looks at two companies from "across". Passenger ships are more glamorous and more accessible than cargo boats, so have always attracted more attention, but without cargo boats, Manx homes would have frozen in winter and would have lacked many of the basic necessities of life. Using documents more that a century old, I have recalled the coal boats run by Glasgow Steam Coasters. They had built up a fleet of no fewer than 29 vessels by the late 1890s, and for a

time, their red and blue house flag was familiar in Manx waters. Every schoolboy is taught the motto, "If you do not at first succeed, try, try, again". The second company to be covered in Chapter 6 epitomises that philosophy in the person of Samuel Wasse Higginbottom. Accorded a couple of lines in history, Sam was a successful Lancashire coal master, who became chairman of the Tramways Committee of Liverpool City Council, and an MP. A modern reader, hearing that he had crossed swords with the legendary Labour leader, Keir Hardie, over the eight hour day, would dismiss him as a stony hearted Victorian autocrat, but that would be wrong. Conscious of the long hours of the tram men, Sam took over a thousand of them at his own expense to the Island, and championed better catering for them out of ordinary hours. When he died, aged just 49, there was a sadness amongst working families on Merseyside.

In this introduction, you will discover a photo of two small paddle steamers from Blackpool. My mother was born in 1906, so remembered the last days before the Great War of 1914. She had told me that in her childhood there was a direct boat between Blackpool and the Island, and that two of her brothers had taken a trip on it, but I had assumed she was referring to the Steam Packet services via Fleetwood. Given her remarkable memory, that was careless, for her comments, though they might differ from printed history, were invariably correct. Eventually, I found that a long forgotten company, The Blackpool Passenger Steamboat Co had indeed run from Blackpool North Pier to the Island, and I even had photos of the vessel that my uncles must have sailed on a century ago. I was chastened to discover that I had the evidence of the boat she was talking about in my hand for thirty years. She had just celebrated her third birthday when the *Ellan Vannin* went down with all hands, but small though she was, she recalled the impact on her parents and on the community as the shocking news filtered through. More than seventy years later, those memories were still vivid, and she recounted them to me. As she did so, I found that I was sharing those horrific hours as hope ebbed away. A century has now elapsed since the events she recalled so clearly, but **Chapter 7** places on record her first hand account of the shock and distress in Ramsey, so that it is not lost.

WRECK OF THE TUG CONQUEROR. RAMSEY BAY. I.O.M.
JAN. 16. 1905.   COWEN.

*I have spoken of the price extracted by the sea. A part of that price was paid in Ramsey Bay over a century ago. On Saturday, 14 January 1905, the steam tug **Conqueror** entered Ramsey Bay under sail. She was on passage from Liverpool to the Orkneys and had suffered boiler problems. She anchored to await assistance from her owners, the Alexandra Towing Co of Liverpool. By Saturday evening, an East-South-Easterly gale had developed, and **Conqueror**, devoid of engine power, was dependent on her cable holding. The gale raged through Saturday night and all through Sunday, but on Monday just before midday, her solitary cable parted, and the **Conqueror** began to drift rapidly towards the North shore and the Mooragh Promenade. She struck ground opposite what was then the Ramsey Hydro hotel, later the Grand Island, some 300 yards from land. Shortly thereafter a boat left the vessel with a single occupant, a 17 year old ship's boy, who made it to the beach. She was in about 6 to 8 feet of water, and within 100 yards that shallowed to two feet or less, as the slope of the beach is very shallow here. The Rocket Brigade tried to get a line on board, and succeeded at the fourth attempt. The crew started to haul the line in, but with waves breaking over the ship, eventually gave up, sheltering in the wheelhouse. With the ship bumping on the sandy beach and the tide rising, it was a catastrophic decision. As darkness set in about 4.00pm, the crew realised their predicament and individually tried to swim for the beach. Four men, including the Captain made it, but six lost their lives. Owing to the shallow water, the strong inshore gale, which would have made a launch difficult, and the initial success of the Rocket Brigade, no attempt was made to launch the lifeboat until too late. Local people did what they could, wading out into the surf, in some cases waist deep to offer help, and were able to rescue some of the survivors as they drifted ashore. This portrait by G B Cowen, a noted Ramsey photographer, captures this tragic episode.*

In **Chapter 8**, I have looked at the extraordinary period between the close of the Great War in 1918 and the onset of the Great Depression in 1929. It included shareholders meetings every bit as explosive as those I attended in 1985. The great difference was that the defenders of the Packet in 1919 had five of the most respected figures in Manx public life on their side, including the chairman of the IOMSPCo itself. Even today, the proceedings of that meeting are dramatic, and it ushered in the 1920s, a decade of unprecedented change in social and economic life. The data permits a true understanding of those momentous times, but if carried through the entire history of the company, such depth would require several volumes.

Chapter 9, "In the air, on land and sea", utilises the rousing words from the United Sates Marine Corps hymn to reflect the diverse nature of the IOMSPCo, with rare views on board some of the cargo boats and of the company's offices and warehouses. Twice, in the twentieth century, the British Isles were plunged into a World War. The impact on the Island and its shipping was drastic. A little has appeared on the exploits of its vessels at war, but next to nothing has appeared in print on the vessels that preserved the vital Island lifeline from 1939 to 1945. **Chapter 10** rectifies that omission, and we encounter aerial mines, HQ Alien Internment Camps, DORA, who despite her homely name, was anything but homely, and some cans of pineapples.

Chapter 11, on the six sisters of the King Orry class, will invoke fond memories in many readers as they dominated Island shipping from the 1940s to the 1970s.

The longest lived Manx freight company is the Ramsey Steamship Co, and in creating a section on this fine Manx company, it was invaluable that Capt. John Kee, the founder, was related to my mother, and Bernard Swales, a long serving manager of the company was a lifelong friend. I have called the final chapter in this book, "Johnny Kee's Legacy", for that is how my mother's Aunt Eliza called her husband. Many other companies were equally deserving of coverage, but to cover them all would mean to cover none in depth. If it were possible to create a comprehensive record of every aspect of how the sea has affected Manx life, it would take many volumes, but much data has been lost.

Even so, the material that survives would fill several books, so selection is inevitable. As I have said, more could be written on one topic, but at the expense of cuts elsewhere. To give one simple example; Porters Directory of 1889 and Brown's Directory of 1894 list the following Manx registered limited companies associated with shipping, their capital, registered office and in most cases their secretary. The official number, on the IOM Company Register, comes first:

29	Laxey Steamship Co., £6000, 2 Bank Chambers, Douglas. *Sec. Jos. D. Rodgers*
50	Port St. Mary Steamship Co. Ltd., £1600, Village of Port St. Mary. *Sec. W. Mylrea*
54	Douglas Steam Navigation Co. Ltd., £6500, 45 North Quay, Douglas. *Sec. R. A. Cain*
73	Isle of Man Steam Packet Co. £82,546 4s, Steam Packet Quay, Douglas. *Sec. T.P. Ellison*
95	Douglas & Port Soderick Steam Ship Co Ltd, £2000, 24 South Quay, Douglas.
100	Mona Steamship Co. Ltd., £4500, 45 North Quay, Douglas. *Sec. R. A. Cain*
102	Manx Steam Trading Co. Ltd., £5000, 48 Athol St, Douglas. *Sec. C. W. Coole*
103	Douglas Steamboat Co. Ltd., £1000, 19 Duke St, Douglas.
109	Peel and North of Ireland Steamship Co., Ltd., £10,000, Stanley Road, Peel.
156	Mona Steamship Co, £10,000, 45 North Quay, Douglas. *Sec. R M Warhurst* (reconstruction of No 100)

No fewer than ten companies are listed with a relevance to shipping. By 1894, companies 29, 95, 100, 103 and 109 were no longer active. English registered companies operating to the Island, such as Barrow Steam Navigation do not appear, nor do partnerships that had not registered as companies. In this book, I have traced the Mona SS Co (No 100) and its successor, company No 156, and the Peel & North of Ireland SS Co (No 109). Their history runs to quite a few pages, even though one of them only ran for a single season, and the other for just over a dozen years. In any historical work, an author is at the mercy of his sources, and where records no

longer exist, there may be gaps that no amount of effort can recover. It can be frustrating when an impenetrable mist, that might have been sent by Manannan himself, envelopes what we seek, yet the pleasure when the mist is pierced, is great. As I have said elsewhere, people are the mainspring of history, so the spotlight shines on Sukie, a pretty Manx girl, who lived more than two hundred years ago, and to whom the sea brought happiness. Teasing out her story from fragments gathered from many sources has been fulfilling and with a fairy tale ending, highly satisfying. William Shakespeare might not have relished the happy ending, but he would have found the story of Isabella Kerr Kayll much more to his liking. Had the bard lived 200 years later, we might be familiar with a classic tragedy entitled *"The Shipwright's Bride"*.

It is a sobering thought that research on this book began when I was in my late teens. Forty-two years later, a period that has seen the appearance of twenty-two other books and two daughters, *part* of that research has seen the light of day! I have spent many hours in the research library of the Manx Museum, and would like to express my appreciation to the archivists and their staff. My earliest researches were conducted when Miss Anne Harrison was archivist, and in recent times, I have been glad to seek the invaluable advice of Roger M C Sims, the Chief Librarian Archivist, who retired in May 2009. Further data has come from Glasgow Museums & Art Gallery, the General Register of Shipping & Seamen, Swansea, Lloyd's Register of Shipping, London, the City of Manchester Museums, the Isle of Man Family History Society, the IOMSPCo, the Harbour & Lights Department, Western Australia, the Western Australian Historical Society, Cammell Laird & Co, Birkenhead, Vickers Ltd, Barrow Shipbuilding Works, Burns & Laird Lines Ltd, Captain S P Carter of the Laxey Towing Company, Mona Creer, J M Dunn, Brian Fisher, Fred Henry, W T Lambden, G E Langmuir, Tom Lee, Pat Pearson, Sue Pedersen, Captain Chris Puxley, Harbour Master, Silloth, J S Quirk, G G M Robinson, Richard Sleigh, William Sleigh, Leo Venn of Tasmania, Jean Webster and many other individuals. Special thanks are due to Professor D B McNeill, who at the height of his own career, took the time to encourage my researches

when I was at the very start of my own writing career. In the days when the Steam Packet was under Manx control, my parents knew many of the company's shore based and seagoing officers, and their help and advice was appreciated. The names of R A Kissack and Geoff Bell spring to mind, as do Captains Bridson, Callow, Corteen, Hall, Kinley and Ronan. Bernard Swales, manager of the Ramsey Steamship Co, was a lifelong family friend, and many other seafarers have helped over the years. I am indebted to Allan Anderson for helping me discover the truth about John Wood, the builder of the first *Mona's Isle*, and of the Manx girl he met and courted.

The handbills, posters, letters and other documents were from a collection started by my father, and continued by myself, and cast a vivid light on the world of yesteryear, and I am glad to share them with you. Sadly, I also know of at least one lorry load of historic paperwork that ended up on the refuse tip. How much irreplaceable material was lost in that way? Apart from the documentary sources, I have been able to illustrate it with a variety of contemporary photographs. The illustrations use some views from public archives, but to a large extent draw on the photo collection that I had believed to have been started by my Grandfather, Robert Applegarth Hendry II (1884-1942), but as I mentioned in a previous book (100 Years of Mann), some views that were taken in the early 1900s that I had attributed to him, turned out to be the work of his father, Robert Applegarth Hendry I, (1855-1921). My father, Dr Robert Preston Hendry (1912-1991) continued that work, and as soon as I was old enough to handle a camera, I was recruited to continue a photographic record that now covers well over a century of Island life. In recent years, my wife Elena has joined me in that mission. That photographic collection has been supplemented by several collections I have rescued over the years, one being the work of William Alexander Mackie, a Lancashire man who moved to the Island as agent for Lancashire Associated Collieries and made it his home. Views by T H Midwood, Charlie Midwood and G B Cowen, who were talented professional photographers from long ago, also appear. I mentioned documents that went to the tip. I rescued one photographic collection that was sitting at the door waiting to go into the bin, but know of another collection of glass plate negatives from the nineteenth century that survived intact into the start of the 1970s, when most of it was consigned to the rubbish dump. What might we have gleaned from such views?

Working with Colin and Gwynneth Brown of Manx Experience has been a pleasure with this as with previous books. If this volume achieves the success that Colin and Gwynneth's commitment to it warrants, then maybe there can be a sequel that will look at some of the themes that were squeezed out of this volume. I sincerely hope so, as I have loved putting it together, and sharing a lifetime's research into things Manx.

Acknowledgement has been made to many people, but a special word of thanks is due to my parents, Christine May Elaine Hendry (nee Brown) and Dr Robert Preston Hendry. My mother was born in Edwardian days, and spent her childhood in Ramsey and Andreas. One of her earliest memories was of the distress in Ramsey when the **SS Ellan Vannin** went down in a gale in the Mersey. Her father was a successful businessman and chairman of the Ramsey Town Commissioners. He was friends with many of the leading figures in Manx life at the turn of the century. Brought up in that society, my mother, who was a perceptive observer of human nature, recalled many of their foibles to me in later years. My father was born a few years after her,

but recalled the morning when a letter was delivered with an accompanying note expressing the Post Master's regret that it had been damaged due to immersion in water, as it had gone down when the **SS Douglas** was rammed and sunk in the Mersey in 1923. When I was a child, they recounted their memories of the Island to me, and that love for the Island was communicated to me. Hearing a first hand account of the impact of those far off events was one of the first steps on the road to this book. Ideally, a historian prefers contemporary documentary evidence for any statement he may make, but in the real world, much is never committed to paper, and what is written down may only tell part of the story. Verbal tradition is eschewed by many historians, and must be weighed carefully, but where it can be compared to written evidence, it can augment and perhaps shed a brighter light on what is otherwise dim. The stories of Sukie Corrin, or the 1919 Steam Packet events, and of the birth of the Ramsey Steamship Co would be weaker without such evidence. Perhaps the most astonishing example of how verbal evidence can turn out to be true is a legend I was told when I was a child, "that one of your ancestors wore a suit of armour". It is the stuff of childhood make-believe, not serious historical fact, but in 2008, I found documentary evidence from 1683 in the Manx Museum that one ancestor left the armour I had been told of to his son! If

a story of 1683 turns out to be correct, then I am willing to give credence to more recent stories from 1760.

Trips to the museum, or to diverse places to photograph, were family occasions, and I recall my mother's anxiety when I was scrambling about on the steep slopes near Douglas head lighthouse in order to photograph the **SS Manxman** with the lighthouse as a setting. As a child, she had been something of a tomboy, and had walked over the top of the swing bridge in Ramsey harbour and climbed the hazardous face of the quarry at the back of the Hairpin, but was far more concerned when I was making a less dangerous climb. In more recent times, I have been accompanied by my wife, Elena, on photographic trips. In April 2008, when our daughter Anastasia was just under six months old, she watched with interest, as a pair of dredgers scooped mud from the bed of Peel harbour. When we called at the Manx Museum Library, one of the assistants looked at Anastasia and quipped, "Library users get younger by the year". I am sure it is a remark she will relish as she gets older! I hope that Anastasia and her younger sister, Alexandra Amy, will read this book later on, and if they should treasure the work started by their great great grandfather, Robert Applegarth Hendry 1st in recording the changing face of our Island, and wish to carry it on, that would be a rich reward. It is a very special place.

This engraving dates from the 1890s, and gives an excellent impression of the world that our Victorian ancestors knew, with Douglas harbour thronged with the large paddle steamers of the Steam Packet, smaller excursion steamers from Blackpool and elsewhere and a multitude of sailing fishing craft. Although the ships had changed, the scene in its essentials did not vary greatly until the 1970s.

CHAPTER ONE
Sukie and her Naval Officer

Generations of parishioners have walked up the path from the main road to Malew parish church. If you make that walk, you will pass ancient memorials on both sides of the pathway. They are a gazetteer of Manx names, Moore, Callister, Cowley and Corrin to name but a few. If, instead of entering the church, you look to your left, a 200 year old stone sarcophagus sits close to the entrance of the church. It is a link with a fairytale romance that starts on the restless waters of the Atlantic and flowers in Malew. Most of the surrounding graves bear the name Corrin, but this one commemorates a Dr Dominique LaMothe. The name is not Manx, and a passer-by might conclude it sounded French, and wonder why a doctor with a French name was laid to rest in Malew churchyard in 1807. Dominique La Mothe was indeed French, and the story begins at Bayonne in the Basses Pyrenees, a few miles north of the Spanish border. Today, Bayonne is overshadowed in popular esteem by nearby Biarritz, the playground of the wealthy. At the close of the seventeenth century, Jean La Mothe, master surgeon, lived in the Place Notre Dame. One of his sons, Arnaud La Mothe, who was born in 1706, followed in his father's footsteps, and in January 1729 married Marguerite Perez, whose Spanish

Generations of parishioners have walked up the path to Malew church, perhaps glancing at the memorials that line each side of the path from time to time. They are a gazetteer of Manx names, but if the worshipper were to turn to the left, instead of to the right to enter the church, he would behold a stone sarcophagus. The couple that lie there were born far apart, one on the Atlantic coast of France, not far from the Spanish border, the other within a few minutes walk of the churchyard where they lie together.

(Inset) Time has made the inscription on the sarcophagus difficult to decipher, but it paints a portrait of a life well lived, "Until the resurrection to eternal life here lieth the body of Dominique La Mothe native of Bayonne, in France and late Surgeon in Castletown where he practiced with unremitting assiduity and with great satisfaction to the public for 47 years. His soul took flight from hence 8th January 1807 to receive his reward for a useful and well spent life of 74 years." The inscription on the memorial goes on to describe the high spirited Manx girl who became this French doctor's companion for eternity, "Here lieth with her husband's remains the body of Susanna La Mothe nee Corrin who departed this life 9th November 1803 in the 63rd year of her age." How the couple met and why La Mothe lies far from his native land, surrounded by his Manx in-laws is the subject of this chapter.

15

surgeon. It was issued by Louis Marie Jean de Bourbon, Duke of Penthievre and an Admiral of France, and to obtain it, La Mothe had to appear before two Naval surgeon-Majors to convince them of his competence.

La Mothe's diary recorded that he sailed off to war on 2 June 1755. A later entry noted "nous avons ete priz, par les Anglais, 13 August 1755". La Mothe's experience of war had lasted just ten weeks before he was taken prisoner. Subsequently released, La Mothe returned to Bayonne, where his father died on 24 May 1760. The seven years war was now raging between England and France, and on 30 June 1760, just over a month after his father's death, he joined the privateer brig, **St Lawrence** of Bayonne under the command of St Martin Le Veron. Privateers sailed under Letters of Marque issued by naval powers in time of war to attack the enemy trade routes, and Le Veron was a skilful commander, capturing six English ships in September and October 1760. Unlike the U boat campaigns of the First and Second World Wars, when merchant ships were sunk without warning and without regard for the life of the crew, the idea in the eighteenth century had been to capture the vessel, place a prize crew on board, and sail to a friendly port where the ship and cargo would be sold, bringing wealth to the captain, his officers and crew. With a crew of only 98 men to begin with, le Veron could not afford to put large prize crews on board the captured merchantmen, and was worried lest the English crews rose up and overpowered their captors to retake the ship. He was a wily bird, and to permit the smallest possible prize crews, transferred his English prisoners to the holds of his own brig. By early October 1760, with his ship in the Atlantic, west of Ireland, Le Veron must have been well pleased with himself. His fortune and that of his officers was made.

We must now leave Dominique for a few moments, and travel to the Island, and to the Parish of Malew. A few years after Arnaud La Mothe had been married, a young man called Henry Corrin stood by his wife-to-be in Malew Church. The date was 14 July 1738, and as he stood before the vicar, he may have reflected that the Rev J Woods had officiated in the same church when his father, also called Henry Corrin, had married his mother, a strong willed and outspoken

*Although we cannot know the precise details, this early nineteenth century woodcut of a ship lying helpless under the guns of a warship captures the excitement that must have been felt as Capitaine St Martin Le Veron prowled the Atlantic in the **St Lawrence** in the autumn of 1760. Six times he pounced, and six times, English merchantmen received prize crews to sail them to France. Did La Mothe join any of those boarding expeditions? As a surgeon probably not, as Le Veron could not afford to lose his doctor in some petty skirmish on the decks of an English merchantman, but as the crew of the **St Lawrence** shrank as another prize crew sailed away with each capture, Le Veron must have become increasingly desperate for officers and men.*

name recalls the mixed heritage of this border area. Their first son, Dominique La Mothe was born in Bayonne on 4 August 1731. Like his father and grandfather, Dominique became a master surgeon, but the middle years of the eighteenth century were a time of frequent wars with England, and on 27 May 1755, he received his commission as a naval young woman called Amy Stevenson back in 1707. Amy, sometimes spelled Aymee, had been born in 1683 and was descended from the Stevensons of Balladoole, a famous and ancient Manx family that could trace their occupation of Balladoole back to the fourteenth century. Amy's first cousin, John Stevenson, SHK, a leading figure in the Act of Settlement of 1704, built the present Balladoole House, which dates from 1714. Her father, Captain John Stevenson was his uncle and the two men are frequently confused, as only a few years separated their birth. He was Constable, or commander of Peel Castle, then still an important military base. To add to the confusion, both men had daughters that were christened Amy ! A family legend had it that Stevenson was an anglicised version of FitzStephen, an Anglo Norman knight who was the son of Stephen, Constable of Cardigan Castle and a Welsh girl, Nesta, daughter of Rhys ap Tewdyr. Not only was Nesta beautiful and clever, she was a Princess, being the daughter of the last independent king of South Wales, and if she was not a nymphomaniac, she came close to it, for as well as bearing five children to her husband,

Gerald of Windsor, she bore children to Stephen of Cardigan, King Henry 1 of England, and at least one other lover. Even if the stories of descent from Nesta were legend, Amy had a glittering pedigree and was not in the least abashed in a male dominated society. Her son, young Henry Corrin was to marry a girl called Susanna Quay, the daughter of Thomas Quay, a Castletown merchant and one time soldier. Unlike the tempestuous Amy, or the long dead Nesta, Susanna seems to have been a gentle but capable girl, much loved by her husband. The Revd Woods, who had served the community since 1695 was now ageing. Even in his younger days, John Woods had been forgetful at times, but as the years pressed heavily, record keeping became ever more haphazard. Henry and Susanna's wedding was notified to the Bishop of Sodor and Mann, but was never entered in the parish register. Even before the Revd Wood's death in August 1739, record keeping had collapsed, so we do not know the exact date when Susanna bore the couple's first children, twin girls, Susanna and Elizabeth. A son Thomas, who died in infancy, was born in August 1740, so

sometime between the spring and autumn of 1739 is likely. The outbreak of the French war in 1756 probably did not mean very much to the teenage girls, but in 1760, shortly after they turned twenty, events were to catapult a handsome young French naval officer into their lives.

In avoiding the risk of the crews of the captured ships overpowering his prize crews, Capitaine Le Veron had been smart, but in doing so, he had created a new problem. With his captures, his own crew was now depleted to around 30 men, although "men" is hardly the right term, as seven were young boys. In an episode worthy of the pen of C S Forester, and in the "Hornblower" mould, the English crews rose up on 31 October 1760, overpowered their French captors, killing the First Officer in the process, and took the ship. Dominique La Mothe was a prisoner of the English for the second time in his naval career. Although the **St Lawrence** was in the Atlantic, and there must have been nearer ports to sail her to, the victors sailed her in to Douglas, where she arrived at 11.00am on 9 November. The arrival of a ship with French prisoners of war presented the

Although this engraving by T Breckell dates from 1822, some sixty years after Dominique LaMothe first set eyes on Castle Rushen, the view he had on the November day in 1760 when he first arrived in Castletown would not have been much different. Today, we can admire the medieval stone towers of this superbly preserved castle, but I doubt if LaMothe saw them in that light, as they were the forbidding bastions of the place that was to be his prison. The engraving shows the Castle prior to the construction of Quay Road with the original gatehouse and guardroom in the centre of the view. The modern entry to the castle, opposite the police station is out of view to the left of the gatehouse. LaMothe would have been taken through the gatehouse, and to the stairs to the dungeons, which were conveniently close to hand. The vault itself was a grim place, the lower parts of which were subject to flooding during the spring tides. It was not the place to be on a cold November day, or any other day for that matter. Susanna Quay, Sukie's mother, had been brought up in Quay House, which was a few yards to the right of the castle, and which was to pass to Dominique and Sukie after her death. (Author's collection)

T. Breckell

When Sukie Corrin was born c1739, her great-grandfather, Captain John Stevenson, had been dead for twenty years, but her grand-mother, Amy Corrin, nee Stevenson, who had been christened in 1683, was still alive, and the little girl was eleven by the time Amy died. As a child, Amy would have remembered the elegant military uniforms worn by her father, and her upbringing at Balladoole and in Peel, when her father was Constable or Commander of the Castle, with a military command equal in size to Castle Rushen itself. John Stevenson must have cut an elegant figure in his blue or scarlet tunics, to judge by his tailor's bills, which still survive! Did Amy enthral the little girl with memories of Peel Castle, which must have looked much as it appears in this engraving? Did she tell Sukie about the gleaming armour that her own grandfather, Major General Richard Stevenson had worn, and recall the days of a proud military elite, of which she was a daughter? No one can tell, but from stories that came down to my mother, that could only have originated with Amy, which, incredibly, included mention of that suit of armour, and were retold to me more than two centuries after Amy died, she must have had a gift with words that was to exercise a powerful hold on the imagination of her descendants. If she could influence a child born two hundred years after she died, and I am sure it is through Amy that I inherited my own love for the history of our Island, what might have been her effect on those who sat at her knee? When a dashing young naval officer entered Sukie's life, did she see Dominique as the living embodiment of the childhood stories recounted by her grand-mother? In fiction, the fairy godmother casts her spell with a magic wand. Amy did so with magic words that lived for quarter of a millennium. Quick tempered and tempestuous she may have been, but I rather like her.

Island authorities with a problem, and the crew was lodged in the dungeons of Castle Rushen. Governor Basil Cochrane informed the Duke of Atholl, then Lord of Mann, and a letter was duly sent to the Board of Admiralty to request their removal, as they were a serious burden on the resources of a small community. Until the early part of the nineteenth century, officers who were captured were usually offered parole, under which they agreed not to escape, or serve against their captors, until exchanged for another prisoner. On 14 November 1760, the officers of the **St Lawrence** duly signed a bail bond, and were allowed to reside in Castletown in the vicinity of the

Castle. Dominique La Mothe found lodgings with Henry, or Hal, Corrin and his family, and met Susanna, who was known as Sukie within the family, and her sister Elizabeth. Over the next few weeks, the Lords Commissioners of the Admiralty started the process of removing the French prisoners from the Island and orders were sent for an RN vessel to call at Douglas to pick them up. On 24 January 1761, **HMS Delight**, under Lieut John Archer, dropped anchor in Douglas Bay and applied to the governor to collect the prisoners. In all there were 27 of them, although Archer's orders had mistakenly told him to collect 26 prisoners, and by chance, that is what he did. Equally "by chance", on the day

that **HMS Delight** arrived in Douglas, Dominique La Mothe had gone exploring in the country, and could not be found. A suitable wind coming on that evening, Lt Archer sailed, and La Mothe reappeared. His parole would have permitted him to be absent during the day, but the Island authorities were not amused, as they had one prisoner still on their hands, and it was doubtful if the Royal Navy would wish to send a warship for just one man. La Mothe was back in his cell that evening.

Thus far, the story I have told appears in the official papers that have survived, and in a history of the La Mothe family written by Dominique's great-grandson, High Bailiff John

Corlett LaMothe. However, I was aware of the outlines of the LaMothe saga long before I read the LaMothe account, or the official records, for my mother was descended from Sukie Corrin's younger brother William, and she had told me the story from Sukie's perspective. Like her grandmother, Amy Corrin, and her possible distant ancestor, Nesta, Sukie was a resourceful and lively girl, and Dominique was a dashing young naval officer, and soon the couple were in love. When the family got wind of the arrival of the ship to take Dominique away, it seems likely that Sukie and her young doctor were packed off to the country post haste. When Dominique was carted off to gaol, Sukie did not collapse in tears, or if she did, it must have been brief. Instead, she dispatched her father to see Governor Cochrane. He was born in 1701, his parents being William Cochrane, Laird of Ochiltree and Mary Bruce. He was related to the Earls of Dundonald, and to the celebrated diarist, James Boswell, who described him as "a man of great common sense and prudence". He was Governor of the Island from 1751 to 1761, when he became Commissioner of Excise in Scotland. High Bailiff LaMothe recounted a legend that Governor Cochrane's wife had been ill for some time, and her condition was deteriorating, and that the local doctors had been ineffectual, so Dominique had been called in to help. In the Corrin story, Hal was dispatched to tell the governor that he had a highly skilled medical man in the cells, who might be able to effect a cure, and Dominique was duly summoned, and cured "the governor's Lady". In the social circumstances, the term "lady" would be entirely consistent with wife, so both stories agreed. Roger Sims of the Manx Museum referred me to papers in the Museum exchanged between two researchers on Manx Gaelic over 100 years ago. They recorded an episode that made no apparent sense to them, that Sukie, in company with some other ladies, had visited LaMothe in prison. They left it at that. Given the story handed down to me, it made perfect sense, and added a missing link. My guess is that Sukie realised that it would be improper for a young girl to visit a man in prison, so had taken along her mama, Susanna, and sister Elizabeth as chaperones, to tell Dominique what was afoot, and suggest that if he cured the governor's lady, it would do his status no harm. Suitably forewarned,

When Sukie and Dominique travelled to Liverpool in 1763, it was to visit St George's church, which was on the site once occupied by Liverpool Castle at the top of Lord Street. It was designed by Thomas Steers, and was provided with arches along one side for the use of local market stallholders. The towers at each end housed the offices of the clerk of the market and the night watch. The church was built for Liverpool Corporation between 1726 and 1734, so was less than thirty years old when the couple exchanged their marriage vows there. Located in the heart of the commercial and maritime part of the city, the original congregation would have consisted of seafarers, local businessmen, lawyers and the Corporation of Liverpool, but this came to an abrupt end in 1863 when the existing incumbent delivered an intolerant sermon denouncing the election of a mayor of Jewish descent. With municipal support ended, the church struggled to find a congregation and closed in 1897. It was demolished in 1901-02 and a memorial to Queen Victoria erected on the site. When I discovered that Sukie and Dominique had married at St George's, I realised that with our family's Liverpool associations, I might well have an engraving of the church, and so it turned out. This portrait was the work of William Gawin Herdman (1805-1882) a celebrated Merseyside artist. Had she been alive, Sukie's grandmother, Amy Stevenson, might well have approved of the couple's choice of church, for she is the one person who might have known that one of Sukie's distant ancestors had visited the same place when Liverpool Castle occupied the site. In fact, he played quite an important role in the city's history, as he granted the City's Charter on 28 August 1207. His name was John "Lackland", otherwise King John of England. Sukie was descended from King John by way of the Stevensons of Balladoole, the Christians of Milntown, the Nevilles and the Percies, a genetic potpourri of some of the most tempestuous families in Manx and English history that might help explain Amy and Sukie's forceful character.

when he was brought before the governor, Dominique offered to see the lady, and soon she was on the mend.

The story, which comes from two separate sources that diverged within living memory of the events, and is supported by the independent report of Sukie's visit to see LaMothe in prison, is logical, except for one small detail. Governor Cochrane was a bachelor, who had on one occasion commented ruefully "none of his women friends would agree to be Governess"! From surviving letters, Basil Cochrane seems to have been a lively and sympathetic character, meriting Boswell's praise. Perhaps it was not the governor's "Lady" but one of the Lady Friends who would not "agree to be Governess", that had fallen ill. Down the years, it would be easy for a lady friend to be transformed to lady and then to "wife", as in the LaMothe account. Indeed in Victorian days, which is when the High Bailiff wrote his account, wife would be seen as far more acceptable than lady friend. No official date survives for Dominique's release from gaol, but his tombstone, which records that he practised medicine in Castletown for 47 years, and that he died in 1807, suggests that it was days at most that he was in gaol. Had Dominique tended Cochrane when he was ill, there would have been no need for a "lady" to enter the story at all, so the inference must be that Dominique tended a lady who was held in high regard by the Governor. Had he merely tended the governor, and been released in gratitude, his position would have been precarious after Cochrane left the Island in 1761, not least because George Moore, an influential member of the Keys, was an inveterate enemy of Cochrane. He was bitterly against naturalising foreigners and Catholics in the Island, and was powerful enough to block some attempts. LaMothe would have fallen foul of Moore on every count, but the records give no hint of any further troubles. The facetious use of the term "governess" may hold the answer, for it only makes sense if Basil Cochrane had courted one or more of the "local" girls when he was governor, and as a scion of the Scottish peerage, that would mean the daughter of one of the leading families on the Island. If Dominique had saved the life of a lady friend of the governor, who was also the daughter of one of the powerful families living in the vicinity of Castletown, he and Sukie

Dominique LaMothe's signature speaks to us across the centuries. Although one cannot read too much into it, due to the differences in writing styles and methods, the strong upper and lower strokes and angular character, suggest someone who is confident, alert and resilient, characteristics that seem to be reflected in his adaptability and adventurous life. Although Dominique could read and write, Sukie was born in an age when it was not regarded as necessary, or indeed desirable, for girls to learn such skills, and from the available evidence it seems that Sukie "made her mark" on any official papers, but she and Dominique ensured that their children, including the girls, were literate. It suggests they were thoughtful parents, ahead of their time.

would have had influential allies to protect them from Moore after Cochrane had left the Island. A chatty letter from John Quayle to Basil Cochrane, after he had returned to Scotland, mentions that "the French Doctor was no sooner released from being a prisoner of war than he became captive to Suky Corrin" This could mean that Dominique remained in gaol from 1760 to 1763, but from the letter, Quayle obviously knew that Cochrane would be interested. That would hardly apply had Cochrane never met La Mothe, or that he had remained in gaol. The official records are silent, but England was at war with France, and Dominique would assuredly be arrested had he set foot in England, so the Island authorities may have felt that the less London knew about it, the better. As Moore had on at least one occasion gone over Cochrane's head to complain to the Duke of Atholl, it would be much safer if Dominique was technically a prisoner of war, albeit on parole, until the end of the war.

Sukie's father, Henry Corrin (1713-1769) was a successful and wealthy merchant, but such was the gap in eighteenth century society between trades people and the ruling elite that

it is at first sight surprising that the Governor, who was descended from the Scottish peerage, would receive a visit from a mere merchant, let alone pay heed to him, where a serious illness was concerned. It is only when we delve into the close connections that grew up between the ruling circle and the wealthy merchant families in eighteenth century Castletown that the story begins to make sense. It is Sukie's grandmother, the abrasive and tempestuous Amy Stevenson who provides the vital clue. Her grandfather, Major General Richard Stevenson of Balladoole, had been Deputy-Governor of the Isle of Man and Receiver general. He was long dead, but in his day he had been one of the most powerful figures in Manx life. Amy's father, Captain John Stevenson (1655-1718) followed in the family tradition, holding military office as Constable, or commander, of Peel Castle. Amy's grandmother had been Isabell Christian of Milntown, and John Stevenson was intensely proud of his descent from Milntown. Isabell had been dead for close on a century when Sukie fell in love, but the Christians of Milntown were the most powerful family on the Island for generations. Amy's mother, Ellin

Dominique and Sukie's romance, which had been nurtured by the restless seas and preserved by Sukie's determination not to allow the Royal Navy or a war to interfere with her happiness, created a dynasty that bulked large in Manx political, medical, legal and literary life for the next century and a half. In looking at the impact of the sea on our Island and its people, it is worth recalling some of the descendants of Dominique and Sukie. Frederick La Mothe, the third son of the couple followed his father's footsteps in medicine and married Margaret Corlett of Glentrammon, Lezayre. It was their grandson, John Corlett Lamothe, (1838-1898), the name also appearing as John Corlet La Mothe, who wrote down the La Mothe side of the family story in 1896. Even as a young law student, J C Lamothe had shown an aptitude with the pen, and his "Statute Laws of the Isle of Man 1853-1861" was a vital tool for the Manx legal profession for decades. He became High Bailiff of Ramsey and a director of the Manx Northern Railway.

Galloway, was the granddaughter of one of the wealthiest men in Castletown, a merchant called Jeffrey Gallowey. Sukie's twin sister, Elizabeth was to marry Deemster John Lace a few years after Sukie's romance, and her younger brother William married Ann Tyldesley in 1766. Her parents were Captain Richard Tyldesley of the Friary, Ballabeg, and Ann Stanley, a descendant of the Earl of Derby. The Corrin family was linked by friendship and matrimony to the most influential and powerful families in eighteenth century Mann, and given that background, Henry's visit to the Governor is no longer exceptional.

As to the identity of the mysterious lady, that must be surmise. The Stevenson, Heywood, Norris, Christian, Parr, Stanley, Tyldesley and Huddlestone families would all have provided a suitable match for a governor who was a younger son of the Scottish nobility. Sukie's grandmother was Amy Stevenson. Her younger brother married a Tyldesley. The family were friendly with the Huddlestones. With those connections, Hal was well placed to have known of an affair with a daughter from those families, but other families cannot be ruled out. When the lady took ill, Hal could have spoken to Cochrane, whose surviving letters show that he had a high regard for the merchant community, which in itself is unusual for that era. One letter typified this. In December 1756, Cochrane had written to the Duke of Atholl, ". . . there is a good deal of money due by the merchants but money is att [sic] present scarce with them and I do not care to press hard upon them as they are all good men". If Dominique had saved the life of a well-connected Manx girl, Cochrane's departure later in 1761 would not be such a serious blow, as Dominique would have earned the gratitude of powerful backers.

By 1763, faced with the overwhelming power of the Royal Navy, French ambitions were in tatters, and on 10 February 1763, the Treaty of Paris ended the war on advantageous terms to Great Britain. It was an important event in the lives of the young couple. Dominique could now return to France, but Sukie accompanied him on the first stage of the journey, as far as Liverpool, where they were married at St George's Church, on 6 April 1763. Had Dominique remained in a prison cell until the

7 M. Lamothe —

Shortly after John Corlett Lamothe wrote his book on the statute laws of the Island, he married Sarah Banks of Liverpool, and their first son, Frederick Malcolm Lamothe, was born in 1864. He became High Bailiff of Ramsey and Peel, and prior to his appointment as Deemster in 1921, he was a director of the Isle of Man Steam Packet. From May to July 1924, he acted as Deputy-Governor during the illness of the Governor, a post that had also been held by one of his ancestors, Major General Stevenson. If Amy's stories, told to her granddaughter, of the pomp and pageantry of the official life she had known as a child, had predisposed Sukie to the handsome young French naval officer, who entered her life in such a dramatic way, I think Amy would have been well pleased with the careers of some of her descendants.

end of the war, it is more than likely that he would have returned to France, taking his young wife with him, as he would have an assured future in his own land. Instead he visited France to collect his share of the prize money from the captured British ships. He invested the proceeds in a cargo of brandy, which he sold in Dublin, returning to the Island in September 1763, which suggests that life had treated him well between 1760 and 1763. His arrival back on the Island was about two months before the birth of the couple's first child on 23 November. Given the dates, one is tempted to conclude that the young lovers celebrated the news of peace with great enthusiasm. Dominique and Sukie were to have eleven children, several of whom rose to prominence in Manx medical and legal circles. Whatever qualities they inherited from Dominique, they also inherited Amy and Sukie's forceful character. At a time when women were not regarded as intelligent enough to witness official documents, one of their daughters, Sophia LaMothe, attended the wedding of her first cousin, another Henry Corrin, in 1793, the year in which a further war broke out with France. Although there were two male witnesses to the wedding, Sophia's bold signature as witness shows that she was no more overawed by a male dominated society than her mother, her great grandmother, Amy, or the long dead Nesta. I have encountered no other wedding witnessed in quite this way, which suggests a young woman who was supremely self-confident. The wedding that she witnessed on behalf of the Lamothe and Corrin families was of my Great-great-great grandfather. Sukie died on 9 November 1803, and was buried in the Corrin family plot at Malew. Dominique passed away on 8 January 1807, joining her amongst her Corrin ancestors and siblings.

I have told the story of Sukie and Dominique, as it is a fairytale romance with a happy ending, which has the added benefit of being true. When I was a child, my mother would recount Manx stories to me, and I would sometimes say to her, "tell me about Sukie". Even the fragment that survived was exciting, and deserved perpetuating, but with access to both the Corrin and LaMothe versions, and the scrap of paper in the museum files, I have explored it in more depth than ever before. It has the drawback of being dependent in part on verbal tradition, with the apparent flaw of the governor being unmarried, but the transition, from lady friend to lady, and to wife, would be easy to make, and whilst the LaMothe version did say "wife", my mother always used the term, "the governor's lady". If the stories bequeathed by Amy to her grandchildren of descent from Milntown and of a suit of armour survived with such accuracy for over 200 years, it is likely that the legend about Sukie is substantially correct, and it fits known facts. I have chosen to open this book with Sukie and her naval officer because it shows how the sea has influenced the lives of generations of Manx folks. Had La Mothe not gone to sea in the service of his country, and had he not been captured and delivered to Castle Rushen when his ship arrived in Douglas, he and Sukie would never have met. Had weather conditions not forced Lt Archer to sail when he did, Dominique might have been apprehended and incarcerated in an English prison hulk, as so many French naval prisoners were. Had the Island been a constitutional part of the UK, instead of a law unto itself, it is unlikely that an enemy prisoner of war would have been invited to treat the governor's lady, or to practice medicine in time of war. The common theme is the influence of the sea on Mann and its inhabitants.

Every book that has been written since A W Moore's outstanding history of the IOMSPCo appeared in 1904 has fostered the impression that prior to the birth of the Steam Packet, the shipping services to the Island were deplorable, and that after 1830, opposition vanished overnight. Writing for the 75th anniversary of the founding of the Packet, and coming from a family that was associated with the Packet from its inception, this was understandable, but a fuller description is called for. The best account of the fraught state of communications in the eighteenth century comes from Governor Basil Cochrane, whom we have already met in Chapter 1. He replied on 11 December 1759 to the Duke of Atholl's complaint about insufficient funds being remitted from the Island to his coffers. I have left the spelling and punctuation as drafted:

> *"My Lord*
> *three days ago I had the honour of your Grace's letter of the 19th of last month and as to not makeing greater remittances. It is very true we have above one thousand pounds due but the last summer and hearvest we were plagued with tenders and cutters pressing about the Island which for a long time putt an end to all trade and a great deal of this winter the weather has been so bad that boats and vessels were often prevented from passing and repassing so that the poor merchants have suffered greatly upon these accounts I was obliged to forbear pressing them too much. The merchants are the bees that brings in the honey so there is a necessity to favour and deal tenderly with them".*

Looking at the imperious deadlines, with their threats of fines for late delivery, that are hurled at the taxpayer today by an allegedly compassionate and democratic government, I think I prefer Governor Cochrane's wise discretion! A few months before that exchange between the Duke and the Governor, the British government had taken the first steps towards ending Atholl rule on the Island, writing to the Duke:

> *"My Lord*
> *We are directed by the Lords Comm'rs of his Maj'ts Treasury to acquaint your Grace that they having received many and frequent complaints of great frauds in the Revenue occasioned by the illicit trade carried on to and from the Isle of Man and it being the opinion of the Boards of Revenue of Ireland and Customs in England that no effectual remedy can be provided while it remains in the hands of a subject. Their Lordships are of opinion that it will be of service to the Crown and the publick that the same be purchased by his Majesty: And to that end their Lordships have empowered their secretaries to receive your Grace's proposals for the sale of the said Island; And to treat with you for the same if it is agreable to your Grace*
> *We are my Lord with the greatest respect*
> *Your Graces most obedient and most humble servants*
> *J West*
> *Saml Martin*
> *Treasury Chambers*
> *23d March 1759"*

Initial reluctance by the Duke to sell was followed with the threat of sanctions, and the result was the Act of Revestment in 1765, which transferred the rights of the Duke of Atholl as Lord of Mann to the British Crown. The act was hated in the Island for the hardship it caused. It was aimed at the profitable smuggling industry, which had grown up in the eighteenth century, as the Island was outside the jurisdiction of British customs officers, but meant that UK customs duties were also levied on local transactions, and the money siphoned off to benefit the UK coffers, and not pay for what was needed on the Island. In simple terms, it was the usual case of officialdom correcting a small abuse by a few by inflicting a bigger abuse on everyone. Clucas Joughin (1854-1921) a talented Manx author, wrote a novel, *Gorry, Son of Orry* which was published in 1903, and which captured the bitterness felt on the Island as a result of the act. The novel is summarised in *A Century of Mann, 1860-1960*. After the Act, the UK government appointed officials to govern its new domain, and as with all governments, then felt compelled to supervise them, so a weekly sailing packet was set up between Douglas and Whitehaven in Cumbria in 1767. Basil Cochrane had moved back to Scotland, but after 1765, his willingness to "deal tenderly" had no place in the hearts of the Island's new rulers. Today, no scheduled services have operated to or from Cumbria for sixty years, but a study of a map of the Irish Sea will reveal why the British government selected remote Whitehaven at that time. The distance from Douglas to Liverpool is some 80 sea miles. From the north of the Island to the Cumbrian coast is around a third of that, and in the days of sailing packets, that was important. Although private travellers were carried, the primary purpose of the Whitehaven Packet was to facilitate communication between the crown officers on the Island and London. It would leave Whitehaven on a Monday, returning from Douglas on a Thursday, unless delayed by weather. David Robertson, who had been a British customs officer, and revisited the Island as a "tourist", gave an account of a trip from Whitehaven in 1791 on board one of His Majesty's cutters, a trip which was interrupted when the cutter spotted a small boat at anchor and investigated. Robertson takes up the story:

> *"I sailed from Whitehaven in one of his Majesty's Cutters; and, as the day was delightfully serene, in a few hours observed the mountains of Mona breaking from the ambient clouds. On a nearer approach they afforded us a sublime and picturesque view: Mountain piled upon mountain,*

extending in a lofty range for many miles; in the centre of which, Snaffield, [sic] with awful grandeur, lifted his brow to Heaven, and seemed proudly to claim the pre-eminence.

The bold and rugged coast next demanded our attention; as even at a league's distance it seemed to threaten us with approaching ruin. In some places it sunk into deep and gloomy caverns; and in others was overhung with frowning precipices: while the solitary screeches of the seamews united with the wildness of the scenery, to fill the mind with an awful melancholy.

In a little, I discovered, under the shelter of Maughold's Head, a small vessel lying at anchor. It proved a smuggling boat, laden with wine, rum, and tobacco; and had sailed from Laxey on the preceding night: but, unable to reach the English shore before morning, had retired under the high land, in expectation that the ensuing night would prove more favourable. But how elusive are the hopes of mortals! Being soon discovered by the cutter, the boat was without any opposition seized, and the crew transported aboard our vessel."

Robertson spoke to the owner, who had been captured. He was an impoverished Cumbrian land owner, who sought to restore a declining family fortune by running a cargo, and instead lost what little he had left, bringing ruin to a young family. Holden's Directory of 1811 recorded that His Majesty's Whitehaven and Douglas packet the **Lady Elizabeth** received the Mail at Whitehaven, every Monday evening, and waited three days after her arrival, in the Isle of Man, for the Isle of Man letters. **The Brilliant** sailed twice a week, between Liverpool and Douglas, her owners being Burrows and Fleetwood of Liverpool. **The Friends** sailed twice a week, between Liverpool and Douglas. (Owners Leece and Drinkwater of Liverpool). Packet boats and traders between Douglas and Liverpool included **Duke of Athol**, (owners, Leece and Drinkwater), and **Duchess of Athol**, (owners, Burrows and Fleetwood). By 1815, there were two regular Packet boats sailing between Douglas and Whitehaven, the **Lady Elizabeth** being supplemented by the **Triton**. There were five

The ramifications of the Napier clan have puzzled many historians, but the story began with Robert Napier (1726-1805). He married Jean Denny, and their children included John Napier, (1752-1813) and James Napier (1763-1848). The two brothers entered into partnership in an engineering business. John married Ann McAllester in 1787, and their five children included David (1790-1869), the subject of this portrait, and Isabella (1793-1875). The younger brother, James, had married Jane Ewing in 1789, their seven children including Robert Napier who was born on 18 June 1791, and married his cousin Isabella in 1818. David Napier, although only a year older than his cousin Robert, was active in steamship work from 1811, whilst Robert did not come to prominence in maritime affairs for another decade. In 1814, David married Marion Smith, after whom he was to name an early steamship, and whose father, Francis Smith, owned an engine works at Camlachie. As with his sister's long and happy marriage to his cousin Robert, David and Marion Napier were to enjoy many years together, Marion dying on 1 February 1867, aged 73. David's last days were saddened by the death of the couple's youngest daughter, Alexina in January 1868, David dying on 23 November 1869. As with his cousin, Robert, and his friend John Wood, David Napier never received the official recognition he so richly deserved in his lifetime. The failure to honour the Napiers or Wood did no dishonour to them, but heaps discredit upon Westminster and Whitehall.

sloops, schooners and packet on the Liverpool run, and two serving Dublin. 1815 also marked the first appearance of a steamer in Manx waters, when a small steamer called at Ramsey en route to take up ferry work on the Mersey. On 7 May 1816, a steamer called **Greenock** called at Douglas en route from the Clyde to

the Mersey, and made a short pleasure trip as far as Laxey, the first recorded passenger sailing under steam as far as the Island is concerned.

The first regular steamer service to serve the Island commenced in August 1819, and is customarily attributed to James Little & Co of Greenock, but the story is more complicated. The driving force behind the new venture was David Napier, who was Isabella Napier's brother, and therefore the brother-in-law, as well as being first cousin to Robert Napier, who was to play a key role in the birth of the Packet a decade later. If any man deserved the title of "The Father of Sea Going Steam Navigation" and the Father of Manx steamer services, it was David Napier. He was the son of John Napier and Ann McAllester, and was born on 29 October 1790, and baptised at Dumbarton on 7 November 1790. He was apprenticed to his father, and was working as an engineer by the age of 15. He had visited the ill-fated canal paddle tug the **Charlotte Dundas** as a boy, and by the age of 20 was manager of his fathers works, and responsible for work on the boiler for another pioneering steamer, Henry Bell's **Comet** of 1812. From foundry work and building boilers, Napier moved into marine engineering and to opening up promising shipping routes. In 1818, he established a steamer service between Greenock and Belfast with the **Rob Roy**, which was of 90 tons burden and 40 hp and built by William Denny of Dumbarton. Although he was still under thirty, Napier was a shrewd businessman, and realising that a service between Liverpool and Greenock for Glasgow would be well patronised, he persuaded Provost Mills of Glasgow and other leading citizens to finance a service. The first steamer in 1819 was the 150 ton **PS Robert Bruce**, which was built by Scott's of Greenock, and received 60 nhp engines from David Napier's works. She was 94' x 18' 7", or about the size of a 20th century tug. With severe winter weather, sailings ended after 11 October 1819. The service resumed on 5 April 1820, the **Robert Bruce** being joined by the 246 ton **PS Superb** in June 1820. She had been launched at Scott's yard in Greenock on 29 April 1820, and was fitted with 72 hp two cylinder engines by David Napier. She was said to be the " finest, largest and most powerful steam vessel in Britain", making the passage from Greenock to Liverpool in around

With James Little & Co of Greenock as agents, David Napier instituted the first regular steamer service to call at Douglas in 1819, the **Robert Bruce**, plying between Greenock, Douglas and Liverpool, the Douglas-Liverpool leg taking around ten hours. The 246-ton **PS Superb**, illustrated here, joined the **Robert Bruce** on the route in 1820. Reputedly the "finest, largest and most powerful steam vessel in Britain", she was used by Napier until 1823, when she was disposed of, operating in Italian waters from 1824. Contemporary sources reveal that at this time, there was delight that the Island was on the premier steamship route in the world.

thirty hours, and was claimed to have had the first copper boiler put into a steamer. After a winter break in 1820-21, both boats returned to the Greenock-Liverpool service. As with most early steamers, she was owned by a consortium, including Little and Napier, but she was sold to Italian owners in 1824 for service between Naples and Palermo.

A Parliamentary Report on steamer services in 1822, contained an account by T. S. Traill:

*"I was exposed to a violent storm in the **Robert Bruce**, and was surprised at the ease with which she wrought in a very heavy sea, and the much less motion she had than a sailing vessel would have had in similar circumstances. Contrary to my expectation her decks were not inundated, we could walk tolerably on them, and even books in open shelves were not displaced, circumstances which also astonished Captain Scoresby junior who accompanied me. In the worst of the gale we made nearly half a mile per hour against a heavy head-sea and a violent gale...in approaching the Isle of Man from Liverpool."*

With the arrival of the **PS Majestic** in July 1821, the **Robert Bruce** switched to the Whitehaven and

Liverpool route and then Belfast and Liverpool, calling at Douglas, but she was lost off Anglesey on 23 August 1821. The 240 ton **Majestic** had been launched at Scott's yard on 19 April 1821, and was provided with side lever engines by David Napier. She was 134' 2" by 21' and managed to cut the Greenock-Liverpool schedule to 25 hours, despite calls at Port Patrick and Douglas.

They were passenger-only boats, the cabin fare, with food, being 31s. 6d; and the steerage fare, 10s. They sailed three times a week from Greenock, calling at Douglas en route. James Little was the Greenock agent, hence the venture being associated with his name, with James Hamilton in Glasgow, and John Richardson in Liverpool. Napier was intensely proud of his steamers, writing on 10 May 1822:

*"I can say with certainty that the **Superb** and **Majestic**, presently plying between Greenock and Liverpool, are far superior in every respect to the **Sovereign** and **Meteor**, and will out-sail them in any kind of weather; as a proof of this, the **Sovereign** was at Liverpool the other day and sailed along with the **Superb**, when the latter out-sailed the former fully one mile in five".*

In June 1822, Napier introduced

the **City of Glasgow**. She was launched at Scott's yard on 9 April 1822 with engines, as usual, by David Napier. She was 110' 4"x 22' 4", and her tonnage was variously calculated as between 191 and 300 tons; She had two cylinder 100 hp engines, and was capable of 10 knots, a remarkable speed at such an early date. In the days before modern companies, vessels were frequently owned by a consortium, and there were 21 owners of the **City of Glasgow** when delivered, the most significant being William Mills, David Napier and James Little. She was registered at Greenock on 28 May 1822, the registry being transferred to Glasgow in 1825, when her multi-partner ownership was cancelled and she became the property of the Glasgow & Liverpool Steam Packet Co.

Delivery of the **City of Glasgow** was timely, for the **PS St George** of the St George Steam Packet Co began sailing in opposition to the Little boats on the Liverpool-Douglas-Greenock station on 8 June. A period of racing ensued, and after modifications to her paddle wheels, the **St George** had the advantage. Napier and the St George Company then came to an understanding, with the St George people abandoning the Greenock route and sailing their vessel from Liverpool to Dublin and Bristol, and Napier agreeing not to compete on that route. Haining's Guide of 1822, which had been written prior to the **City of Glasgow** or the **St George** entering service, gave a summary of shipping services at the dawn of steam propulsion, the reference to steam vessels building at Liverpool including the **St George**, which was completed in 1822:

*"The intercourse with the surrounding kingdoms has been greatly facilitated lately, by means of the steam packets, and the trading vessels; the regular traders to Liverpool are - the **Duke of Atholl**, the **Duchess of Atholl**, and the **Douglas**. To Whitehaven – the **Triton**, and the Post-office Packet. To Dublin – the **Earl of Surrey**, and to Ardglass in the north of Ireland – the **Peel Packet**. During the last two summers we have had a great influx of visitors, computed about three thousand. Many come for pleasure, and a few to recruit their shattered constitutions. They circulate considerable sums of money, but have not*

improved the morals of the inhabitants.

*The steam packets are large, are elegantly fitted up, and generally make very expeditious passages. The **Superb** leaves Liverpool on Tuesdays, and the **Majestic** on Friday morning, call at the Isle of Man, Port Patrick, proceed to Greenock and return the same week. The **Highland Chieftain** plies between Liverpool and Dumfries, calling at Douglas, Whitehaven, Workington and Maryport. A vessel of a larger class, and of superior power is to be employed by the same company during the ensuing summer, which will afford a direct communication with the north of England and the Scottish capital. Two steam vessels are building at Liverpool, which are to run to Greenock, calling at Douglas, and the fares are to be greatly reduced."*

The 53 ton **Highland Chieftain** had been built by A McLachlan of Dumbarton in 1817 as the **Duke of Wellington**. She was 71' 4" x 14' 10" with a draft of 5' 5" and her engines from D McArthur & Co developed 16 hp. She was lengthened to 81' by William Denny in 1820, and her original engines replaced, doubling her power output. After a spell at Fort William, she came south and operated between Dumfries, Whitehaven, Douglas and Liverpool in 1821. She subsequently returned to the West Highlands. She was probably the oldest vessel to be employed on regular sailings to the Island. With at least four owners, she survived until 1838, a remarkable age for a pioneer steam ship.

In August 1822, the Liverpool shipping agent, John Richardson obtained the IOM mail contract for the **Majestic**, **Superb** and **City of Glasgow**, mail having previously been sent via the Whitehaven sailing packets. This necessitated an all year service, and from 6 November, a dedicated Douglas-Liverpool mail run was provided by the **Superb**, but this was so uneconomic that Douglas was made a call on the main Greenock route from 17 February 1823. **Superb** was disposed of in 1823, the other two boats maintaining the mail contract in summer until it was lost in 1827.

Lord Broughton left an account of a voyage in 1823:

The 350 ton **PS Majestic** of 1821 replaced the **Robert Bruce** of 1819, and cut the passage time between the Clyde and the Mersey from 28 to between 22 and 25 hours. With relatively slow speeds, passage times in those days could be markedly altered by a favourable tide or wind, allowing exceptionally fast or slow runs. My father found this sort of variation easy to believe, for as a young medical student, he used to cycle the 120 miles between Liverpool and Rugby, usually in around 12 hours, but depending on wind, it could vary from 9 to 15 hours. The **Majestic** was built by John Scott & Sons, and was 135' x 22' 8", and was provided with a two cylinder, 100 horse-power Napier engine and a copper boiler.

---

*"September 12, 1823. Left Lord Grosvenor's and went from Liverpool to Glasgow in the **Majestic** steamboat. Sept 13, within six miles of Greenock the pipes of one of the boilers burst, and our vessel stopped immediately. Had this happened last night we must either have made for Ramsay harbour, or have been lost. I cannot think, after all, that the steam-boats are or can be made secure in a heavy sea off a lee shore. They are very large for their depth. Watt had no idea that his invention could be applied to the sea, and Napier of Glasgow, who made the sea engines, was laughed at, at first. Now three steamboats leave Liverpool for Glasgow every week. The breeze carried us to Greenock just as the **Post Boy** steamboat came up to tow us. We encountered a great many steamboats full of passengers".*

There was fierce rivalry between the Scottish ship owners and the influential businessmen in Liverpool and Manchester, and a Manchester-backed service, known as the Merseyside & Clyde Steam Navigation Co, commenced Liverpool-Clyde sailings in 1823, with the

Henry Bell, and **James Watt**. At first these services did not call at the Island, but from 1824, regularly put in to Ramsey. The reason for selecting Ramsey was that whilst a Douglas call entailed a significant detour, calling at Ramsey involved very little additional mileage. Unlike the 1819 Little service, they carried passengers and goods. They sailed from Greenock, to which passengers and the mails were sent by river steamer on the morning of departure, with goods going down by lighter the previous evening. In October 1826, a new and better vessel, the **William Huskisson** entered service, the company often being referred to as "The Huskisson Co". thereafter. Unlike the previous vessels, she had been built on the Clyde by Scotts of Greenock, and was launched on 10 July 1826. She was 137' 10" x 23' 9" and of 227 tons, and was named after a leading politician of the day, who, tragically, was run down and killed on the opening day of the Liverpool & Manchester Railway in 1830. In 1831, she was transferred to G&J Burns, and was later switched to the Dublin-Liverpool route, sinking in January 1840. The indiscriminate contemporary use of official names, unofficial names and the names of the agents greatly complicates the history of this period, not least because local agents might represent more than one line. With the Napier boats only running in summer from 1824, the Merseyside boats conveyed the mail in winter for John Richardson.

The *City of Glasgow*, which had been built for the Little & Co's Glasgow-Liverpool run in 1822, and was regarded as outstanding at that time, suffered two misfortunes in 1825. The first was to her reputation. The *PS Ailsa Craig* of 1825, which had come from R & A Carsewell of Greenock, was engaged on the Glasgow-Belfast service, so was not in fact a rival, but both boats sailed down the Clyde. One day, the captain of the *City of Glasgow*, recalling the many victories of his ship, deliberately slowed down to give both craft a level start at the Cloch Light. Sadly, all this sporting gesture did was to reveal the inferiority of the older vessel, as the *Ailsa Craig* steadily pulled away until the two vessels separated, one heading for Ireland and the other for Liverpool. In October 1825, the *City of Glasgow* nearly met her end. After engine damage en route from Greenock she was undergoing repairs in Douglas bay, when she was driven ashore. At first regarded as a wreck, she was salvaged and taken to the Clyde for repairs, not resuming service until May 1826.

In the autumn of 1826, Mark Cosnahan, who apparently had homes on the Island and on Merseyside, formed the New National Steam Packet, placing the *PS Victory* on the Douglas-Liverpool route. His service ran until June 1827, during which time, he offered shares in it to the Manx people, but did not receive much backing. Two and a half years later, when a public meeting was held to discuss the formation of a shipping line, it was very different. Why was this so? Public resentment had not boiled over in 1827, as it was to before the end of the decade, which suggests that there was still general satisfaction as late as 1827. Secondly, although Cosnahan came from an old and highly respected Manx family, he

had been a brewer, then a farmer, then a brewer, and finally a grocer, and had gone bankrupt in the process. When a local man did that, it left a stain. In a small community, where the leading figures, whose financial support would be essential, all knew one another, that sort of background would be common knowledge, and was not calculated to win backers, unless there was serious discontent. How was it that the situation changed so dramatically and so quickly?

*In 1822, the **City of Glasgow**, was added. She could do the Douglas-Liverpool run in around nine hours. The **City of Glasgow**, 123' x 22', was 300 tons and 106 hp. It was on 24 July 1825 that the legendary race between the **City of Glasgow** and the brand new **PS Ailsa Craig** took place, with the older boat slowing down to wait for her rival off Cloch Point, just west of Gourock on the Clyde. Alas for this sporting gesture, the newer boat won convincingly, a clear indication of how quickly marine engineering was progressing, as the three-year-old boat had been a crack ship when new! From 1793 to 1828, John Murray, Duke of Atholl, was governor of the Isle of Man on behalf of the British government, and was a periodic passenger on the boats operated by James Little & Co. On one celebrated occasion, he arrived at Douglas with so much baggage, including carriages and furniture, that the boat was badly delayed whilst it was all unloaded, prompting vociferous complaints from through passengers to Liverpool.*

Napier and the Merseyside "Huskisson" people had done a good job, given the limitations of the technology at their disposal, and lack of

proper harbour facilities in Douglas, but all this was to change. The St George Company had competed with Napier in 1822, and then come to an agreement over spheres of influence. In April and May 1825, they returned to Manx waters, operating a thrice weekly service with the *Prince Llewellyn* and *St David*, the boats then returning to their usual Welsh haunts. Of all the early shipping companies, the St George group is the most confusing, as it was a loose confederation of allies, but often just the names of the agents and vessels appeared. In 1826 and 1827, the St George group ran a seasonal Liverpool-Douglas-Dublin service with the *PS Kingston*. She returned in 1827 with a Liverpool-Douglas route. By the autumn of 1827, Napier/Little boats were providing a seasonal service between Greenock and Liverpool, the Mersey & Clyde (Huskisson) boats were slower, but sailed all year, calling at Ramsey, but from August 1827, when Napier lost the mail contract to them, making a Douglas call as the mail boats, until August 1828. The St George boats were still seasonal from Liverpool, but in 1828, a new name, that has clouded the issue ever since, appeared on the Manx scene, "the St David Company". It was a part of the St George confederation, and placed the *St David* on the Douglas-Liverpool run that spring, securing the mail contract in August 1828. At first, highly thought of, as she was a dedicated Liverpool-Douglas boat, so entered Douglas harbour, unlike the Scottish sailings, the loose structure of the St George confederation meant that there was no suitable replacement ship, and with three weekly round trips in summer, she was "worked to death". Defects were patched up or ignored with dire effects on reliability. The first winter was not too bad, but at the end of the following summer, when reliability had suffered, she was belatedly taken off service for a long overdue overhaul in September 1829, and a small Mersey ferry, the *Abbey* utilised. She had been built by Charles

Grayson in 1822, for the Liverpool-Birkenhead ferry service, and was 76' 4" x 16' 10". Although she was adequate for a short ferry trip across the Mersey, her lack of covered accommodation meant she was hopeless for the IOM route, and even the return of the **St David** in late November did little to appease the Island. Months of unreliability, culminating with the deplorable **PS Abbey** had brought the Island to boiling point. Had the St George group operated as a more centralised venture, with replacement tonnage available, the **St David** could have been overhauled before she became unreliable and despised, and a totally unsuitable replacement would not have been needed.

In May 1830, by which time it was too late, as the company had done everything they could to make themselves hated and the **Mona's Isle** was almost ready for launching, the **Prince Llewellyn** relieved the **St David**, and in June the **St George** herself appeared briefly, before giving way to the **Sophia Jane**.

Meanwhile, another legendary name had appeared on the Manx shipping scene, and had events followed this course a year earlier, it might all have been very different. Two brothers, James and George Burns had entered into partnership as produce merchants in 1818. Travelling between Glasgow and the major Irish Sea ports, they soon became well known, and in 1824 became agents and partners in an existing sailing ship line. By 1828, they had a dozen sailing smacks, but the brothers saw that the future was in steam, and joined forces with rivals to found a new venture, known as J Martin and J&G Burns. The first sailing of the new steam service was by the **PS Glasgow**, of 280 tons and 250hp, which was one of no fewer than four paddle steamers built on the Clyde with the same name in 1828 ! The Burns vessel was built by Caird & Co of Greenock, and was their yard No 2. The inaugural sailing from the Clyde was on Friday 13 March 1829, but the first call at the Island was not until 30 April 1829. The **PS Ailsa Craig**, of 1825, 297 tons and 250hp, was added, followed by the **PS Liverpool**, 330 tons and 340hp some months later. Meanwhile the Whitehaven route had been resurrected. The *Manx Sun* for 10 August 1830 carries an advertisement placed by the Douglas agent, David Forbes, for the **St Andrew** of the Whitehaven Steam

Navigation Co, which:

"will arrive here from Whitehaven every Saturday for Dublin and return every Monday from Dublin for Whitehaven".

If the illustration that accompanied the advertisement was accurate, the **St Andrew** was a typical two-mast paddle steamer with the funnel abaft of the paddle box, and virtually no rake to it. She was under the command of Captain M Banks, and Professor D B McNeill records that the service had commenced in 1830, although the 90 ton Dumbarton-built **St Andrew** dated from 1826. Her first couple of years had been spent sailing between Belfast and the Clyde, interspersed with some of the first cruise ship activities in history, with a weekend cruise from Belfast to the Giant's Causeway in June 1826, and a more spectacular cruise from Glasgow to the Giant's Causeway, Iona, Staffa and Tobermory in 1827. The Whitehaven venture suffered from the competition that was building up in the Irish Sea. There was still a demand for a service to the Cumbrian coast, and for a time in the 1840s, some Dublin to Douglas sailings of the IOMSPCo **Mona's Isle** and **Ben-my-Chree** were extended to Whitehaven.

The same issue of the *Manx Sun* carried an advertisement by John Clark of the Steam Packet Office at the corner of the Parade in Douglas for David Napier's **Majestic** and **City of Glasgow**, which sailed from Douglas for Liverpool every Wednesday, Friday and Sunday morning, from 6.00am to 8.00am, and returned every Tuesday, Thursday and Saturday evening, sail-

THE MAJESTIC,
Captain OMAN,
AND
THE CITY OF GLASGOW,
Captain CARLYLE,

Sail from GREENOCK every MONDAY, WEDNESDAY, and FRIDAY, at One o'Clock in the Afternoon, and from LIVERPOOL, every MONDAY, WEDNESDAY, and FRIDAY, at Ten o'Clock in the Forenoon, calling off PORT PATRICK, and at DOUGLAS, ISLE OF MAN, both in going and returning from LIVERPOOL.

These Packets carry no Goods, being expressly fitted up for the comfort and accommodation of Passengers.

FARES.

For the First Cabin, including Provisions and Steward's Fees.				
	To Port Patrick.	To Isle of Man.	To Liverpool.	To Greenock
From GREENOCK,	£1 1 0	£1 10 6	£2 5 0	£0 0 0
PORT PATRICK,	0 0 0	1 1 0	1 11 0	1 1 0
ISLE OF MAN,	1 1 0	0 0 0	0 17 6	1 10 6
LIVERPOOL,	1 11 6	0 17 6	0 0 0	2 5 0

For the Second Cabin without Provisions.				
	To Port Patrick.	To Isle of Man.	To Liverpool.	To Greenock
From GREENOCK,	£0 10 0	£0 10 0	£0 10 0	£0 0 0
PORT PATRICK,	0 0 0	0 10 0	0 10 6	0 10 0
ISLE OF MAN,	0 10 0	0 0 0	0 9 6	0 10 0
LIVERPOOL,	0 10 6	0 9 6	0 0 0	0 10 6

Children under Twelve Years of Age Half Price.

ON DECK.

A COACH,	£4 15 0	A HORSE,	£2 10 0
A CHAISE,	4 0 0	Dogs, per couple,	0 10 0
A GIG,	2 10 0		

Parcels Forwarded to the Isle of Man and all Parts of England.

The Proprietors will not be accountable for the Delivery of any Parcel of the Value of Two Pounds and upwards, unless entered, and paid for accordingly.

Passengers are put on Board and landed at Greenock, Douglas, and Liverpool, free of expence. The Passage between Greenock and Liverpool is generally made within Twenty-five hours.

May 1, 1826.

JAMES LITTLE, Agent, Greenock.

*This advertisement from May 1826 for the **Majestic**, (which is illustrated), and for **City of Glasgow**, reveals the difficulty in unravelling ownership of these early steamers, as it lists the masters and the local agent, James Little of Greenock, but does not detail the owners. It relates to the boats put on by David Napier and managed by James Little as agents at Greenock.*

ing for Greenock, calling at Port Patrick, weather permitting:

"These superior and well known packets are expressly fitted up for the comfort and accommodation of passengers, carry no goods, and generally make a passage in 7 or 8 hours to and from Liverpool".

John Clark also advertised the Burns steamers.

"The safe commodious and

swift steam packets Ailsa Craig, Captain Carlyle, and Glasgow, Captain Hepburn, call regularly at Douglas and land and take on board passengers for Liverpool every Sunday and Thursday at high water, and from hence for Greenock and Glasgow every Sunday and Thursday morning, calling at Port Patrick. . . . These well known packets are of the first class, have superb accommodation for passengers and are propelled by 2 engines of 100 hp, make the passage in 8 hours and combining comfort and speed render them superior to any other packet on the station. . . . A new packet, called the Liverpool, of 160 hp will shortly join Ailsa Craig and Glasgow. They will then call three times a week, of which due notice will be given."

John Clark first inserted this advert in the *Manx Sun* on 17 May 1830. When she entered service, the **PS Liverpool** was under the command of another renowned master, Hugh Main. The differing horsepower figures quoted for these early steamers are a source of confusion and usually relate to nominal horsepower and indicated horsepower. Length and tonnage is also calculated in various ways, whilst the duplication of names in the early days poses further problems.

Thomas Sayle, of the Market Place, Ramsey, was agent for yet another vessel:

"The superior and fast sailing Steam Packet, Enterprise, Captain Crawford, will sail alternately at Ramsey every Wednesday morning for Liverpool, and every Saturday morning for Greenock. Captain Crawford is an experienced navigator, and nothing has been spared to render the said vessel as commodious as possible".

The **Enterprise** was a small steamer owned by the New Clyde Shipping Company, the Liverpool agent being David MacIver, a native of Greenock, and had started running in 1827, with the **Solway** chartered as well in 1827-28. In 1827-28 the weekly calls were at Ramsey, but in 1829, the **Enterprise** had visited Douglas, resuming its Ramsey calls the following year.

In May 1830, the Merseyside-owned **Henry Bell** under Captain Wilson, the **William Huskisson** under Captain Chaplain and the **James Watt**

James Burns, who was born in Glasgow in June 1789, so was a contemporary of John Woods and the Napiers, started as a produce merchant with his younger brother George in 1818, moving into sailing ships in 1824. In 1829, the brothers switched to steam, and achieved a commanding position on the Glasgow-Belfast route and also between Glasgow and Liverpool, calling at Douglas en route. A pioneer of Irish Sea shipping services, Burns decided to concentrate on their core routes when the Isle of Man Steam Packet was formed, and later worked with Samuel Cunard to serve Halifax, Boston and New York. A capable businessman, he was shrewd enough to realise that the Manx route was better served by a dedicated service, which would also speed up his Liverpool sailings when they were under threat from competition. He was married twice, leaving one son, and died on 6 September 1871.

under Capt Spiers, also known as the War Office Steam Packets, were listed as sailing regularly from Ramsey to Liverpool on the morning of every Wednesday, Friday and Sunday, and for Glasgow (rather than Greenock) every Tuesday, Friday and Saturday evening, calling at Port Patrick when the weather permitted. Josiah Heelis was the Ramsey agent, whilst Thomas McMeiken was the Douglas agent. Such was the rate of progress that they were now outclassed, and Glaswegians were convulsed with mirth when Captain Spiers of the Sassenach steamer, the **PS James Watt** reported to his owners that when he was en route to Glasgow, he had encountered the Burns steamer, **PS Ailsa Craig**, which had left Liverpool for Glasgow at about the same time as he had, on her way back south on her

next passage. A move to place the Manchester boats under Burns control collapsed due to dissentions amongst the Manchester owners. The "War Office" title did not mean the boats were owned by the War Office, but was inherited from the sailing packet era when government owned sailing packets had provided services, and a decision of 1815, when the Post Office were given powers to insist that steamers carry mails, and legislation in 1818 allowing the Admiralty to appoint half pay Naval officers to the command of mail boats as a way of reducing unemployment of naval officers. Apart from the **Henry Bell**, **William Huskisson** and **James Watt**, which were referred to in Josiah Heelis' advertisement as "War Office Steam Packets", the **PS Kingstown**, ran a Dublin-Douglas service under the title of "St George War Office Steam Packet" in 1826. Finally, although not related to the Isle of Man, the St George Company was locked in a battle with a company actually known as the War Office SPCo on the Dublin-Bristol route in the 1820s and 1830s. The St George Co eventually gave birth to the City of Cork SPCo, whilst the War Office SPCo became the Bristol Steam Navigation Co. Confusingly, the title St George War Office Steam Packet was used on the Bristol route for the St George owned **PS Severn**! The best way to translate this apparent anomaly would be 'a steam powered mail boat commanded by a half pay naval officer and owned by the St George Company'.

The profusion of vessels and routes that predated the Packet, with Dublin, Ardglass, Glasgow, Greenock, Port Patrick, Dumfries, Maryport, Whitehaven, Workington and Liverpool all served once or twice a week, indicates remarkable progress in the eighteen years since the **Comet** first took to the waters of the Clyde, and a greater variety of destinations than is possible today, even in summer, let alone in winter. Perhaps the ultimate paradox is that the journey between Ramsey and Port Patrick in May 1830 was easier and much quicker than it is today! Why, with this abundance, and considerable improvements in performance, was there such dissatisfaction on the Island? It has been customary to point to high fares, and to give quotes about crazy and rejected craft, and to assume that there was constant dissatisfaction on the Island from 1819 to 1830. This was far from the case, as the negligible support for

Prior to the invention of Edmonson card tickets, passengers travelling on the boats that plied between Greenock, Douglas and Liverpool were issued with brass tokens, Liverpool & Isle of Man and Greenock & Isle of Man options being known. They do not give an operator, but the engraving of the vessel and reference toGreenock on this token from the Alan Kelly collection confirms they relate to the pioneering period before the birth of the IOMSPCo. The closest match would seem to be David Napier's PS Majestic of 1821. Photo: Alan Kelly

The PS Liverpool, 137' 6" x 22', was launched by John Wood at Port Glasgow in June 1830, so was a near contemporary to the IOMSPCo Mona's Isle, which was slightly smaller at 116' x 19'. She was intended for the J&G Burns's Glasgow & Liverpool service, and was of 330 grt. She was transferred to Dublin in 1835 and to the Peninsula & Oriental Steam Navigation Co in 1842. She is seen in P&O ownership standing by a sailing ship off the coast of Portugal. She stranded off Tarifa in November 1845, and although refloated, was not worth repairing, so was broken up. It was a good job for the infant Steam Packet Co that J&G Burns decided to concentrate on their core traffic between Glasgow and Liverpool, and that the PS Liverpool, which was in every respect the equal of the Mona's Isle, and strikingly similar in appearance, was not deployed against the Manx company, for that would have been a far different contest compared to the St George. James Burns would have seen the Steam Packet boat under construction at the same time as his own vessel, and must have realised that competing for the Manx traffic would be a tough fight for very little benefit, so it suited both companies to leave the other well alone. It is notable that the Steam Packet did not make any serious effort to open up a Scottish service until after railway competition had persuaded Burns to abandon the Glasgow-Liverpool service in 1856. It may well be that there was a tacit understanding not to poach in one another's preserves.

Cosnahan in 1826-27 demonstrates. The Scottish boats, put on by David Napier and Little from 1819 onwards offered a summer service, with the slower Lancashire-owned Huskisson boats providing all-year facilities. These early steamers were very costly to operate, and were only viable on the busiest routes, and Douglas was either tagged on to a more important route, or would not have been served at all, as the attempt to run the **PS Superb** as a Liverpool-Douglas steamer in 1822-23 revealed. Had Burns entered the fray early in 1828 rather than 1829, they might have picked up the mail contract from the Liverpool boats, and as a well run company with new vessels, would have provided a satisfactory service. Instead, the Post Office decision to award the mail

contract to the **St David**, as a dedicated Liverpool-Douglas vessel, was initially a success, but the chaotic nature of the St George group meant that no adequate cover was available. Mismanagement led to unreliability due to lack of maintenance, and a

well-run rival was sure of support. Because it was local, many Manx people would pay higher fares to the Mona's Isle Company to get back at the St George group, and in winter that meant it was anything but a level playing field.

Many years ago my father was sent a photo from Australia of a painting of the PS Sophia Jane. After her exploits in Manx waters for the St George Steam Packet, she was sold to Edward Biddulph in 1830, and sailed to Australia on a speculative venture. Although most of the voyage was under sail, she was the first steamship to arrive in Australian waters, so earned a special niche in maritime history. She was 256 gross tons and was a wooden hulled paddle steamer, 120' 3" x 20' 1" x 10' 3", with 50 hp side lever engines and had been built in 1826 by Barnes & Miller at Rotherhithe. She arrived at Sydney on 13 May 1831, and began sailing on the Hunter River in New South Wales. Biddulph sold shares in her to local people, but in November 1833, she was bought by J H Grose. By 1839, she was owned by J T Wilson, who got into debt and fled. She was sold to General Steam Navigation Co of Sydney in 1840, sailing on the Illawarra River. She was broken up c1845. In the understandable absence of photographs of vessels of this date, we have to rely on paintings, but as commented elsewhere in this book, the artist has placed the funnel too far forward, as it is almost in line with the crankshaft, which turns the paddle wheels. The chimney was probably much closer to the main mast, but the artist has either got his perspective wrong, or moved it forward as it looks more aesthetically pleasing in this position!

The circumstances behind the birth of "The Mona's Isle Company" as the Isle of Man Steam Packet Co was known until 1832, have been recounted many times. To an island community that was moving out of the isolation that had gripped it since the dawn of history, adequate shipping services had become the overriding issue. A sailing packet service had commenced in 1767 two years after the Act of Revestment, but in winter, days or weeks could pass when the island was lashed with storms, and no sailings were possible. The first of the new fangled steamboats had visited the Island in 1815, just three years after Henry Bell's diminutive paddle steamer, the **PS Comet**, had taken to the waters of the Clyde. Steamer services to and from the Island commenced in 1819, but delight at being on a steamer route had given way to frustration at the poor service provided by St David Company, which was an offshoot of the St George's Steam Packet in 1828-29. Because of the disjointed structure of the St George's group, only one vessel, the **St David** was available, and it ran month after month without proper repairs. Unreliability in the summer of 1829 was followed by a two month absence for major repairs, during which time a totally inadequate replacement was provided, and local resentment towards the St David company, which had been mounting, boiled over.

On 17 December 1829, a meeting took place at Dixon & Steele's sales rooms, which then occupied a part of the site later acquired by the Steam Packet. James Quirk, High Bailiff of Douglas presided. £4,500 was subscribed on the day, which was over half of what was needed, a remarkable start. Amongst those present were Edward Gawne of Kentraugh, G Geneste, James Moore of Cronkbourne, Dr Philip Garrett, Lewis Crebbin, W Quiggin, J Wulff, and Edward Forbes, Captain Banks of Balnahow (Howstrake), and a "W Wood (shipbuilder, Glasgow)". As there does not seem to have been any member of the shipbuilding family

with the initial W, it must have been John Wood himself who attended that meeting. Of all the people present that day, John Wood (1788-1860) was the most important, for it was his professional skill that was to set the seal of success of the new venture, yet accounts of the Steam Packet say little of this remarkable man. John Wood is renowned as the builder of the **Comet**, which was the first commercially successful steam ship in the British Isles. It was with Wood's father that Henry Bell had placed the contract, but the yard at Port Glasgow was taken over by his sons, John and Charles, after their father's death in 1811. Port Glasgow is on the south bank of the Clyde, a short distance up river from Greenock. John Wood's parents were John Wood (the elder) and Elizabeth Household who were married at Port Glasgow on 28 January 1786. They had two sons, John who was born on 10 October

John Wood (1788-1860) inherited his father's shipyard, and took the building of wooden hulled ships to new levels of excellence. He was shrewd enough to leave engine design to his friends, David Napier, and subsequently to Robert Napier, and concentrate on what he could do brilliantly. Until the age of the iron hulled ship, which was not something that Wood really cared about, the combination of Napier and Wood was without equal anywhere in the world.

1788, and Charles who arrived on 27 March 1790. A painstaking man, John Wood was renowned for building sound vessels, often referred to as "Wood's yachts" on account of their fine workmanship. John Scott Russell, one of the leading Victorian naval architects said of Wood that he was "a consummate artist in shipbuilding".

During his visits to the Island in conjunction with the **Mona's Isle**, John Wood must have met John James Kayll, a master brewer and maltster, with premises in Wellington St/Castle St in Douglas. Kayll, who had been born in Douglas on 14 January 1787, a year and a half earlier than Wood, may well have attended the 1829 meeting, as he was a substantial businessman in town, and was married to a Scots lass, Isabella McClure, of Kirkcudbright in Marown on 20 April 1807. Kayll had strong personal and business reasons for being interested in good communications with the outside world. His own father, James Kayll, had been born in Paisley in 1752, and had been brought to the island as a child by his father, so John James Kayll's family had originated not far from where John Wood was born. Wood soon became friends with the Kayll family. Although a brewer, so in regular contact with the innkeepers, J J Kayll does not seem to have run an inn or hotel directly, nor does the family name appear in any lists I have seen of boarding houses. However, a number of inhabitants did offer private rooms to visitors, which would be superior to the hotels. It may be that John Wood stayed with the Kayll family as a paying visitor to begin with. If so, it was a momentous decision, and their common Scots background probably made for a friendly atmosphere. Before long, the Scots ship builder had more interest in the island than just the ship he was building, for he had met Kayll's second, but oldest surviving daughter, Isabella Kerr Kayll, who had been born in Braddan parish, which included much of Douglas, on 10 April 1809. Despite the twenty year gap in their ages, John and Isabella must have become very fond of one another, for just over a year after the **Mona's Isle**

If Napier and Wood guaranteed the technical success of the Packet, it was the integrity and acumen of Edward James Moore, the company's first Douglas agent that guaranteed its commercial success. He had been born in 1800, his parents being Edward Moore (1762-1835), and Elizabeth Beck of Whitehaven (1762-1834). He became secretary of the Mona's Isle Company on its foundation in 1830, and held that post until his death in 1865, when he was buried at Braddan. By then the fleet had grown from a single steamer in 1830 to five vessels at the time of his death, three of them less than five years old. His father, Edward Moore, and James Moore of Cronkbourne Mills, who was one of the founder members at the 1829 meeting, were brothers. Apart from being associated with the mills, they had also acted as bankers from c1804, to facilitate their Linen manufactory, as there was a shortage of currency on the Island at the time. When forged Five Shilling notes were discovered in circulation, the brothers offered to redeem them if surrendered by holders who could prove they had accepted them in good faith. It was a testimony to their integrity. James Moore's son, William Fine Moore (1814-1895) was Edward Moore's first cousin. The company's first historian was, of course, A W Moore (1853-1909), who was Edward Moore's second cousin, and also served as a director, indicating the close connection between the Moore family and the Steam Packet during its first eighty years. The Hughes-Games family, one of whose members was Chairman of the Steam Packet in the 1920s, was related by marriage to the Moore family.

It was the technical brilliance of Robert Napier, 1791-1876, that provided the engineering foundations for the Isle of Man Steam Packet Co and Cunard Line, and made Glasgow the ship building capital of the world for generations. Although foreign governments honoured Napier for his services to ship building, his own government disgraced its own honours system by showering rewards on lesser mortals, whilst ignoring Napier and Wood. Robert Napier stands by his beloved Isabella at Shandon, their magnificent home.

entered service, the 22-year old Isabella, by now engaged to be married, travelled to Port Glasgow to meet her prospective in-laws. Fate now played a cruel hand, for Isabella contracted a fever, dying on 5 November 1831. John Wood was devastated, and requested permission to bury her in the Wood family plot near his father, where he could tend both graves, which he did for the rest of his life, never marrying after the death of his sweetheart. Back on the Island,

Isabella's mother, although she was now 44 years old, was expecting another child, and when the little girl was born on 18 November 1831, they named her Isabella Wood Kayll in memory of their departed daughter and of her fiancé. They must have thought quite a lot of him. John Wood outlived his fiancée by almost thirty years, dying on 22 December 1860, aged 72, and his coffin was carried by some of his carpenters. They were dressed in clothing that John Wood supplied to his workmen for church on Sundays, viz blue cloth suits with brass buttons and cloth caps, but with white kid gloves in tribute to their chief on this sad occasion. He was laid to rest in Newark Parish Church in Port Glasgow beside his father and Isabella. For many years, details of Wood's love affair were lost, and when the story resurfaced, his fiancée became "Elisabeth Kyall." In 1912, to mark the centenary of the **Comet**, a service was held at the church, at the conclusion of which, his great niece

Edward Moore was a meticulous man, his precise signature usually in the form Edw Moore, but occasionally giving Edward in full, graced most Steam Packet documents until his death in 1865. He married Elizabeth Greaves of Bakewell in 1826, but sadly she died in 1833. He remarried in 1834, his second wife being Susannah Lucas of Knockrushen. The couple had four children prior to Susannah's death in 1844. It is a sobering reflection on the life expectancy of the day that out of the three people responsible for the success of the Packet, John Wood, Robert Napier and Edward Moore, that Wood lost his fiancée when she was aged 22, and Moore lost his first and second wives within eleven years of one another. Only Napier was to enjoy a lifelong partnership.

placed a laurel wreath bound with purple silk on the graves of her uncle John and his fiancée.

Important though Wood was to the infant company, he was to introduce an even more significant character. Robert Napier, who has often been described as 'the father of Clyde shipbuilding' was three years younger than Wood, and was first cousin to David Napier, whom we have already met. He was born on 18 June 1791, to James Napier (1763-1848) and Jean Ewing (1761-1846), at Walker's Close, High Street Dumbarton. His father was from an established Dumbarton family of engineers, blacksmiths and mill-wrights, and was in partnership with his brother John. Robert was sent to the Burgh School and his father had hoped he would enter the ministry of the Church of Scotland, but the boy's interests lay in the family business. At sixteen Robert became apprenticed to his father. His five-year apprenticeship completed, he worked in Dumbarton for a while and also for Robert Stevenson, the founder of the great dynasty of lighthouse builders. In 1815 he went into business on his own, and on 22 December 1818 Robert married his cousin Isabella, daughter of John Napier (and David's sister) and moved to a house in Weaver Street near Glasgow Cathedral. She had been born in Dumbarton on 28 March 1793, so was two years younger than Robert. He produced pipes for a Glasgow waterworks and a 12 h.p. steam engine for a Dundee mill. In 1823, he built a 33 h.p. side lever steam engine for the Paddle steamer **Leven**, for the Dumbarton ship-builder and ship owner James Lang. It was so good that it was later fitted to another ship, **Queen of Beauty** and finally presented to Dumbarton by Napier's heirs. It survives to this day. John Wood soon recognised Robert Napier's expertise, and the two men worked together closely for many years. Apart from the inaugural ship for the newly formed Mona's Isle Company, the Isle of Man Steam Packet title not emerging until 1832, Napier and Wood supplied an armed paddle-sloop **Berenice** to the prestigious East India Company, Napier building the engines, with the hull sub-contracted to John Wood at Port Glasgow. In 1838, Napier and Wood advised Samuel Cunard on establishing the line that was to bear his name, and Napier helped in raising finance as well. As Wood, who was a maestro with timber construction, was not attracted to building the iron ships required by the early 1840's, Napier established his own yard at Govan on the south bank of the Clyde in 1841. In the 1850s, Napier built a magnificent mansion at West Shandon, on the Gareloch. Throughout his life, Napier retained many of the Regency customs

Dr Philip Garrett was another of the founding directors of the Steam Packet, an unusual case of a medical man being involved in a commercial enterprise. There was a connection through marriage between the Kayll and Garrett families. Given Dr Garrett's significant role in the formation of the Packet, I wonder if he had introduced John Wood to John James Kayll? After his death, some of his shares in the Steam Packet were held by his son Philip Lewis Garrett.

of his childhood, including the celebrated Shandon salute, which was a kiss on the cheek for all female visitors to the mansion. That even included Princess Louise, a daughter of Queen Victoria who was married to the Marquess of Lorne, later the Duke of Argyll. No offence was taken, for none was meant. Isabella Napier, his beloved cousin and wife, whom he had known since they were both children, died in 1875, after 57 years of marriage, and Robert Napier was grief stricken, losing the will to live. A serious illness followed her death, which is not uncommon with the surviving partner after a lifetime together, and Napier died on 23 June 1876. He was buried at the family plot in Dumbarton, and as the funeral procession made its way from Shandon to the town, ships in the Clyde flew their flags at half mast, church bells tolled, and fourteen hundred of Napier's employees marched behind the coffin for the last mile. Nowadays, it is fashionable to characterise nineteenth century business leaders as inhuman

*Edward Gawne, a wealthy land owner in the south of the Island, was highly respected, and a measure of that confidence is that he was one of the founding directors and also one of the trustees in whose names the **Mona's Isle** and other ships bought by the Steam Packet were registered up to his death in October 1837. Unlike many contemporary one-man banks, which over-extended and collapsed, his "Mount Gawne" bank only ceased business on his death, settling its debts in full.*

autocrats. The lives of Napier and Wood, the respect accorded to them by their workforce, and their devotion to the two women who entered their lives, one for such a short spell, show it was not so. Would a thousand workers follow the coffin of some of the tycoons or bankers of today to the churchyard? Somehow I doubt it. Napier was not present at the December 1829 meeting, but given the brief interval between the meeting and the launch of the **Mona's Isle** in June 1830, it is certain that preliminary discussions must have taken place long before the public meeting, and that Napier must have been involved from an early date.

What about some of the other people present on that December day? As I delved into the records, I found how closely linked by family, by marriage and by business, the founders of the Steam Packet were. It is a remarkable tale that has been obscured by the passage of the years. James Quirk, who presided, was High Bailiff of Douglas from 1820 to 1841, and in his official role, was well placed to summon a meeting and to interest the powerful and influential of the Island. That he had certainly done, as the attendance list revealed. One of the original directors was Dr Philip Garrett, who was present at the 1829 meeting. Garrett had been born c1786, and had married Helen Miller at St George's church on 15 January 1807. In 1811, he was listed as a surgeon and apothecary in Douglas, the name then being spelled Garrat. By 1823, it had changed to Garrett, and he was in Gt. George St. By 1841 he had moved to Athol St, and was living with his wife Helen and their three surviving children, Charlotte, born c1815, Helena Margaret, christened 17 November 1816, and Philip Lewis, christened 18 April 1824. A daughter, Isabella Jane, had died aged eleven months in 1819. Dr Garrett died on 26 June 1845, and was buried at Braddan on 2 July 1845, aged 59. His son, Philip Lewis, a dentist, inherited some shares in the Steam Packet. As J J Kayll's cousin, Isabella Kayll, was married to John Garrett of Peel, the two families may have been related by marriage, and Garrett may have introduced John Wood to the family.

Edward Gawne of Kentraugh had been born c1772, and had married Catherine Moore at Braddan on 9 July 1801. A brewer and landed proprietor, Edward Gawne had also become a banker in the early 1800s, with card money in circulation as early as 1805. He acquired Kentraugh House in the 1820s. It was one of the finest houses on the Island, and still survives. It is a remarkable structure in freestone from Mostyn, Denbighshire, fronted by a colonnade some ninety feet in length supported by eight massive Ionic columns. He was another of the original directors of the company. Edward Gawne passed away on 4 October 1837, the house going to his son, Edward Moore Gawne, who with 130 shares, was the largest proprietor in the Steam Packet in the 1850s. Just as his father had backed the Steam Packet, to provide external communications, E M Gawne put no less than £400 into the fledgling Isle of Man Railway to transform land communications on the Island when the railway was built at the start of the 1870s. Because Manx law at that time did not permit a normal joint stock company, as in England, the vessels had to be vested in trustees, and a policy of separation of directors and trustees evolved at the time of the 1838 deed of Association, so E M Gawne was a trustee but not a director. He was phenomenally wealthy by the standards of the day, and on his death at Kentraugh on 8 February 1872, left a life interest in Kentraugh to his wife, with a pension of £1000 per annum, equal to perhaps quarter of a million pounds today! Apart from several properties in the south of the Island, and generous bequests to the poor and to servants, family legacies totalled over £50,000, which indicates an estate which in modern terms would exceed £15m excluding the properties!

Apart from E M Gawne, the other trustee appointed in 1838 was John Anderson. He had been christened at Braddan to William Anderson and Mary Callister on 2 January 1796, and married Sophia Thomas, the daughter of Dr James Thomas RN and Ann Cosnahan. His wife was distantly related to Mark Cosnahan, who had "set the ball rolling", so far as Manx ownership of a steamer was concerned, when he acquired a paddle steamer called **Victory** in 1826 and operated her along with another steamer, the **Harriet** until 1827. Cosnahan had offered shares in his venture to the public in November 1826, but there was not sufficient support. The Andersons were living in Douglas at the start of the 1830s, where their son, William James Anderson was christened on 17

August 1831, but before their daughter Sophia Ellen was born in 1838, they had moved to Kirk Michael. Sadly John Anderson died in 1843, his shares in the Steam Packet passing to his widow Sophia, and to his son William, who became a Lt-Colonel, and Receiver-General of the Isle of Man. The couple's other children included a son James and a daughter Louisa. Sophia Anderson died at Patrick in 1870, ending a 40 year association with the Packet.

As with the name, LaMothe, the name Geneste was of French origin, and Louis de Geneste forfeited his estates in Guienne as a Huguenot, during the wars of religious persecution in France. He joined William of Orange in 1686, who became King William III of England in 1688. Geneste was with him at the battle of the Boyne in 1690. He settled at Lisburn outside Belfast, but lived in the Isle of Man from 1724 to 1731, establishing a Manx connection that endured for over a century. George Geneste was a great grandson of old Louis, and was to publish *Statute Laws of the Isle of Man* in 1832, but was to pass away two years later in his mid twenties. The name Louis, sometimes spelled Lewis, was passed down for several generations in the Geneste family, and it is a measure of the tight ramifications of Manx society that the Geneste family were to marry into another powerful Manx clan, the Howards. Louis Geneste Howard was to marry George W Dumbell's sister. Dumbell was the chairman of the Laxey Mines, and creator of the bank that was to bear his name. Although I have found no evidence that G W Dumbell was present at the 1829 meeting, he could have been, for he would have been 25 years old at the time. Within a few years, he was one of twenty-two investors to hold 20 or more shares in the Steam Packet.

James Moore of Cronkbourne was another prominent Manxman, and was related to Edward Gawne's wife, Catherine Moore. Owning Moore's Tromode works, James was the leading industrialist on the Island at the time. A nautical connection existed, as it was an important sailcloth manufactory. James Moore married Elizabeth Jeale, and their youngest son, William Fine Moore, (1814-1895) was too young to have attended the 1829 meeting, but after his father's death in 1846, he took over the family business, and was

(turn to page 36)

William Fine Moore, who was born on 7 July 1814, and died on 29 May 1895, was the son of James Moore, (1772-1846), one of the founders of the Steam Packet, and Elizabeth Jeal (1775-1851) of Kent, who had Manx connections in her own right, being the daughter of Dorothy Wattleworth. His middle name, Fine, came from his grandmother, Elizabeth Moore, nee Fine, of Ballahot, Malew, who married Edward Moore (1734-1810) in 1757. The youngest of seven sons, he purchased Cronkbourne Estate and the mills from his eldest brother, Archdeacon Joseph Moore. He was an MHK from 1858 to 1875, and was appointed as a director of the Steam Packet in the 1850s.

William Fine Moore was also one of the largest investors in the Packet. In 1862, some of the shares that had been held by John Wulff, the banker who was present at the inaugural meeting, came into his hands by way of George W Dumbell. A deeply pious man, the provisions in the 1838 deed prohibiting Sunday sailings, although such voyages had been common with other companies just a few years previously, would have received his endorsement. This, and the use of fines on shareholders, should they refuse to chair a meeting, for the benefit of sick and poor servants of the company, have a close counterpart in the "Rules and Regulations for Government of Tromode Manufactory" which was owned by W F Moore, who adopted the same paternalistic father-figure role to his employees that other noted Victorian employer-reformers pursued.

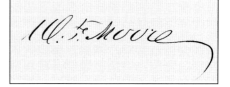

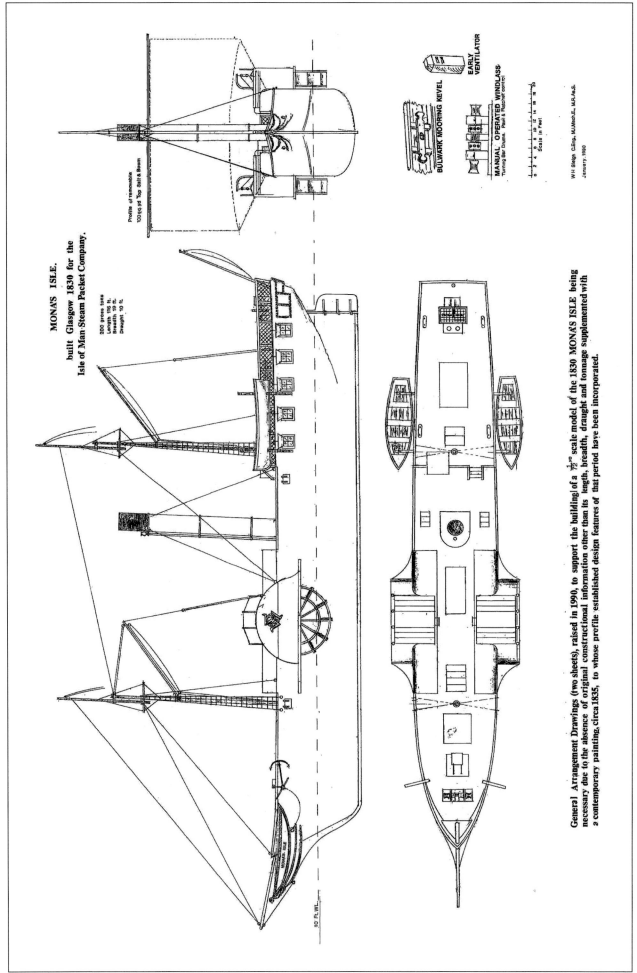

MONA'S ISLE,

built Glasgow 1830 for the
Isle of Man Steam Packet Company.

200 gross tons
Length 116 ft.
Breadth 19 ft.
Draught 10 ft.

Profile of removable
100 sq-yd Top Sail & Boom

BULWARK MOORING KEVEL

EARLY
VENTILATOR

MANUAL OPERATED WINDLASS·
'Turning Bar Drums. Pawl & Ratchet control'

0 2 4 6 8 10 12 14 16 18 20
Scale in Feet

W H Sleigh C.Eng., M.I.Mar.E., M.R.I.N.A.
January 1990.

10 Ft.WL.

MONA'S ISLE

General Arrangement Drawings (two sheets), raised in 1990, to support the building of a $\frac{1}{72}$"° scale model of the 1830 MONA'S ISLE being necessary due to the absence of original constructional information other than its length, breadth, draught and tonnage supplemented with a contemporary painting, circa 1835, to whose profile established design features of that period have been incorporated.

No known drawings have survived of the **Mona's Isle,** *so W H Sleigh set out to rectify that deficiency with GA drawings that conform to the known dimensions and then follow contemporary engineering practice. Unless the original GA drawings should turn up, it is the closest we will ever get to this momentous vessel.*

34

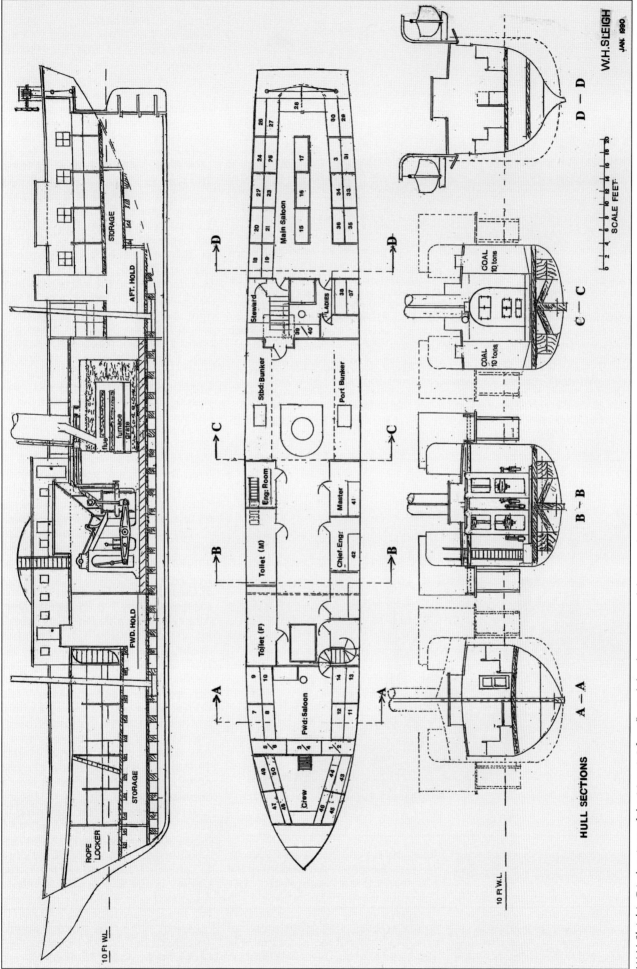

HULL SECTIONS   A — A   B — B   C — C   D — D

W.H. SLEIGH

JAN. 1990

SCALE FEET

*W H Sleigh's GA drawings of the **Mona's Isle** reflected the dimensions of the vessel available at that time. They represented the vessel's characteristics and, as closely as possible, indicated the advances she offered in marine travel in relative comfort.*

*The 1/72 scale model of the **Mona's Isle** of 1830 produced by Mr W H Sleigh gives us the chance to study what this important vessel in the history of the Island and of steam navigation was like, and is a fitting tribute to the Manxmen who had the courage to put their money into a venture that was for the good of their homeland and to the two brilliant Scottish engineers whose professional skills created a remarkable ship.*

W Sleigh

*This elevated view of William Sleigh's magnificent model of the **Mona's Isle** shows the deck houses that would provide illumination and ventilation to the below deck saloons, the way in which the lifeboats must have been secured, and the extended paddle box structures with their cabins and toilets. The precise details must remain conjectural, but known practice on other early vessels and basic engineering principles mean that they must have followed the general arrangement of the model.*

Richard Sleigh

(from page 84)

responsible for the terraced model village at Cronkbourne, which was unique to the Island. He was associated with the Isle of Man Banking Company Ltd, the Isle of Man Telegraph Co and the Steam Packet. In 1851, W F Moore, who held 40 of the £25 shares in the Steam Packet, was one of the five leading shareholders in the company, and also a director. A W Moore, (1853-1909) who wrote an excellent history of the Steam Packet in 1904, and who also became a director,

was his son. To add to the tangle of family relationships, Captain Anderson's daughter married into the Moore family, so that the Moore, Gawne, Anderson, Thomas and Cosnahan families were all distantly related. To raise finance, bankers were obviously going to be important, and the report of the meeting noted the attendance of John Wulff and Edward Forbes. They had formed the Isle of Man Bank (Wulff & Forbes) in 1826. This was not a predecessor to the later Isle of Man Banking Co Ltd, but a partnership between the two men. It operated successfully from 1826 to 1833, but over-extended and from 1833 was in difficulties, but continued in business until 1836, when the business was transferred to the Isle of Man Joint Stock Banking Co, which was formed with a nominal capital of £50,000. Edward Forbes became manager, whilst John Wulff was one of the directors. Edward Forbes was married to Jane Teare of Corvalla, Ballaugh, and lived at Thornton Lodge, which was near Belmont, the house built by G W Dumbell in the 1830s, and which is on the Peel Road, whilst John Wulff lived at Ballaughton, an elegant mansion that was later owned by Dumbell as well. The company remained in business until 1843, by which time John Wulff had passed away. Wulff's executor was none other than G W Dumbell.

Conscious of the hatred that had been generated towards them in the autumn of 1829, the St George Company had replaced the discredited **St David** by the **St George** in 1830 and subsequently by the **PS Sophia Jane**. Although the **Sophia Jane** was, in reality, an excellent ship with a first class master, it was a case of "too little, too late". With sound technical expertise on the Clyde and good financial support from the Island, the Mona's Isle Company got off to a good start, and had the backing of the insular press. The *Manx Sun* eulogised the **Mona's Isle**, when on the morning of Tuesday 17 August 1830, she made her first passage to Liverpool. Her rival, the **PS Sophia Jane** of the St George's Company, was under the command of Captain Tudor, RN. The "Sun" paid tribute to Tudor, as "a good sailor and a polished gentleman", but those kindly sentiments did not extend to the owners of the **Sophia Jane**, or those associated with them. Any misfortune that befell them was a cause for public rejoicing, and on the day that **Sophia Jane** faced her rival at Douglas, slapstick comedy was to triumph.

Within a few months of the **Mona's Isle** arriving, the proprietors of the Mona's Isle Company were delighted with their purchase, and thoughts had turned to a second slightly smaller and cheaper boat for the winter service. Once again, John Wood and Robert Napier were to supply the new vessel, but as ideas were thrashed out during 1831, I have no doubts that the two people who were the most excited were John Wood and Isabella Kayll, as the need to discuss the new boat would have provided a splendid excuse for John to travel to the Island frequently. Their courtship must have been going well, and as Isabella's parents clearly approved, the couple must have seen a bright future. Isabella arranged to travel to Port Glasgow to meet his family, which is when tragedy struck, and she took ill and died. John launched the **Mona** on 27 July 1832, but I suspect the excitement of 1830-31, when everything seemed so bright, had crumbled away on a terrible November day in Port Glasgow. **Mona** was faster than the **Mona's Isle**, but at 98 feet, was very small and was sold in 1841, becoming a tug.

'An unpleasant catastrophe occurred while the **Sophia Jane** was getting ready for sea, by the falling overboard of her agent, Mr Corlett. Fortunately he was not much hurt. We may be however allowed to consider it as an auspicious omen".

Mr Corlett probably saw it in a very different light! Napier's role in creating an outstanding vessel was recognised, and at a celebration dinner held at Dixon's on Saturday 21 August 1830, there was fulsome praise for Napier, and round condemnation for the opposition. The *Manx Sun* reported the event:

"We take much pleasure in recording this dinner, as the occasion is one which will form a memorable era in the history of Manx independence. It comprises a well merited tribute to the builder, who has turned out our Island steamer which may be considered as the brightest star amongst the numerous steamers that traverse the Irish Channel. In structure, as a sea boat, in machinery to propel her, and in accommodation, she floats in proud and triumphant rivalage. It is the superior ingenuity and science of Glasgow, crowned with the laurel of victory, over

In 1833, the directors of the Isle of Man Steam Packet, as the company had now become, returned to John Wood and Robert Napier for their third steamer, **Queen of the Isle**. She was launched on 3 May 1834. At 128 feet, she was twelve feet longer than the **Mona's Isle**, and her 350hp engine produced the same power as her two predecessors combined! She arrived in Douglas on 10 September 1834, and Captain Gill took command, establishing a tradition whereby the senior master took the largest and most prestigious ship. Edward Quayle now commanded the **Mona's Isle** and John Kermode had the **Mona**. No doubt, John Wood had occasion to visit the Island. Although there is no evidence to confirm it, I would be very surprised if he did not visit his friends John and Isabella Kayll, and meet little Isabella Wood Kayll who would be almost three years old. She was the last of their thirteen children, ten of whom were daughters. The oldest girl, Mary Booth Kayll, who had been born in 1808, had died a month after John's fiancée, Isabella Kerr Kayll, had been born in 1809, so she had been the oldest surviving girl when he met the family. Four of her sisters were to live into the 1880s or beyond. How he must have wished that he could have brought his Isabella with him to see her parents and siblings.

*Although the engraver has positioned the funnel too far forward and between the paddle boxes, which would place it in line with the crankshaft driving the paddle wheels, and omitted the ship's boats, this vignette of the **King Orry** offers much of interest. The funnel should be aft of the paddle boxes, whilst the cabin structure should also extend aft. Interestingly, she is flying the "White Ensign" rather than the Red Ensign. Until 1864, all three flags, the red, white and blue were flown by the Royal Navy, the colour of the ensign being determined by the seniority of the Admiral commanding the squadron, but in that year, the White Ensign was reserved for the use of the Royal Navy, the Red Ensign for the merchant service, and the Blue Ensign for the Naval reserve. This view of 1842 predates the 1864 Act by many years. When the wind was favourable early steamers did hoist sails, partly to steady the ship, but also to take advantage of a free source of energy. The **King Orry** was rigged as a topsail schooner, with a mixture of square rigged and fore and aft sails. The master has set a flying jib at the bow, but the outer and inner jib sails have not been set. The foretopsail has been set, but the fore sail below it, and the fore topgallant sail above it are both furled. The main mast is not square rigged, and providing square sails here would run a serious risk of fire from cinders ejected from the funnel. Instead the mast is provided with booms for the lower and upper Spankers, both of which have been set. The engraving also depicts the figurehead at the bow, of King Orry himself.*

Liverpool, whose best steamers will vainly pant in her rear to accompany her.

Another strong and noble feature was developed at this dinner; and that is, the united and permanent spirit which every one felt to establish the independence of the Island, against the usurpation of a gang of strangers and adventurers who have long assumed, as their exclusive right, to convey the Island mail and passengers at their own extravagant prices in any of their crazy and rejected craft; and in addition to treat the inhabitants with contumely.

Mr Napier's health was given, and he replied and testified his zeal and good wishes by declaring his readiness to subscribe £100 towards a fund to preserve the proprietors from any additional loss arising from the opposition to which they are now exposed.

It is well known that the primary object of building the Island steamer, was the honourable and patriotic desire to benefit the interest of the inhabitants of every class. Let therefore, the inhabitants of every class unite to support the honourable intentions of the proprietors. Let them find the vessel, but whatever may be required to support the loss to which they may be exposed by the St David's Co, let the contributions of the inhabitant supply."

The reference to the St David's Co, rather than the parent St George's Steam Packet was a hangover from 1828-29 when the St David arm of the larger organisation mismanaged its service to the Island, and converted initial approval into hatred. Those sentiments were prompted by the news that fares on the **Sophia Jane** had been slashed on the very first day of competition to 5/- (25p) cabin, and 3/- (15p) steerage, as against the initial fares charged by the **Mona's Isle** of 10/- and 5/- respectively. Hopes that the superior accommodation and Manx nature of the vessel would counter the cheaper fares soon faded, and the Mona's Isle Company had to match the St George Company until the latter offered a frantic 6d (2.5p) fare, which the local company decided not to emulate. With the **Sophia Jane** outclassed, the St George's Company struck back, drafting in their crack steamer, the **St George**, but wisely placing it under the command of the popular Lt Tudor, RN. (In the Royal Navy, an officer is accorded the honorary title of Captain if in command of a ship, regardless of his substantive naval rank, so Tudor was Captain of the **St George** but a lieutenant on the Navy list. This was not uncommon, and no reflection upon Tudor's abilities, for the Navy List had become bloated during the French Wars with thousands of lieutenants spending decades in that rank. With military duty unlikely, civilian work was their best chance. On 20 November 1830, the two vessels arrived from Liverpool, and Captain Gill of the **Mona's Isle**, correctly predicting a south-easterly gale, put to sea as soon as he had discharged his passengers and cargo, to give himself sea room. Lt Tudor opted to anchor in the bay, but the **St George** parted her cable, struck the Conister rock and was wrecked. Sir William Hillary, the founder of the Royal National Lifeboat Institution, mounted a heroic rescue, so no lives were lost. Although the St George's Company continued to struggle until July 1831, the loss of their finest vessel had crippled them.

What was the **Mona's Isle** like? She was driven by a two cylinder side lever engine, with the paddle boxes mounted forward of the centreline. Mr W H Sleigh, C Eng., M.I.Mech.E.,

M.R.Ae.S., a professional engineer with a distinguished career in research, with Manx ancestry going back many hundreds of years, studied the two portraits by Samuel Walters that are said to depict the **Mona's Isle**, and noticed discrepancies between them. Walters was not a marine architect, but his paintings provide an invaluable starting point, and conform to known practice in most respects. William Sleigh's research in Glasgow, Liverpool, London, and on the Island, revealed that no builder's drawings are known, and unlike the 1840 Cunard vessel, there were no known accurate models either. Using data on ship building practice and engine design of the day, and applying a professional engineering background, he set out to create new General Arrangement drawings and a model. The most obvious difference between the two paintings is the position of the lifeboats. In the 1831 painting, a single boat of about 14 feet length is slung over the stern. Whilst suitable for river steamers, the keel is only about six feet above sea level and would be vulnerable to damage in the open seas. The 1835 painting shows one boat slung from davits on each side of the vessel abaft of the funnel, and resting in shaped seatings, a much more satisfactory answer. Whilst an alteration is possible, William Sleigh rejects this, as it would have required costly strengthening of the wooden hull to support the localised weight transmitted through the davits. As John Wood was an experienced builder, it would be surprising had he made such a mistake at the outset. The 1835 boat also shows a skylight structure aft that would be needed to provide ventilation for the accommodation below deck, but this is missing on the 1831 painting. With the delivery of the **PS Mona** in 1832, to spare the **Mona's Isle** the arduous winter crossings, she could have been returned to the builders for these alterations, but it is more likely that whilst the 1835 painting is of **Mona's Isle**, the 1831 painting is of a similar vessel, perhaps built for the more sheltered waters of the Clyde, but embellished by Walters with the Manx three legs.

Early wooden steamships such as the **Mona's Isle** comprised a wooden schooner hull, into which the boiler and engine were inserted in a central location to maintain the vessel's fore and aft trim. They were bolted to par-

*This share certificate of 1842 must have given the shareholder to whom it is made out justifiable pride. The vignette is of the **King Orry (I)**, which was the fourth ship to be ordered by the Steam Packet. She was launched at John Winram's Bath Building Yard in Douglas on 10 February 1842. The yard occupied the site of the later Bath Place, in close proximity to the modern Imperial Buildings. The man to whom it is made out is John Winram, so it suggests that part of the purchase price for the only IOMSPCo vessel to have been built on the Island, may have been paid in shares. This particular holding remained in the family for almost thirty years. From this, and the length of time that other early shares were held, it seems that families regarded their shares not as something to make a quick buck out of, but as a long-term investment in the community. The signatories include P Garrett, one of the original directors, Edward Fleetwood, James Lewin, Lewis Crebbin and Francis Matthews, most of whom had been present at the 1829 meeting.*

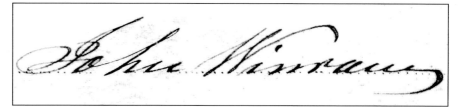

*John Winram came from an Ulverston family that were in quite modest circumstances in the mid-eighteenth century, but steadily improved their lot through hard work. He was born on 5 February 1807, his father being John Whinram (Senior), the spelling of the name varying at this time. His father seems to have been a ship builder, launching wooden schooners at Ulverston for a variety of owners. Some time prior to 1837, John Winram (Junior) had moved to the Isle of Man and had become manager to James Aiken's yard at Bath Place in Douglas, although he was not yet thirty. The yard had been established in 1826, to take advantage of low timber import duties in the Isle of Man, and by 1831 was employing some 80 men. By the late 1830s, Winram was quite well off, as he held six of the £25 shares in the Steam Packet, whilst his wife Margaret, who was one year older than he was, held one share. Although James Aiken retained ownership of the yard, it had become known as Winram's yard by the start of the 1840s, and in 1841 Winram built the hull of the **King Orry**, the only Manx built ship in the history of the Steam Packet. It seems likely that technical advice came from Aiken's yard on Merseyside, and it is interesting to note that Rawson, Aiken & Co held no fewer than 100 shares in the Packet by 1856. In 1841, Winram's son, also John, who was born in England, was 14 years old, the couple's other children including Frances, 10; Margaret 6; and Agnes 3. John Winram was also a director of the Steam Packet, whilst another member of the family, George, who had trained as a shipwright, had become the Lloyd's surveyor in Liverpool by the 1840s. It is probable that the family also had connections with the Brocklebank family who established a sailing ship line about 1770, and whose vessels flew their houseflag at the foremast rather than the mainmast, as is almost universal. After his death, Winram's shares passed to his widow Margaret, and some shares then went to their daughter Margaret.*

allel beams located each side of the keel, the separation being dictated by the engine's fixing points. The beams ran the length of the engine room, and were attached to each of the hull frames. The paddle wheels on early beam engine steamers were forward of the boiler room, which gives a characteristic appearance to these pioneer steamers. The illustration in Chapter 2 of the **PS City of Glasgow** of 1822 shows this very well. The position of the boiler determined the location of the hopper type coal bunkers, which were replenished through deck hatches. In the absence of frame contour drawings, the General Arrangement drawing for the model used frame contour drawings of a schooner of similar size. The masts would have been bedded in a socket at keel level, so would not intrude on the boiler room or engine spaces, another important aspect in the design.

Deck level cabins were provided by extending the paddle box structure fore and aft, with doors and windows facing the deck. This added structural strength, and gave protection to passengers and crew on the deck. A passenger berth diagram of the 1834 **Queen of the Isle**, but which was intended to serve for the **Mona's Isle** and **Mona** as well, suggests all three vessels were similar. This contemporary drawing shows an access on the

port side to the forward below-deck accommodation and on the starboard side to the aft below-deck accommodation. Apart from these companionways or "staircases" in non-nautical language, the deck accommodation would have included toilets for both sexes, a VIP cabin, and facilities for the chief engineer and master, both requiring secure accommodation for their necessary documentation. The external and internal General Arrangement drawings were based on these considerations, and I am delighted to include them, and illustrations of the model built from them. In the absence of any original drawings, they give us the best opportunity of studying what John Wood and Robert Napier created for the Island. After twenty-one years of service, a commendable lifespan for such an early vessel, the **Mona's Isle** went for scrap. Until William Sleigh's meticulous research, what she must have been like had vanished from human consciousness. He has brought her back to life, and with his permission, it is a privilege to include this tribute to Napier and Wood in these pages.

What was it like to travel on the **Mona's Isle**? Oswald's Guide of 1831 surveyed the situation after she had arrived:

"Before steam vessels were introduced, the communications

*of the Island were kept up by means of sailing packets to Whitehaven, Liverpool, and Dublin, which still continue to sail frequently, and to carry on the whole trade of the country. But it is by the steam packets that visitors now make the passage. These vessels were first established between Liverpool, Douglas, and Greenock, by a Glasgow company in 1819. They carry nothing but passengers and luggage, horses and carriages. Since the extension of steam navigation, the passage between Liverpool and Douglas has been supplied by vessels expressly appropriated to it alone. The last year there were the mail packet and the **Mona's Isle** three times a week in summer, and once a week in winter. The **Mona's Isle**, Capt. Gill, is a very superior vessel of her class, and was built last year by subscription, expressly to supply this passage regularly. She is one of the most beautiful vessels that has yet appeared on the coast, and makes her passage in the most expeditious, safe, and comfortable manner. The following vessels also touch at Ramsey, on their passage between Glasgow and Liverpool, when the weather will permit, and occasionally call at Douglas for passengers, all very excellent and safe vessels, **Huskisson**, **Ailsa Craig**, **James Watt**, **Henry Bell**, **Enterprise**, **Glasgow**, and **Liverpool**. The **Scotia**, which plies between Greenock and Dublin, calls frequently at Peel; and the **St. Andrew**, between Whitehaven and Dublin, regularly passes through Douglas bay once a week. These are worked, even in rough weather, with the most astonishing precision, and an experience of twelve years has proved them worthy of confidence.*

The commanders and the stewards give universal satisfaction; and the matrons that wait in the ladies' cabins, are humane, active, and attentive women. The number of passengers between Liverpool and the Island, besides those for Scotland, is often numerous; and an early attention is, therefore, necessary to secure a berth in the cabin. But the passage being often made during the daytime, and the deck spacious and pleasant, a bed, unless for

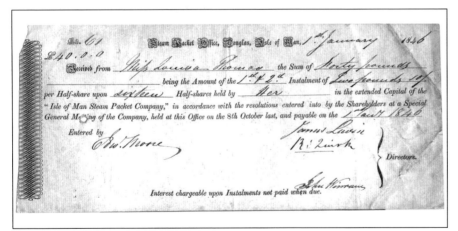

In 1845-46, the Steam Packet acquired two more vessels from Robert Napier's yard on the Clyde. The names **Ben-my-Chree** and **Tynwald** entered the Packet lexicon for the first time, and to pay for this rapid expansion, the proprietors passed a resolution on 8 October 1845 to increase the capital. Investors customarily paid for the shares they had agreed to buy by instalments every few months. This receipt acknowledges payment of the first and second instalments due on the new shares by one of the proprietors on 1 January 1846. Today, when the weekly shopping trip to the supermarket often comes to more than this, £40 may seem trivial, but in 1846, an agricultural labourer would regard himself as fortunate if he were to receive £1 as his weekly wage. If you regard it as forty weeks wages, the size of the investment becomes clearer. It is signed by Edward Moore, who was the Douglas Agent, and therefore Manager & Secretary of the Company, from 1830 to 1865. The directors include James Lewin, one of the directors when the 1838 Deed of Association was signed, Richard Quirk, Receiver-General of the Isle of Man, and John Winram, whom we have already encountered.

invalids, is of the less importance. The packet anchors inside of Douglas-head, a few hundred yards from the pier, and frequently when the tide answers, comes into the harbour. The passengers are immediately brought ashore with care and safety, by boats stationed for the purpose; but it is proper to remark, that there is sometimes a confusion, occasioned by a rush to get into them; and it is recommended, especially if ladies are in the question, to wait till the hurry is over. The landing boats are regularly numbered, and a constable is sent from the town on board the packet, to regulate their coming alongside; but when there is a disposition to irregularity, unless his endeavours are seconded by the passengers themselves, his utility, in contributing to their safety and satisfaction, must be much limited."

Oswald's Guide is invaluable as it summarises the position soon after the birth of the Steam Packet. Apart from popular sentiment on the Island, technical progress also favoured the new line. William Sleigh has pointed out that an Admiralty analysis of 1843 showed the cost of repairs per day on two ships engined by Robert Napier had been 10d and 17.25d per day. By contrast, engines from other builders varied from 6/6d to almost £1 per day, giving more than a 23-fold variation in the worst case. Robert Napier's engines were outstanding in cost terms and reliability. The **Mona's Isle** received one of the first ten engines built by Robert Napier. Having selected Wood and Napier, the Mona's Isle Company had much lower running costs, so could tailor a service to suit the Island. This would not have been possible even three years earlier, or with a different builder. However, the established operators helped seal their own fate. Steamers were costly, so there was an understandable desire to keep an "old" boat in service, but in the 1820s, two or three years marked the difference between modernity and antiquity. The latest word in 1823/24, the **Henry Bell** and the **James Watt**, were archaic by 1830, yet they continued to serve the Island, attracting increasing scorn. The **St George**, brought in by the St George Company, after the **Sophia Jane** had been defeated, dated back to 1822 and was the company's first ship. Astonishingly fast for her day, she was also out-

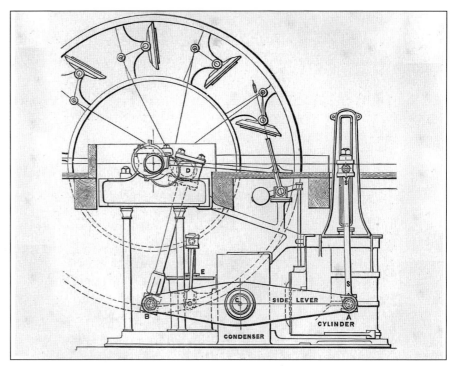

*In the absence of drawings of the engines of the **Mona's Isle**, this drawing of a 900 ihp side lever engine developed by William Denny of Dumbarton in 1854 explains how these engines operated. They were developed from the stationary beam engines used to pump water out of mines on land. A casting above the cylinder on the right guides the crosshead, which is attached to the piston rod. Side rods, S, pass down each side of the cylinder to a side lever at A. The side lever is pivoted at C, and at B a connecting rod is attached to a large crank D to turn the paddle wheel. The little connecting rod works the pump, E. Unlike the early Newcomen stationary pumping engines, where steam was condensed in the cylinder, the side lever engine used the separate condenser that had been developed by James Watt in 1765, as this avoided the waste of heating and cooling the cylinder on each stroke. It was further developed for marine use by Samuel Hall in 1834. Another benefit, though probably not appreciated at the time, was avoiding the stresses inherent in repeated rapid heating and cooling of the precision-engineered cylinders. Without the economy of the separate condenser and more reliable performance, steam propulsion at sea would have been uneconomic. Napier's contribution was to develop the side lever engine to far greater standards than anyone else. An 1840s analysis by the Admiralty showed the low downtime and cost per day of repairs to Napier's engines compared to his rivals. The comparisons almost defied belief. It took years for other builders to catch up. If ever someone deserved official recognition and honours, Napier did, but he did not receive them. It seems that the Honours system in Victorian days was not much better than in our own time, when civil servants, politicians, sportsmen and media figures rank far above those who do something worthwhile for Society.*

classed, and when she was driven on to Conister Rock, it broke the heart of the St George Company. With older boats outclassed, any prospective rival would have to go to Robert Napier to acquire a comparable vessel, and then fight it out. With limited winter traffic, the St George company decided it was not worth it, and the relentless competition on the Glasgow-Liverpool route persuaded the Scottish and Lancashire owners to come together in March 1831 with a unified service, under Burns management, so that the **Glasgow**, **Ailsa Craig** and **Liverpool** and the three Mersey & Clyde packets, **James Watt**, **Henry Bell** and **William Huskisson**, worked together. By then, David Napier and Little had wisely dropped out, to con-

centrate on more profitable areas.

What of David Napier himself, the true father of Manx steamer services, and a man who has never been given just recognition on the Island ? He was a brilliant marine engineer with a string of inventions to his credit, and a first class businessman seeing the possibilities of the Belfast and Liverpool routes early on. He was shrewd enough to know when to drop a venture if competition became too fierce, and that is what he did. In 1836, he moved to Millwall on the Thames, seeing profitable opportunities there. When he left the Clyde, he sold the celebrated Lancefield foundry that he had founded in 1821, to his cousin Robert Napier. He died in London on 23 November 1869, aged 79.

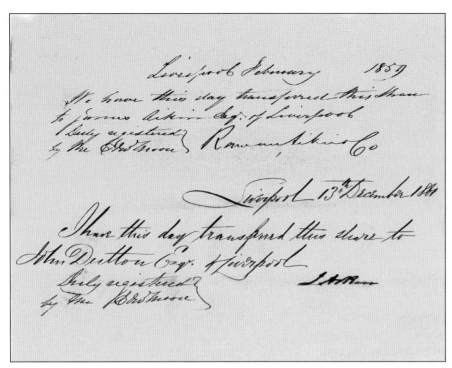

Rawson Aiken & Co, sometimes spelled Aikin, was a long-term major investor in the Steam Packet, the only larger investor in 1856 being Edward M Gawne. As owners of the Bath Place yard in Douglas when John Winram built the **King Orry** in 1842, it is probable that they had provided technical guidance, and part of the cost may well have been paid in shares. Because of constant pressure to expand the dock estate, ship builders on the Mersey faced problems in long term use of a site which meant that with the exception of Laird's yard in Birkenhead, later Cammell, Laird, the Mersey shipbuilding industry never achieved the prominence of Glasgow, Barrow or Tyneside. These two manuscript share transfers of February 1859 and December 1861 record the transfer of a share from the shipyard to James Aiken personally, and his disposal of it two years later. Apart from the firm's official signature, "Rawson, Aiken & Co" the transfer includes James Aikin's signature to the second transfer, and both have been registered by Edward Moore.

For a time, Burns advertised a daily service, but a new rival appeared on the scene. David MacIver, the energetic Liverpool agent of the **Enterprise**, was vexed at the loss of his job, when the ship he represented was sold. He persuaded a sailing smack owner, David Chapman of Glasgow, to join forces with him, and roped in James Donaldson, a wealthy Glasgow cotton merchant, James Thomson, and other Glaswegians to form the City of Glasgow Shipping Co. As David Napier's 1822 **City of Glasgow** was now up for sale, she was purchased by David Chapman and John Thomson in 1831, being transferred to the City of Glasgow Steam Packet Co in 1832. Contemporary reports use "Steam Packet", "Shipping" and "Steamship" almost at random in company titles. She was joined by a formidable new steamer from John Wood's yard in 1832, named **John Wood**. The **PS Vulcan** followed in 1833, and the old **City of Glasgow** was sold to a Goole owner in 1834, being replaced by a new vessel of the same name the following year. Remarkably for such an early steamer she remained afloat until 1855. Rivalry resumed on the main Glasgow-Liverpool run, and the former Manchester boats were put into the hands of Laird's for sale in May 1831. With the **Mona's Isle** taking the bulk of the Manx traffic, G&J Burns and the City of Glasgow companies decided to concentrate on their core traffic between Liverpool and the Clyde. After a period of fierce competition, MacIver and his colleagues were won over by the Burns, MacIver becoming a partner and lifelong friend. To avoid too much delay, the Anglo-Scottish boats anchored in Douglas bay, making them less attractive to passengers, and as the Douglas call was no longer economic, Ramsey became the venue, but by the 1840s, the traffic was so light, that the Liverpool-Glasgow boats had little enthusiasm for an Isle of Man call at all. The growth of the UK rail network resulted in G&J Burns abandoning the service altogether in 1856. The awkward structure of the St George company, which led to a deplorable service during the autumn of 1829, after a promising start the previous year, had provided the spur to creating the Mona's Isle Co, The loss of the **St George** in 1830 was a serious blow to their immediate rival, whilst David Napier had decided to pull out due to competition, and the rivalry between G&J Burns and the MacIver meant that these well run companies, who would have been formidable competitors, had more pressing matters to attend to. This combination of circumstances, and the decision to use Napier and Wood changed the course of history.

Sir Winston Churchill once said that if the case of St George and the dragon had arisen in modern times, that St George, instead of being equipped with a lance, would be equipped with a flexible formula, and the whole matter would be referred to the League of Nations. In 1830-31, the Manx dragon had decisively vanquished St George. There was to be an extraordinary sequel to the defeat of the St George Company that was played out in Westminster in 1833, and which has seemingly been ignored by Manx writers. Although the company had been soundly defeated on the Douglas route, it remained a powerful force in the Irish Sea, operating at different times between Dublin and Liverpool, Dublin and Bristol, Dublin and Glasgow, Liverpool and Newry, and out of Cork. On many routes, St George was facing severe opposition, and in 1833, decided that it was time to vanquish the numerous little dragons that were snapping at his heels. Combat had not succeeded, so St George decided that a flexible formula might be a better answer, and the place to obtain it was in the Houses of Parliament. A private act of parliament was sought, and at the third reading of the St George's Steam Packet Company's bill on 19 June 1833, Lord Sandon put forward a glib explanation of the purpose of the bill:

"it is simply to enable the Company to sue and be sued, and to make some other regulations for the management of its concerns. The only reasonable objection that can now be made to it is, that it places the Company in competition with others; but in my opinion, so far from it giving the Company greater powers than others were invested with it, in fact, contains less provisions to

that purport than other Companies have."

A Scottish member tore holes in the bill, pointing out that far from being an Irish Company as it had claimed, to win sympathy due to the depressed state of the Irish economy, whilst 87 subscribers did reside in Ireland, another 74 lived in England. Apart from powers to raise immense amounts of capital, it was pointed out that the bill included:

"the power of chartering all other vessels that professed to go on the same line as their vessels, and therefore a monopoly would be established, by which they might charge what prices they pleased. A more predetermined system of monopoly was never heard of".

It had been suggested that railway companies came before parliament for exclusive rights to build specific routes, and this was no different, but the Earl of Ormelie pointed out:

"The object and the practice of the Company has been to throw out every competitor, and the parties now come to Parliament to enable them to perpetuate the system. I draw a marked distinction between bills for Steam Packet Companies, and those for Railways: in the former, all parties can plough the ocean without hindrance; in the latter, it is necessary that the sanction of the Legislature should be given before the grounds of private individuals can be cut through".

Having failed in battle, St George had sought a formula that would allow him to steal the claws of not one dragon, but all dragons that might wish to challenge him in perpetuity. The proposal was decisively rejected by Parliament, and with it the hopes of the St George company of creating a monopoly in the Irish Sea by legislative means if it could not do so by the quality of its services. Had the vote gone differently, the St George's Steam Packet might well have come back to the Island, armed not with a boat but with an Act of Parliament permitting it to seize the vessels used by its rivals. To suggest that the bill was targeted at the Isle of Man Steam Packet would be wrong, but the St George company must have realised that its defeat in

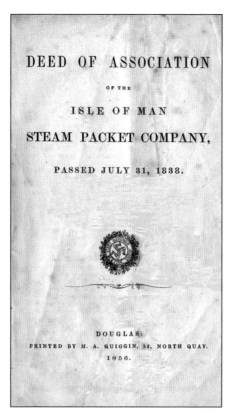

The Deed of Association of 31 July 1838 governed the company for decades. It was printed in a slender booklet with a deep blue paper cover, some printings including a complete list of shareholders.

1830 had become widely known in the steam ship world, and must have encouraged its many competitors elsewhere. The St George Company eventually became the parent of the City of Cork SPCo, which was to operate for many decades. When I read of St George and this unsporting attempt to vanquish his rivals, I could not help a wry smile. As a small child I took part in a school play in which I vanquished St George in knightly combat. It was a fair fight, and meant that I got to hold hands with the damsel, who was a charming young lady, and who was in no apparent distress at the demise of St George. Alas, an interfering wizard came along, restored St George to life, and I was duly dispatched, the wizard declining to restore me. To a child, this seemed totally unfair, but my eminently logical request for permission to do what any sensible person would do in such circumstances and to slay the wizard for unsporting behaviour was turned down, much to my displeasure. It is a good job that parliament was more reasonable than my teachers, or that interfering wizard. I still wish I had slain the Wizard on the "Opening Night"

Cannell's Guide of 1843 provides a snapshot of how shipping services had developed over the next twelve years:

"When the tide answers, the packet invariably comes into the harbour, at other times it anchors inside of Douglas Head, about 100 yards from the pier, and the passengers are immediately brought ashore, with care and safety, free of any charge, by boatmen stationed for the purpose. The landing boats are regularly numbered, and each boatman has also his respective number attached to the arm by means of a brass plate, without which, no porter or boatman is allowed to approach the vessel, and the police are always in attendance, on the arrival of the packet, to put in force these regulations, and to prevent confusion and imposition. The trip on a fine day, is really delightful; except to a few the effect of the motion of the vessel, steadily directed by powerful machinery, is much less than that usually produced by the swell caused by the wind and the tides in sailing packets. The mails are conveyed by these packets; every day in the summer, and twice a week in winter; and one of them carries goods, which is found to be a great accommodation to persons in business. The fare from Liverpool to Douglas, during the summer is only 7s. 6d. cabin, 3s. steerage. There is also a steam communication kept up with Whitehaven, Douglas, and Dublin, during the summer season; and the Scotch packets call at Ramsey on their passage to and from Liverpool. There are also several regular trading vessels to Liverpool, Whitehaven, and the Scotch and Irish ports."

Josiah Heelis, who had been agent for the "War Office" Packets at Ramsey in 1830, had now become the Steam Packet agent in the town. As the Steam Packet acquired more vessels, the capital was enlarged to fund the expansion. It had commenced at £7250 in 1830. In 1831 the capital was increased to £12,000. By 1846, it totalled £40,688. In 1884, the capital stood at £82,500, and by 1896 had reached £200,000, in varying denominations including £25, £12 10s and £5. The first formal

STEAM COMMUNICATION
BETWEEN
LIVERPOOL & DOUGLAS,
Isle of Man.

THE ISLE OF MAN STEAM PACKET COMPANY'S powerful and first-class Steam Ships

	Tons.	Horse Power.
Mona's Queen (new steamer)	550	280
Tynwald	750	320
King Orry	450	200
Ben-my-Chree	400	150

Will ply between LIVERPOOL and DOUGLAS, with her Majesty's Mails and Passengers,

DAILY, DURING THE SEASON,
From the 1st of JUNE to the 30th of SEPTEMBER,

Leaving Liverpool at 11 a.m.,
And Douglas at 9 a.m.

There will be EXTRA PASSENGER STEAMERS *throughout* JULY *and* AUGUST, *from Liverpool every* MONDAY *and* SATURDAY *Afternoon, about 2 o'clock, and from Douglas about 7 a.m.*

From September to June.—The MONA'S QUEEN, or TYNWALD, will leave Liverpool every TUESDAY, THURSDAY, and SATURDAY Morning; and leave Douglas every MONDAY, WEDNESDAY, and FRIDAY Morning, with her Majesty's Mails, Passengers, and Goods. *Average passage 5 to 6 hours.*

Pleasure Excursions Round the Island, and to the adjacent Ports in ENGLAND, SCOTLAND, and IRELAND, take place frequently during the Season from Douglas.

The times of sailing can be obtained in *Bradshaw's Guide*, page 151, and of the Agents at

LIVERPOOL: THOS. ORFORD, 32, James-street.
MANCHESTER: JNO. WALKER, 77A, Market-st.
DOUGLAS: EDWARD MOORE.

xix.

*Although undated, other paperwork dates this advertisement for the Steam Packet to 1857. This is confirmed by the composition of the Steam Packet fleet, as the **Mona's Queen** entered service in 1853 and **King Orry** was sold in 1858. It is of particular value as it gives the sailing times and frequencies, and reveals that in the 1850s the **Mona's Queen** and **Tynwald**, the two largest and newest boats were to handle the winter sailings. Thomas Orford, whose name was to be associated with the Packet for almost 120 years, had become the Liverpool agent.*

ALL the partners owned the property jointly, which is unwieldy when there are dozens or hundreds of them, the 1838 deed confirmed that the property was vested in two trustees, who were Edward Moore Gawne, who had taken over this role from his late father, and John Anderson. Any lawsuit, whilst it would be under the management of the directors, was to be in the names of the trustees, and individual shareholders, who would have a right to conduct the case in an ordinary partnership as suited themselves, renounced such rights in the deed. Under the 1838 deed, the capital was £12,000 British, divided into £25 shares, the word British being inserted, as the Manx and English currencies were not uniform, there being 14 Manx pennies to the English shilling, and approximately 21 Manx shillings in an English pound. An Act of Tynwald ended this bizarre anomaly in 1840. The capital could be increased by a majority vote of the shareholders at a general meeting, but no shareholder could be compelled to subscribe to any increase.

Five shareholders were to act as directors, and required a qualification holding of two £25 shares, which sounds very little today, but was some hundreds of times its current value in those days. Modern directors might not appreciate article 11, which specified the qualification for directors, but added "and his services to be gratuitous". Serving as a director was to contribute to the common good, and was not seen as something to make a personal profit from. Although Tynwald was not yet elected by popular universal vote, democracy was prized in the island, and the modern corporate raider would not appreciate clause 12:

"That each proprietor of one share shall have one vote; four

"deed of association" was drawn up in 1838, and is illustrated, as is an 1842 share certificate, the earliest I have seen relating to the Steam Packet. This reveals several unusual features about this early Manx company. Although it refers to a share of £25 and "directors", which is the terminology of 'company speak', the title is "Isle of Man Steam Packet Company". The word "Limited" does not appear, and the certificate refers to a Deed of Association of 1838. Limited Liability legislation did not exist in the Isle of Man until the 1860s, long after it did in the United Kingdom. Companies were, in effect, partnerships, but with the member's interest expressed in units of £25, with half shares of £12 10s offered later on. The Steam Packet operated as if it was a joint stock company, but until the deed of association of August 1838, it was on a very loose footing, and rights were obscure. The new deed confirmed that it was a "Partnership Company", but because an ordinary partnership means that

DEED OF ASSOCIATION.

This Indenture, made the thirteenth day of August, in the year of our Lord one thousand eight hundred and thirty-eight, between the Owners of certain Steam Vessels, belonging to the port of Douglas, in the Isle of Man, called the "Mona's Isle" and the "Queen of the Isle," and Shareholders in a certain Steam Packet Company, carried on under the style and title of "The Isle of Man Steam Packet Company,"

Witnesseth, that whereas the said several persons have for some time been jointly interested in the said Vessels to the extent of their respective shares therein, as entered in the Company's books; and the said Vessels have for some years past been employed in conveying Goods and Passengers, to and from the port of Douglas, to such other ports and places as have heretofore been deemed advisable; and the said several Proprietors and Shareholders have heretofore carried on business as a Joint Stock Company, under the management and superintendence of a Board of Directors, by the said style and title of "The Isle of Man Steam Packet Company." And whereas the said Company hath hitherto been governed by certain Rules and Regulations agreed to by the Proprietors, or a majority thereof, and by such

ISLE OF MAN STEAM PACKET COMPANY.

I illustrated the title page of the 1838 Deed of Association on page 43. The Deed itself opened with a recital of the situation as it was in August 1838. Many millions of passengers have sailed to and from the island in the years since then, and countless sea miles have been marked off, but the basic purpose as enshrined in the 1838 deed, to convey goods and passengers "to and from the Port of Douglas", remains as true today is it did on 13 August 1838. In the chapter we have just read, we have learned of the people whose vision, foresight and resolve made it all happen. The Moore and Gawne families, Philip Garrett, Robert Napier, John Wood and his doomed fiancée, Isabella Kerr Kayll, and many others. At first sight, their legacy may seem elusive today, and of little relevance to us. The ships they built are long gone. The places they worked from have fallen victim to the developer, and even the paper trail they left is fragmentary and elusive. A few forgotten memorials, their inscriptions weathered by the hand of time, and scattered across churchyards in England, Scotland and Mann would seem to be all that endures. It is easy to believe that, but if we care to look, their true memorial is all around us, for they laid the foundations for the success that the Island and its people enjoyed from the 1830s down to modern times. Their memorial is the island as we know it. That is not a bad legacy to leave behind, when you come to think of it!

of "One for All, All for One" immortalised by Alexandre Dumas in "The Three Musketeers" reigned:

"That any Proprietor refusing to act as Chairman at a General Meeting when required by a majority thereof, shall be fined twenty shillings, British, which sum shall be disposed of for the benefit of sick and poor servants belonging to the Company".

Having trained in company law in the 1970s, when I first read through those rules of so long ago, my thoughts were "how wise and how just". As a corollary I might add, "how arrogant and foolish are the rules we use today in comparison". It would be reassuring to believe that the present economic crisis will bring a return to the wiser values of the past, but I shall not hold my breath.

By Millennium year, 2000, Glasgow, Greenock, Ardrossan, Stranraer, Port Patrick, Garliestown, Silloth, Workington, Whitehaven, Piel Pier (near Barrow), Ransden Dock in Barrow, Morecambe, Fleetwood, Blackpool, Llandudno, Bangor (Co Down), Ramsey, Peel and Castletown had all been added to the list of places you could once have sailed to or from. In some cases routes operated for many years. In other cases for a year or two, and a few routes had the melancholy distinction of closing more than once. I believe that Whitehaven, which seems to have been the earliest steamer service to close in the early 1820s, holds the blue riband in this respect as the route was reopened for a single season in 1929, more than a century after its first closure. In 2005, the **MV Lady of Mann**, in her last year of service with the Steam Packet paid a single visit to Whitehaven and since 2007, there have been annual day excursions by Steam Packet fast craft from Whitehaven to Douglas, a fascinating resumption of a link that goes back more than 200 years. Fleetwood closed at the start of the 1960s, and after re-opening, closed again as a result of the Sea Containers take over of the Packet in the 1980s. Ardrossan was another victim of Sea Containers, but reopened briefly when CalMac operated a service to the Island in 1998 and 1999. When you add the Douglas and Peel harbour ferries, coastal sailings from Douglas to Laxey and Ramsey, and Round-the-Island cruises, the list becomes formidable.

---

shares, two votes; ten shares, three votes; twenty shares, four votes; and that no shareholder shall have more than four votes."

By these wise provisions, the original subscribers ensured that larger shareholders, who had put more into the company, and might be expected to have a better idea of what was prudent, did have a larger voice, but it was not possible for one man or a small group of shareholders to outvote the majority of individual members. They were wise provisions, and must have contributed to a sense of unity and fair play. Today, they would be an anathema to the bankers, the city, the institutional investors and corporate raiders, whom we may thank for the economic

blizzard that is sweeping the world as these words are being written. Our ancestors had a better and a fairer system. Sadly, the recent antics of a few so-called celebrities who attempt to hijack the AGMs of leading companies to promote their own particular causes mean that such a democratic principle, if applied today, would be exploited. This democratic and wise structure survived until 3 March 1885, when the Packet became a conventional Limited Company.

Other clauses in the rules prohibited a proxy holder voting more shares than he had in his own name, so that the proxy system could not be used as a steamroller, forbade the sailing of vessels on a Sunday, and in the case of clause 23, emphasises how the spirit

Like many children with a Manx background, my mother regaled me with stories of "themselves", or the "Little People". I knew of the "Buggane", the "Phynnodderree", the "Glashyn", the "Moddey Dhoo" and the many other amazing beings that simultaneously enchanted and terrified our forefathers. The words of that beautiful and touching ballad, *Ellan Vannin*, speak of the Mermaids, who might be described as the nautical cousins of the fairies. Years later, I heard tell of two nautical fairies that swapped their traditional Manx homes along the east coast of the Island for the Pacific and Indian Oceans. Fairies are not renowned for providing documentary evidence of their existence, but one of the sisters had left quite a paper trail, and it was when my father and I were looking at a piece of card that measured 2.35 ins by just over an inch that we had our first evidence of this aquatic Manx fairy. As the evidence piled up, we found not one but two sisters, one three years older than the other. Both girls had been born in Scotland, had spent their youth on the coasts of Mann, and then ventured far afield. To my surprise, one of these Manx fairies ended up in Bombay, whilst the other fairy emigrated, as many Manx folk had, to Australia, to explore the waters of the Swan River, before finishing her days in Hobart harbour in Tasmania.

In pursuit of the two sisters, I was drawn into the long forgotten world of the Mona Steamship Company. It was a small company, or rather three small companies, with five separate share structures, and three ships. The human side included a renowned Scottish ship builder who specialised in steam yachts, tugs and small pleasure craft, a retired English investor, the son of the High Bailiff of Douglas, and a galaxy of other Manx worthies. The paper trail officially commenced with the Memorandum of Association of the Mona Steamship Co, which was drawn up on 16 April 1888. The company's registered office was at Lloyd's office at 45 North Quay, Douglas, and the company was formally registered as IOM Company No 100 on 4 May 1888. The initial capital was to be £4,500 in £5 shares, and the first secretary was Richard A Cain, a shipbroker of Loch Promenade, Douglas IOM. He was the son of Matthias and Catherine Cain, and had been christened on 21 March 1855 at St Matthews Church in Douglas. His middle name was Alma, which is more commonly a female name, but comes from the River Alma, which flows into the sea north of Sevastopol in the Crimea. It is not a big river even in winter, and in the drought of a Crimean summer, a child could cross it with ease, so why did a Douglas couple, with the solid Manx name of Cain, christen their son after this river in the far off Crimea ? In the 1850s, one of the biggest events to capture public interest was the Crimean war of 1854-55, the only time that Britain and Russia have gone to war. It was an absurd war fought to protect the inter-ests of the Turks from Imperial Russia, and led to a strange alliance between Britain, France and Turkey. A British army was dispatched to the Crimea. Battles such as Inkerman, or the charge of the Light Brigade at Balaklava, left a strong impression on public opinion, and many streets built in the 1850s, public houses and children, including the infant Richard Alma Cain, acquired names from this remote part of Imperial Russia. The Alma was the site of the first major battle, soon after the Anglo-French forces landed north of the town, and carried out a long flanking march to besiege the defences south of the town. In doing so, they met a Russian force occupying a strong defensive position on a ridge south of the Alma. After a difficult battle, where the outcome was frequently in doubt, the Russian forces retired. The war itself dragged on, and neglect of the wounded catapulted Florence Nightingale to fame as she transformed army nursing. Although the public at home were full of enthusiasm for these stirring deeds, the soldiers in the far off Crimea detested their French and Turkish allies, and developed admiration for their stoic Russian foes, many saying they would prefer to fight alongside the Russians, and against their French and Turkish allies! At the end of the war, when the British troops left, their farewell

This illustration is said to portray the **Manx Fairy** *shortly after her arrival on the Manchester Ship Canal, but unless the background has been touched out, the open sea suggests that the Isle of Man is more likely. As there seem to be no passengers on board, it could be a view produced for publicity purposes before the* **Manx Fairy** *had even entered service, or might have been taken from the Iron Pier in the middle of Douglas Bay prior to an excursion from that long forgotten pier.*

Photo c/o Manchester Museums

*This evocative commercial card of the **Manx Fairy** dates from the late 1880s, and is taken in the early afternoon, as she discharges passengers at Ramsey after a pleasant cruise. It shows the wing platforms on each side of the upper deck, and passengers discharging via a wooden gangway, which is clear photographic evidence of alterations that must have taken place prior to her moment of glory in Australia as a Royal yacht, when a portion of the upper deck railings had to be removed with a hacksaw. One of the officers supervises disembarkation. As only a small crew was carried, all hands had to be versatile. It may be a purser, but is quite likely to be the mate, William Charles Corrin, who served as Captain when Captain Cannell was promoted to the **Fairy Queen**. Attention is drawn to the single lifeboat slung at upper deck level on the starboard side, the fashions, especially the bearded onlooker in the striped blazer and cap, and the apparent absence of anyone who is bare headed.*

parade was before a Russian general who expressed his admiration for them.

The MSCo was formed to run excursions up the east coast of the island from Douglas, but its Memorandum & Articles of Association provided much wider powers, allowing it "To purchase, build, hire or in any other way acquire steam ships". They could convey passenger or goods, and passenger ships were authorised to sell intoxicating liquors, whilst the vessels could ply between "such ports and places of the Isle of Man and elsewhere as the company may from time to time determine". A cynic might conclude that the company was empowered to steal ships with which to take inebriated passengers to Australia, and whilst the MSCo never sailed to Australia, one of its boats reached India, and another got to Australia via the Manchester Ship Canal! The chronology is interesting, for whilst the company had not been formed until April 1888, the vessel they were to acquire, the **Manx Fairy** (register no 76309) had been launched in 1887 at T B Seath's shipyard at Rutherglen in Lanark, and registered in Douglas in January 1888. As late as 28 September 1888, some months AFTER she had been delivered, only 639 of the £5 shares had been placed, giving a paid up capital of £3195, of which £80 still remained to be paid. The biggest holding of 100 shares was in the name of Thomas Seath, a ship builder of Glasgow, the remaining holdings being for 20 shares or less. These dates, and Seath's sizeable holding, reveal that preparations to form the company had commenced long before the official papers were drawn up. In the early 1880s, the yard had been busy, with 14 and 11 ships launched in 1883 and 1884, but there seem to have been just a couple of launches in 1885 and in 1886. It seems likely that the **Manx Fairy**, the sole vessel launched in 1887, was a speculative venture by Seath, who saw the east coast of the Island as a possible venue for one of the small passenger steamers he specialised in building, and to keep his yard at work.

According to his monument in Glasgow's Southern Necropolis, Thomas Bollen Seath was born on the 23rd September 1820 at Prestonpans, East Lothian. When he was five years old, Tammsy, as he was known, injured his spine in an accident whilst playing. He started work as a cabin boy for Thomson and McConnel, the agents for the City of Glasgow Steam Packet, sailing between Glasgow and Liverpool, and to Belfast and the Highlands. Later he worked for the Largs Steamboat Co, and opened his own ship yard at Meadowside, Partick on the north bank of the Clyde in 1853. By 1856, he had only built a

The **PS Lancelot** was built by Robert Duncan of Port Glasgow, yard No 30, in 1868, for Graham Brymner & Co of Greenock, and in common with other ships in their fleet was given a name from the legends of King Arthur. In 1874, she was sold to Gillies & Campbell of Wemyss Bay for their Rothesay and Millport services. By the late 1880s, relations between Captain Alexander Campbell and the Caledonian Railway were bad, Campbell complaining that the CR were unfair in the split of receipts on through tickets from Glasgow via Wemyss Bay to Bute and Great Cumbrae, and the CR criticising the elderly vessels that were usually on the service, such as the twenty year old **Lancelot**. With his lease due to end that autumn, Campbell tried to bounce the CR into a new deal, but merely hastened the demise of his service. In 1890, the River Cart, a subsidiary of the Clyde, which ran through Paisley, was being improved, and the **Lancelot** sailed from Paisley to Millport and Rothesay on 14 August 1890, but was later sold to the Isle of Man, running between Douglas and Ramsey in 1891 and 1892 but was then disposed of to Turkey. This portrait, taken at the Broomielaw in Glasgow, shows her as the middle of three vessels, the nearest being the **PS Sultana**.

few ships, one being the revolutionary **PS Artizan** which drew just 27 ins for the Glasgow to Rutherglen service. Seath was captain, owner and chief engineer, working the engines by controls from the bridge to the engine room, an idea that other shipbuilders did not copy for well over a century. In 1856 he moved upriver to Rutherglen, then a small town on the Clyde two miles south-east of Glasgow. With the small ships needed at that time, the move was no problem, but later on, it limited the size of vessel that could be built to about 200 feet, due to the width of the river at this point. He saw the difficulties as a challenge to be overcome, and produced some 300 vessels in all. He built the first six 'Cluthas', which were small river ferries operating on the Clyde, and which played a role in popularising river trips with Glaswegians. The **Esperance** of 1869, and the **Raven** of 1871, still survive and sail regularly in the Windermere Steamboat Collection. He married Helen Young of Glasgow, who was a few years younger than he was, but sadly she passed away in London on 3 November 1873 at the early age of 46. Infant mortality was high well into the nineteenth century, but the couple were exceptionally unfortunate, for at least eight of their children died by the age of ten, one living for just four hours. Thomas Bollen Seath passed away at his home, 'Sunny Oaks' at Langbank, on the 3rd February 1903, a year after the yard had its first idle period. The yard subsequently passed to Wm Chalmers & Co, and closed c1920.

Unless an overdraft was taken out, some deal must have been struck with

The late Fred Henry sent me this photo of a paddle steamer off the Dhoon many years ago. Said to have been taken in August 1888, but probably taken three years later, it was once believed to be the **PS Minnow**, but the height of the passengers on deck indicate it is much longer than the 119' of the appropriately named **Minnow**. It conforms in all respects with known views of the **PS Lancelot**. The radial slots on the paddle boxes, position of the ship's boat at the stern, the location of the funnel ahead of the paddle boxes, and the row of portholes to the dining saloon beneath the raised quarterdeck are all identical to the Clyde steamer. A name, which is indecipherable, but which is longer than six characters is faintly visible at the bows; and the last letter resembles a "T". The funnel appears to be white or yellow with a black top, which would distinguish her from the red and black of the IOMSPCo. A photograph of an unidentified but small paddle steamer that may well be the **Minnow** appears alongside Blackpool North Pier in 1867 in Lancashire Coast Pleasure Steamers by Andrew Gladwell, but no definite views of this vessel have come to light.

Photo c/o late Fred Henry

Seath, as the capital was insufficient to allow the company to meet the £3,500 bill for the **Manx Fairy**. She was 128' 6" x 16' 6" x 9' 3", and was yard No 254, She was a twin screw steamer, and was driven by a pair of compound engines by Huston & Corbett of Glasgow which delivered 300 ihp, and could propel her at 14 knots. Captain S P Carter has commented that her hull was unusually narrow for a twin screw steamer, with the result that the tips of her screws projected beyond the hull line, which could result in their fouling a jetty if she turned on a stern rope or spring. To avoid this, special guards were provided. At the time, most pleasure steamers were still paddle driven and it has been suggested that **Manx Fairy** was built with conversion to paddle propulsion in mind if the screw layout was unsuccessful. She was a single decked ship with a steel framework, of 120 gross register tons (net register tonnage 24.62), and arrived in Manx waters on her delivery voyage from Glasgow via Greenock on 26 June 1888, under the command of Captain John Tarbet. Her first port of call was Peel, but she sailed for Douglas later the same day. The Board of Trade records her first master as John Tarbet, but only from 29 June 1888. This may well be the start of operations. Tarbet was probably a Scottish master, employed by Seath for the builders' trials and the delivery voyage, and remained with the vessel until a local master was familiar with her. He was replaced by John Cannell on 25 July 1888. Cannell had a home trade master's certificate dating from January 1884. In 1888, the company's receipts were £1236 and expenses £764, leaving a surplus of £472, which was sufficient to declare a 10% dividend on the first year's operations.

In 1889, the MSCo acquired a second vessel, the **Minnow**. She was very small, being under 100 tons, and had been in Manx waters for at least a year. A potential candidate would be a vessel built at Birkenhead in 1858 for the Blackpool, Lytham & Southport S P Co. She was an iron paddle steamer, 119' 8" x 19' 3" x 7', of 68 grt and with 40hp engines, and is recorded as being sold out of service sometime after 1886. In 1888, she had been operated by the Douglas Steamboat Company Ltd, a small company with a capital of £1,000 with a registered office at 19 Duke St, Douglas. It had been registered soon after the Mona Steamship Co, the companies being

No's 100 and 103 on the Manx register. In 1889, the Island enjoyed a fine season, with less rainfall than usual and long periods of warm dry weather. With Manx tourism developing rapidly, 1889 was a good year for the company, with both vessels often running to capacity, and revenue increased by over 50% to £1,860, with expenses rising to £950, leaving a surplus of £910, which permitted an interim dividend of 10%. With this excellent start, it was hardly surprising the company was considering adding a larger vessel to the fleet by the start of 1890. The offer of a 160 foot long twin-screw steamer that could carry 400 passengers, or twice as many as **Manx Fairy**, prompted the board to seek approval to increase the capital.

On 10 February 1890, the MSCo held an Extraordinary General Meeting at Butterworth's Hotel on Prospect Hill, Douglas, to sanction an increase from £4,500 to £12,000 and a prospectus was issued at the start of March. The chairman was Edgar Robinson of 12 Queens Ave, Douglas IOM, the other directors being R B Brierley, S J Harris, F W Spencer, J S Evarard, C W Coole, J Barron and G S Cain. Robinson, who was a widower, seems to have been born c1821 in England, and was a Commission agent, drawing income from railway and dock investments. Amongst the other directors, S J Harris was the son of High Bailiff Samuel Harris, who had been born in Douglas in 1815. Sam Harris had been admitted to the Manx bar in 1842, becoming High Bailiff of Douglas in 1864, and Registrar of Deeds. He had been a key figure in the formation of the Isle of Man Bank in 1865, and in many other important public projects. He was a legend in his own long lifetime, and did not start relinquishing his many official posts until 1900, dying in 1905. Sam had married Anne Bateman Craig in 1839, and Samuel Joseph Harris was the third of their eight children, four of whom died in infancy. Samuel Joseph had been christened at Onchan on 25 April 1844, and showed signs of emulating his father in his attainments. By 1881, he was Deputy Registrar of Deeds under his father. A conscientious young man, indeed a "high flyer" in today's argot, and keenly interested in shipping, Samuel Joseph Harris was a valuable addition to the board. John Sawrey Evarard, although less well known, was another ambitious young man in a hurry, and was to rise to

prominence in the company. Unlike the elderly Robinson, Evarard was quite young, having been christened at St Matthews Church on 10 November 1861, his parents being Joseph and Mary Ann Everard (the spelling varies). His father kept apartments on Prospect Hill, John following him in this business, with accommodation on 7 Loch Promenade by the time the MSCo was being formed. His elder brother, Myles Posthewhaite Everard, who had been born in October 1854, was christened on the same day as John, and was proprietor of the Gaiety Theatre by 1887. This was not the present Gaiety Theatre on the Promenade, but was located on Prospect Hill. It had been opened in 1862 by his father, Joseph Everard, as the Victoria Hall, and no less a figure than Sir Henry Irving was to appear there. It later became the Prince of Wales Theatre, the United Services Theatre and the Gaiety Theatre on 4 July 1881.

R A Cain was secretary. The revised capital was to comprise the existing 900 shares of £5 each and 7,500 new £1 shares. Five shillings would be payable on application, 5/- on allotment, 5/- on 16 May 1890 and the balance on 16 June 1890. It was common to have a local and a UK bank, Dumbell's handling the work on the Island, whilst the Manchester & Liverpool District Bank dealt with business "across". The proposed additional vessel, which dated from August 1888, had originally been offered at £7,000 as against a new cost of £15,000, and by March 1890, the asking price had come down to £6,500. From differing figures quoted at the time, she was between 160' and 168' long, with a beam of approximately 22'. The next firm progress is on 21 January 1891, when the shareholders again met at Butterworth's Hotel to approve the creation of another 1000 £1 shares, increasing

Unlike the IOMSPCo, or the Peel & North of Ireland Steamship Co, where the cast list was largely Manx born, the majority of the leading figures in the Mona Steamship Co, throughout its existence, including the chairman, Edgar Robinson, had come to the Island from England during the boom years of Manx tourism from the 1870s onwards.

The **SS Fairy Queen** is alongside the South Pier at Ramsey in the 1890s. The photograph came from the late Fred Kinnin of Ramsey, whose family owned the well known fishing boat, the **Master Frank**. Legend has it that there was a family connection with the Mona Steamship Co, and that the family may have acted as boatmen at Ramsey, ferrying passengers to and from the shore when the tide was too low for the steamers to enter the harbour. The view has been made available by Captain Stephen Carter, of the Laxey Towing Co, who started operating a pleasure vessel along the Manx Coast in the 1990s, about a century after this view must have been taken.

Photo courtesy of Capt S. P. Carter

the nominal capital to £13,000. From this it would seem that the original proposal to acquire the 1888 steamer, had fallen through. The new capital was to finance the acquisition of another ship from T B Seath's yard at Rutherglen. Despite his three score years and ten, "Tammsy" was keen to combat low orders, for the yard had remained quiet since 1887. Of the 11 vessels launched in 1890, four had been barges, whilst four had been electrically powered launches. They were small, but showed Seath was as progressive in his seventies as he had been when the yard was first opened. The order book for 1891 was lean, just four vessels, and the price quoted by Seath, which was little more than for a second-hand vessel, suggests that keeping the yard in work was a major factor. The new ship was the **Fairy Queen**. She was 170 feet in length, with a beam of 22 feet and drew 9.4 ft. The register tonnage was 136.38. She was powered by a 70hp triple expansion steam engine. **Fairy Queen**, official No 98629, was initially registered in Glasgow, but quickly transferred to Douglas under the ownership of John Sawrey Evarard, one of the directors of the MSCo. The "Queen" which was yard no 278, was launched on 31 March 1891, ran her

trials on the Clyde on 16 May 1891, and then sailed for Douglas. On 26 May 1891, the **Fairy Queen** took the Directors of the MSCo and friends on a trip from Douglas to Isle of Whithorn in southwest Scotland. A bill of sale of 2 November 1891 transferred **Fairy Queen** from Evarard to the MSCo. As no fewer than seven ships bearing the name **Fairy Queen** were launched on the Clyde between 1831 and 1923, confusion has sometimes surrounded these vessels. Perhaps the best known 'Fairies' were the three vessels owned by James Aitken of Kirkintilloch, which were distinguished by suffixes I, II and III. Even more confusingly, Seath had launched no fewer than three **Fairy Queens**, in 1859, 1878 and 1891. The builder's numbers, 254 for the **Manx**

Fairy of 1887 and 278 for the **Fairy Queen** in 1891 give some idea of Seath's output at this time.

A 1960s reminiscence of the pleasure trips from Douglas to Ramsey claims there were two small steamers, **Lancelot** and **Fairy Queen**, sailing twice daily from Douglas, calling at Laxey, Dhoon Glen where a local fisherman took passengers off by rowing boat, and Ramsey. The vessels were said to leave Douglas for the 75 minute sail to Ramsey at 10.15am and 2.45pm, returning from Ramsey at 12.15pm and 4.45pm. A restaurant was opened on Dhoon beach, the foundations of which were still visible in the early 1960s. The situation was much more complex than that, and the panel below tabulates the vessels and operators involved.

Year	MSSCo	Evarard#	DSCo	Roper
1888	Manx Fairy		Minnow	
1889	Manx Fairy/Minnow			
1890	Manx Fairy/Minnow			
1891	Manx Fairy*	Fairy Queen		Lancelot
1892	Fairy Queen			Lancelot
1893	Fairy Queen			

* Possibly only for part of the season
\# On behalf of Mona Steamship Co

In 1888, the MSCo had faced competition from the **PS Minnow** of the Douglas Steamboat Co, but acquired the **Minnow** prior to 1889. This seems to have been the situation in 1890, but the **Minnow** was apparently broken up after the 1890 season. Unfortunately for the MSCo, a new operator, J & W Roper had appeared on the scene, with the **Lancelot**. Clearly the MSCo felt there was now overcapacity, so disposed of their older vessel prior to the 1892 season. The writer of the 1960s reminiscence spoke of just two ships, the **Fairy Queen**, and the **Lancelot**, but this only related to a single year, 1892, and they were rivals, not working together. Although the **Lancelot** is not a part of the Mona Steamship Co story, it is sensible to deal with her here. She had been constructed by R Duncan & Co of Port Glasgow in 1868, and was 191' 2" x 18' x 6' 9", with a Haystack boiler working at 40 psi. She had been built for Graham Brymner & Co, and was sold in June 1874 to Gillies & Campbell of Wemyss Bay, for their services to Millport and Rothesay. The position of the independent steamship operators on the Clyde worsened at the start of the 1890s with the expansionist policies pursued by the Caledonian Railway and the other railway operators, the North British and the Glasgow & South Western Railway. Captain Alexander Campbell, who owned the Wemyss Bay steamers, had connected with the Caley trains for many years at Wemyss Bay, but realised he was going to be squeezed out. His contract was due to expire in September 1890, but he ended operations with a month's notice from 30 April 1890, seemingly in an attempt to force the CR to give him an extension rather than face a summer without connections. It was a mistake, as the CR rose to the challenge, and Campbell had to find odd work for his boats during the summer. Most of the fleet was elderly, and there was no prospects of using it on the Clyde, so at the end of the summer, the **PS Lancelot** was put up for sale. By May 1891, she had moved to the Isle of Man, and was competing with the MSCo boats. The Ropers promoted her qualities "a Lady's cabin, a Dining Saloon, Refreshment Bars and both instrumental and vocal music on all Sailings . . . celebrated artistes from the Grand Hotel, Leeds." By 1892, she was listed as belonging to J & W Roper of Stanley House, Union Mills,

With the close connections between the Mona Steamship Co and the Manx Sun newspaper, due to the presence in both companies of Frank Spencer, the company AGM was always reported in full in the paper, additional copies being run off to circulate to shareholders. This is the opening page of the AGM for 1897, the first AGM of the third and final company. The ornate title lettering was typical of the typeface used by local printers in Victorian times for this sort of work.

but she was 25 years old, with an old style haystack boiler, and was sold to Turkey in 1893, becoming the **Erenkieui**. Handbills for the **Lancelot**, printed by the *Times* office rather than the *Manx Sun* said she was capable of 18 knots.

By May 1891, the **Manx Fairy's** master was given as William Charles Corrin, but with the greater carrying capacity of the **Fairy Queen**, the **Manx Fairy** was now surplus, and in 1891, the company decided to dispose of her. The timing was fortuitous. At this time, the Manchester Ship Canal was under construction. It was seen as one of the wonders of modern engineering, and a heavy excursion business up and down the canal was expected. The new owner of the **Manx Fairy**,

from 25 February 1892, was The Ship Canal Passenger Steamer Syndicate Ltd, of 46 Brown St, Manchester. It is possible that the **Manx Fairy** may even have left Manx waters in 1891, as there is evidence that she may have sailed on the ship canal in the latter part of 1891. If so, this would be on charter. Up to 1891, the MSCo had been successful, but problems were beginning to arise. In 1892, MSCo receipts stood £2,362, which was up on 1889, but expenses had almost doubled to £1,800 so the profit was little more than in 1888 when the capital stood at about a third of its 1892 levels. By the end of the summer, the Board had concluded that the capital was too great to receive an adequate dividend, and had decided

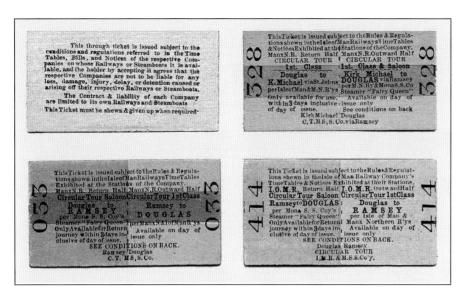

It was a set of circular tour tickets that were jointly issued with the Isle of Man Railway and the Manx Northern Railway which first put us on to the track of the Mona Steamship Co. The MNR, under its innovative manager, John Cameron, had made repeated efforts to establish a joint service from 1889 to 1895, but it was only in 1896 that the IMR finally agreed, the tickets being entered in stock in June 1896. Passengers could travel clockwise or anti clockwise, from a variety of MNR stations, but only from Douglas on the IMR. They were headed MNR, IMR or MSS depending on which company issued them, and were to a common design, but sadly the MSS issues have all vanished, so we can only illustrate the surviving railway issues, but the files make it clear that they would have followed the same format.

Dr R Preston Hendry

to reconstruct the company by winding up the original MSCo, and returning some of the capital to the investors. An EGM to approve these changes was held at Butterworth's Hotel on 23 September 1892. It seems that Richard Cain, the secretary to the original company, had died. A Richard Cain, aged 37, was buried at Braddan on 12 May 1892, his middle name being recorded as Alma, but this may be an incorrect rendering of his unusual middle name, Alma. To deal with the changes, Allen Brocklehurst Johnson, who had been born in 1848 in Douglas, was appointed liquidator of the original MSCo, and secretary to the new company. He had married Emily Clague at St Barnabas church in 1871, and in 1881 listed his occupation as a grocer, but the Victorian era was one of rapid change, and Johnson moved into shipping, acting as shipping agent for the Douglas Steam Navigation Co as well, from the 45 North Quay offices.

The Memorandum & Articles of a new Mona Steam Ship Co (as opposed to the Mona Steamship Co title of the first company), had already been prepared, and were registered on 10 October 1892, as Company No 156 on the Manx register. Edgar Robinson had also passed away, and was buried at Braddan on 14 August 1891, so F W Spencer became chair-

man, the other directors being J S Evarard, R B Brierley, S J Harris and W A Rayner. Frank William Spencer had been born in Hereford, and christened at St Owens in Hereford on 2 July 1858, his parents being Robert William and Jane Spencer. By 1881, the family were living at 6 Whitmore Place, Stretford Road, Stretford, Manchester, where Robert William Spencer, was working as a journalist, his two eldest sons, Frank William and Wilfred Robert, both being reporters. Towards the end of 1881, Frank Spencer moved to the Island, and in conjunction with Louis G Hannay ran the highly reputed Manx Sun newspaper from 1881 to 1898. Hannay was one of the victims of the Dumbell's affair, declaring bankruptcy with debts of £15,000, and losing the paper in 1900. It limped on with various owners until taken over by the IOM Times in 1906. A B Johnson was now secretary, and the capital was given as £10,400 in 13,000 shares of 16 shillings (80p) each. A tripartite agreement between the MSCo (1st), A B Johnson as liquidator of the MSCo, and C W Coole, advocate to the new MSSCo, transferred the company's assets to the new company and existing shareholders received new stock in proportion to their old holdings. The largest stock holding was still Thomas Seath's and this had risen to

1000 shares, the next largest holding being William Rothwell of Eccles with 450 shares. The registered office remained at 45 North Quay, Douglas.

1893, the first year of the reconstructed company, saw some improvement, and further problems. Revenue climbed from £2,362 to £2,747, but expenses increased from £1,800 to £1,900. The reason was due to an early Easter, for as the chairman, F W Spencer explained at the AGM on Thursday 16 November 1893, "when you work three weeks longer than you have done, you must expect to pay three weeks' more expenses". With Spencer owning the Manx Sun newspaper and printing facilities, the company could be sure of good coverage for its proceedings in the Sun, and most of its printing seems to have been done there as well. R B Brierley, a director of the original company and briefly of the second company had stood down, but was at the AGM, and from the tenor of the meeting it had been an amicable parting. He had been replaced by Oswald Edmondson. The meeting was a friendly occasion, for L G Hannay, who was Spencer's partner in the Manx Sun was present, as was Miles P Evarard, the proprietor of the Gaiety and elder brother to John Sawrey Evarard. A coal strike in the latter part of the season had added to the fuel bills, and the season had not been a good one for the island, not least because of the uncertainty generated by the coal strike. The balance sheet showed just the one steamer, **Fairy Queen**, which, with sundries, was now valued at £9,315, or more than her acquisition cost! This provoked some questioning, during which the board explained that the vessel had been kept in excellent condition, and the only interruptions in sailings had been due to weather, not mechanical failure. Her master, Captain Cannell, whom we met earlier on the **Manx Fairy**, was obviously highly thought of. S J Harris had been ill for some time and had passed away, his death at the age of 49 cutting short a life of great promise. The vacancy in the board was not filled, reducing the number of directors to four, their remuneration being settled at £50. A 7% dividend was declared on the reduced capital. A development that was not even mentioned, took place on 7 September 1893, when the first section of the fledgling Manx Electric Railway opened between Douglas and Groudle. It was not yet perceived as a threat, but within seven years was to bring the Steamship Co to its knees.

In 1894, the electric railway reached Laxey, and competition began to bite into Mona Steam Ship Co receipts, as many tourists preferred the novelty of electric traction to the familiar sea excursion that was available around the coasts of Britain. Concurrently with the electric railway expansion, Allan B Johnson stood down as secretary, from 27 June 1894, but remained closely connected with the company, and in 1901 was still listed as shipping agent for the Mona Steamship Co and Douglas Steam Navigation Co. Johnson, who was 53 years old in 1901, and living in Braddan, died aged 56 and was buried at Braddan on 5 October 1904. The new secretary, R M Warhurst, moved the registered office from 45 North Quay to 28 Athol Street, a venerable Georgian building in the heart of commercial Douglas. Robert Morledge Warhurst had been born at Gorton on the east side of Manchester in 1866, and was the son of Thomas Morledge Warhurst and his wife, Amelia. By 1881 he was training as a solicitors clerk, and later moved to the Island, marrying Elizabeth Helena Lofthouse at St Thomas' Church, Douglas on 21 April 1895, soon after he became secretary of the MSSCo. With competition from the electric tramway, the MSSCo began a slow decline. During this period, J S Evarard succeeded F W Spencer as chairman, but was unable to reverse the trend. The trouble was that the electric railway was siphoning off passengers and revenue, but operating costs varied very little. In 1893, expenses had stood at £1,900. In 1895 with considerably lower traffic, they still stood at £1865, but fell by £100 in 1896. Apart from the main Douglas-Laxey-Ramsey run, the *Fairy Queen* would make Sunday excursions to Port St Mary, and was even to venture as far as Kirkcudbright, leaving Douglas at 9.30am and offering three hours ashore. One useful development in June 1896 was the introduction of round trip tickets with the Island's steam railways, whereby a passenger could sail from Douglas to Ramsey and return by train, or vice versa. John Cameron, manager of the MNR, had been a keen advocate of such circular tour ticketing from the earliest days of the Mona Steamship Co, but the IOMR was reluctant to get involved. The tour could be 1st or 3rd class rail, and go clockwise or anti-

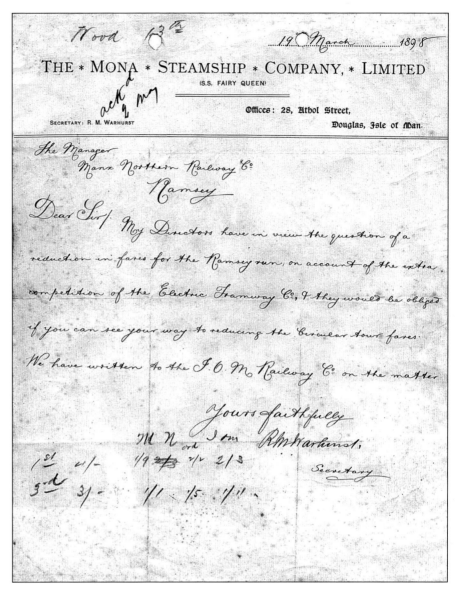

With the completion of the electric railway to the outskirts of Ballure expected in 1898, R M Warhurst, secretary of the MSSCo, wrote to the two railway companies on 19 March, prior to the commencement of the season to suggest a reduction in fares.

clockwise, with starting points at Douglas, Kirk Michael, Ballaugh, Sulby Glen and Ramsey.

MSSCo profits continued to fall, and in an attempt to restore the company's finances, it underwent yet another reconstruction. At an Extraordinary General Meeting on 2 February 1897, at the Salisbury Hall in Fort Street, it was agreed that Robert Morledge Warhurst be appointed liquidator of the existing Mona Steam Ship Co, and that he consent to the establishment of a new Mona Steamship Co, thus resurrecting the original title of 1888. As in the 1892 reconstruction, the MSSCo (2nd), the liquidator, and the new MSCo (3rd) were authorised to enter into a series of agreements. In those days, company law required that such resolutions be confirmed at a second

EGM. This took place on 25 February 1897, the new company being registered two days later. The first ordinary AGM of the new MSCo (3rd) took place at the Salisbury Hall at Fort Street on Wednesday 10th November 1897. Apart from the three directors, Evarard, Edmondson and Windsor, and the secretary, R M Warhurst, just four shareholders turned up. Edmondson's name reveals a fascinating paradox. In the 1881 census, Oswald R Edmondson is listed as residing with his wife, Alice, and family which included three sons Oswald, Arthur and Frank and a daughter Elizabeth, at 50 Bury New Road, Broughton in Salford, Lancashire. He was aged 45 and his son Frank, the youngest of four children was 5 years old. Moving to the Island, and living at Laureston Avenue, Douglas,

Oswald Edmond-son's son Frank was to carve out a remarkable career for himself. The 1890s saw the birth of practical electric traction in the British Isles, the few earlier lines being little more than novelties. When he was still in his twenties, Frank became chief engineer to the Isle of Man Tramways & Electric Power Co, which was building the electric line up the east coast of the Island that was to bring his father's shipping company to its knees! In 1911, to celebrate the coronation of King George V, Frank Edmondson was asked by Douglas Corporation to arrange electric illuminations in Victoria Street and on the Loch Prom. There is some evidence that they were the first seaside illuminations in the British Isles. His father, Oswald Richard Edmondson outlived the MSSCo by several years, and was buried at Braddan on 9 July 1913, aged 77, whilst Alice is recorded as being buried on 28 January 1919, although no age is given. Their daughter Elizabeth died unmarried in 1916. Their son, Frank Edmondson was buried at Braddan, on 26 January 1936. For most of the previous thirty years, Frank had been the highly respected manager of the Manx Electric Railway. Interestingly, it was Frank Edmondson who was to design the only locomotive ever built for commercial railway service on the Island, IOMT&EPCo, later MERCo, No 23. Almost eighty years after Edmondson designed it, my father and I were involved in preserving it when it was under threat of scrapping, little realising the Edmondson connection with the Mona Steamship Co.

The other director, Frank Windsor, was a shipping agent, representing White Star and American Line to New York; and Castle Line to South Africa, and worked out of Athol Street. Unlike the 1892 reconstruction, when 4 shillings (20p) had been returned per pound, to create 16s shares, there was no mention of capital being returned to investors in the first annual report. The capital now stood at 13,000 shares of 10 shillings (50p) each, of which 25 had been forfeited years before for non-payment of calls, reducing the capital to £6487 10s. The **Fairy Queen** had been revalued to this precise sum, and the balance of £268 represented the profit for the season. Expenses had been pared to £1,591 to make this possible, and a 4% dividend was declared. In admitting a decline in receipts, Evarard, who was now termed managing director, a revolutionary new transatlantic concept in British business life, mentioned that the "Llandudno & Liverpool Co", presumably the Liverpool & North Wales Steamship Co, which had been formed in 1891, also referred to a "falling off of visitors during June and July". In August 1897, there had been a couple of good weeks and then bad weather. He ruefully commented "we know that if people have a rough passage in crossing they have had enough sailing until they go back". A feeling that the fates were aligned against them was beginning to grip the little company. One of the directors, O R Edmondson, commented, "I must say that everyone connected with the steamer has deserved our best thanks. It is said it is not in mortals to command success, but they may deserve it, and, I think, in this case, we deserved much better results than we have obtained . . ." Joseph Drake Rogers, who had been auditor of the previous companies, had been appointed auditor, and was a popular and well-respected figure in the community. His reappointment went through without demur.

With the completion of the Electric railway to the outskirts of Ramsey in 1898, the MSCo board decided that drastic action was called for, and fares were cut to 1s 6d return. The policy

Joseph Drake Rogers, who was born in England in 1842, worked for the commercial department of the Liverpool Daily Post in his early twenties. However, he spent most of his professional life as an accountant associated with businesses in the Dumbell sphere, acting as secretary to the Great Laxey Mining Co, auditor to the bank itself, and being involved in the Brewery Syndicate, the Mona Aerated Water Co, IOM Tramways & Electric Power Co, Snaefell Mountain Railway Association, and other ventures. He was also associated with the erection of the Central and Woodbourne Hotels in Douglas. Some of the participants in the Mona Steamship saga were also associated with Dumbells, though none of the three directors at the close were shareholders in the bank. Mystery and tragedy have always surrounded Rogers. Alleged by some to be an illegitimate son of G W Dumbell, he lost two children and his first wife within a few years of their marriage. He later remarried, but went to jail for his part in the bank affair. He died at Blendellsands, near Liverpool, aged 69, on 1 January 1912, and was buried locally, but his memorial is in Braddan.

was a success with revenue rising to £1950 and profits to £333. Even so, it was a sad contrast to the halcyon days of ten years before with its 10% dividends. A perennial source of concern was harbour dues, for the company, on a 1/6d fare (7.5p) paid 2d at Douglas and 1d at Ramsey, whilst the Steam Packet, on a ten shilling fare, paid the same at Douglas. J D Rogers, auditor to the MSCo and its predecessors, was a popular figure in Manx society with a finger in many pies. He had been secretary of the Great Laxey Mining Co for almost 30 years, and secretary to Dumbell's Bank for 24 years. He had been a member of the Snaefell Mountain Railway Association, reaping a handsome profit when the mountain line was sold to the IOMT&EPCo. Rogers had very strong views about Laxey, where boatmen were alleged to charge extortionate amounts for landing passengers at low tide.

"Now, I am very intimately connected with Laxey, but intimately connected as I am, I believe you might go away among the Zulus and you would not get among a more barbarous lot than you find in Laxey. I feel very greatly ashamed of Laxey men, to think that they will take advantage of little endeavours of this sort to put bread into their mouths. They were not satisfied with what they were paid in an orthodox way by the officers of the Company, but they laid a system of blackmail upon all the visitors, whenever there was a chance".

A 5% dividend was declared, and as was customary, fulsome praise was accorded to the secretary R M Warhurst, whose long hours of work and devotion to the company were recognised by the shareholders. Another popular figure was Captain Cannell, whose habit of going down to the ship if the wind got up when she was moored in Douglas harbour was praised.

In 1899, despite the completion of the electric railway into its town centre terminus in Ramsey, the MSCo achieved remarkable results. Revenue rose to £2151, and profits to no less than £518, and a 6% dividend was declared. There were just three directors left now, J S Evarard, Frank Windsor and O R Edmondson. The registered office had moved to St George's Chambers, 1 Athol Street, Douglas on 6 February 1899. In his opening remarks at the AGM on 20 November 1899, Evarard commented, "Of course, this year we have had great opposition to meet in the tramway, but I am very pleased to say we have held our own and have actually done better with the opposition of the tramway than we did the previous year without it." Had it not been for dreadful weather in the last two weeks of September when the boat was at the pier ready to sail but weather precluded it, results would have been even better. The question of depreciation was raised once again, and Evarard explained that £80 would be put aside that year, which would make a fund of £800 to date. He went on to explain a novel concept of depreciation, "We have already reduced our shares from 16s to 10s a few years ago, which, we think, was enough to allow for depreciation for several years to come." One shareholder asked where the money set aside for depreciation was kept. The chairman proudly explained "I think that has been stated at every meeting. The money is in the bank at interest." The shareholder was satisfied, for the company's bank was a revered part of the Manx financial establishment. G.W. Dumbell had founded Dumbell's Banking Company Limited many years before. Apart from the irony of the Edmondson family, where father and son were associated with rival concerns, no one thought of the irony that their bank's energetic general manager, Alexander Bruce, was also chairman of the Isle of Man Tramways & Electric Power Co, their most deadly rival.

Rumours had been circulating that the company had received offers for the **Fairy Queen**, and Evarard admitted they had received several offers, but declined to go into details. Earlier in the year, the long serving Captain Cannell had been offered a good appointment "across" and had taken it, ending his connection with the company. It had been an amicable parting, and the mate, Captain Quinn had taken over. George Quinn had been born in Douglas on 29 June 1863, and had received his home trade mate's certificate in December 1886, and his master's ticket in June 1890. The experiences he listed when applying for his master's ticket included spells on the IOMSPCo **Mona's Isle** and **Mona's Queen**, and the **Herald** and **Manx Queen** of the Barrow SNCo, along with several weeks on

The ramifications of the Manx Business community in the Nineteenth century have not received the attention they warrant, for it was a closely-knit group. In researching the Evarard connection with the Mona Steamship Co, I discovered a link with one of the best-known businessmen on the Island. William Thomson was born in Castletown of a Scots father in the late 1830s. His father was an auctioneer, and William followed suit, marrying Annie Boyd of Castletown, who was a little older than her husband. In the mid seventies the couple moved to Douglas, where Thomson worked for John Taggart, the leading auctioneer on the Island. By the early 1880s, they were living at 2 Gelling's Court and Thomson had set up as an auctioneer in Duke St, Douglas, and with Manx company promotions mushrooming in the 1880s, the business expanded to include share dealing as well as auctioneering. By now, they had three children, Maud, Frederick, who became a seedsman, and Lilian Eva, the youngest child, who had been born in Douglas in 1877. After he left school in the 1890s, Douglas Evarard trained with William Thomson as an auctioneer, marrying his daughter Lilian on 19 March 1900, and becoming a partner in the firm. It was a difficult time for Thomson, for he had invested heavily in Dumbell's bank, and his holding of 140 shares made him one of the 40 largest shareholders when the bank crashed. In those days it was common for bank shares to be part paid, Dumbells £5 shares being £1 paid. This was to provide a cushion to reassure depositors in the event of a bank collapse as the shareholders would then have to pay up the balance of £4 per share. Annie Thompson died in January 1915 and was buried at Malew. William, although in poor health, continued to attend the business, which had moved to Athol St by 1910. Remembered for his ready wit at auctions, and ability to make light of his own financial misfortunes, he took ill early in 1917, passing away on 20 February 1917, and was buried at Malew.

the 62 ton Douglas schooner **Blue Bell**. He also listed two months as master of the **SS Minnow**, from July to September 1889, even though this

was several months before gaining his master's ticket. This is further evidence that the **Minnow** was sufficiently small to sail under a boatman's license, avoiding the need for a qualified master. Evarard was a popular chairman, and collected two pats on the back at the close of the meeting, one shareholder proposing a vote of thanks for, "the business-like way he has conducted the meeting and explained the accounts". Another member commented, "I think, considering the time that Mr Evarard has given to this Company, he deserved all that he will get out of the directors fees. I do not know how they are paid – whether they are divided equally… but I am sure that Mr Evarard deserved all the £50 himself for the time he gives to the concerns of the Company". Evarard expressed his thanks, and the hope that with fine weather, next year would be as good, if not better.

The MSCo entered the New Year in good shape, with more money in the bank than had been the case for many years. On Saturday 3rd February 1900, Dumbell's Bank collapsed, throwing the Island into financial panic. One MSCo figure to face immediate problems was Joseph Drake Rogers. As well as auditor to the MSCo and its predecessors, and to Dumbell's Bank and secretary to the Great Laxey Mining Co, he had a role in the Breweries Syndicate as well, the story of which appeared in "100 Years of Mann". The Brewery Syndicate, which was Alexander Bruce's latest venture, had sucked in vast amounts of cash. By the summer of 1899, Dumbell's was in a parlous state. In July 1899, Rogers was worried about Dumbell's accounts, but had not objected. He was to go to jail for that in 1901. In the wake of the Dumbell collapse, the Brewery Syndicate and the IOMT&EPCo crashed into ruin as well. The Mona Steamship Co limped into the first summer of the new century, but Island confidence was at a low ebb, and on 28 May 1901, an extraordinary general meeting was held to confirm the action of the directors in disposing of the **Fairy Queen** at £6,000 a few weeks previously. It was an acrimonious meeting attended by about 50 shareholders, the biggest turnout in many years. J S Evarard was supported by fellow directors Edmondson, and T J Halsall, who had recently joined the

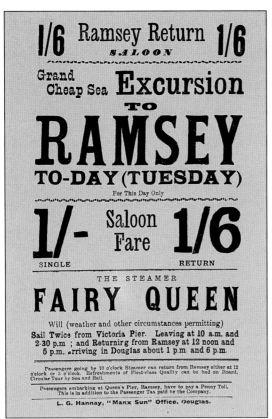

1/6 Ramsey Return 1/6

SALOON

Grand Cheap Sea Excursion

TO

RAMSEY

TO-DAY (TUESDAY)

For This Day Only

1/- Saloon Fare 1/6

SINGLE   RETURN

THE STEAMER

FAIRY QUEEN

Will (weather and other circumstances permitting)
Sail Twice from Victoria Pier. Leaving at 10 a.m. and
2-30 p.m ; and Returning from Ramsey at 12 noon and
5 p.m. arriving in Douglas about 1 p.m. and 6 p.m.

Passengers going by 10 o'clock Steamer can return from Ramsey either at 12
o'clock or 5 o'clock. Refreshments of First-class Quality can be had on Board.
Circular Tour by Sea and Rail.

Passengers embarking at Queen's Pier, Ramsey, have to pay a Penny Toll.
This is in addition to the Passenger Tax paid by the Company.

L. G. Hannay, "Manx Sun" Office, Douglas.

Mona Steamship Co handbills seldom seem to have carried a year of issue, but as this handbill is printed by L G Hannay of the Manx Sun, rather than Spencer & Hannay, it suggests that it was after Frank Spencer had left the paper in 1898, and prior to Hannay going bankrupt in July 1900, as a result of the Dumbell's bank crash. The usual fares were 1/6d single and 2/0d return for Douglas & Ramsey, with the Douglas and Laxey fares being 1/0d and 1/6d.

board. Evarard explained that the reason for selling the steamer was competition from the tramway, and also the Round-the-Island cruises of the IOMSPCo and Barrow Steam Navigation Co. They hoped to return between 8s 6d and 9s per 10s share to stockholders. Apart from approving the sale of the ship and return of money to the shareholders, the meeting had to consider a resolution proposing a payment to the directors and secretary as compensation for loss of office. The 10/- shares of the third company had been selling recently for as little as 4/6d, and one member, relieved at the improvement over the market value proposed 6d per share compensation, which would come to £324 in total. This provoked the ire of two shareholders, a Mr Mates, who had bought stock at 13 shillings, so stood to lose heavily, and Mr Light, who felt the directors should not have sold the vessel without consulting the

shareholders. Against this backdrop, the proposed compensation of 6d per share was trimmed to 3d per share. The meeting was now to get even stormier. Shares had recently been selling for as little as 4s 6d each, and it was remarked that the chairman's son had recently bought large numbers of shares at 4s 6d, when his father must have known of the likely return on capital. Many shareholders were suspicious of what they perceived as "insider trading", and this led to an acrimonious exchange.

The chairman: *"We have earned our salary already"*

Shareholder: *"I think you have earned it by sending your son round to buy shares at 4/6d"*

Chairman: *"It's not polite to call a man a liar, but I call it you all the same . . ."*

This bitter exchange prompted a further line of investigation. John Sawrey Evarard and his wife Annie Collins had seven children; Douglas born 28 Feb 1881: Annie, 26 August 1882: Edith 12 Sept 1884: Arthur 12 Sept 1885: Myles 13 August 1889 (buried Braddan aged 7 weeks 30 Sep 1889): May Avondale 30 Dec 1891: and William 23 January 1897, (died 24 Jan and buried at Braddan 26 Jan 1897). For events that took place in 1901, the only son who would have been old enough was Douglas, who was working as an auctioneer by 1901. He married Lilian Eva Thomson, who died at Cardiff aged 62 on 3 February 1941. They had one daughter Maude, who was born on 1 June 1900, and never married. Although his involvement with the Mona Steam Ship Co was controversial, Douglas Evarard retained links with the sea, and on 9 March 1906 was appointed Hon Secretary of the Douglas branch of the Royal National Lifeboat Institution. In 1910, he and his father, J S Evarard, were amongst the mourners at the funeral of a leading Douglas builder, George Preston (1848-1910). After my grandfather, Robert Applegarth Hendry II passed away in 1942, my grandmother, Emily Hendry (nee Preston), who was George Preston's daughter, returned to live in Douglas. She had known Douglas Evarard ever since they were children, and as they were both wid-

owed, they married in the early 1950s. As Douglas Evarard was the youngest character in the Mona Steamship story, I had, as a child, met the last surviving figure in that episode in Manx life. He was buried in Douglas Borough Cemetery on 27 July 1957, aged 76.

The motion for winding up the company named R M Warhurst as liquidator, but this was challenged. Despite the controversy, the secretary, R M Warhurst remained popular, as his devotion to the company was widely recognised, and he was appointed liquidator at a fee of £30. The resolution was confirmed at a 2nd EGM on 12 June 1901, and registered on 14 June 1901. Warhurst returned the money to the shareholders, and the MSCo vanished into obscurity for the next twenty years. In 1922, the IOM Company Registry decided it was time to tidy up its records, and trace defunct companies. The Registry sent out a request for information. On 17 May 1923, a note of impending dissolution was sent to the company's office. It was sent back marked "Not Known Return to Sender" stamped on the envelope. On 18 August 1923, the Mona Steamship Company was struck off the register. Robert Morledge Warhurst had pre-deceased the company by a few months, being buried at Douglas Borough Cemetery on 29 August 1922, at the early age of 57, but John Sawrey Evarard, who had been associated with the company from first to last, survived to the age of 85, being buried at Douglas Borough Cemetery on 14 October 1937. The Mona Steam Ship Company was dead, but some of its registered offices lingered on until the drastic rebuilding of Athol Street in the last 30 years of the 20th Century. A few round trip tickets survived, for tours by Mona SS Co, the Manx Northern Railway and the Isle of Man Railway, and most surprising of all, its two best-known vessels long survived its demise.

As we have seen, **Manx Fairy** exchanged the rocky east coast of Man for the waters of the Manchester Ship Canal. The 36 mile long ship canal ran from the Mersey at Eastham Locks to Manchester and was authorised by parliament in 1885, and opened to through traffic on 1 January 1894. As early as 1891, the Manchester Ship Canal Passenger Steamer Syndicate Ltd was operating day trips on the western end of the canal, and in February 1892, purchased **Manx Fairy** to operate excursions from Eastham Locks to the River Weaver, a distance of about 10 miles. When **Manx Fairy** officially entered service with the Syndicate at Easter 1892, Ellesmere Port was still under construction, and passengers had a remarkable view of this mammoth engineering project that was to cost over £15m. As the cruises commenced from the Liverpool Landing Stage, her passengers had the chance to see the upper reaches of the Mersey between the Stage and Eastham Locks as well. For the **Manx Fairy**, it meant that she was still "rubbing shoulders" with the IOMSPCo boats, but at the Liverpool end of their much longer voyages. On 22 April 1895, **Manx Fairy** was transferred from the Ship Canal Passenger Syndicate to the Ship Canal Passenger Steamer Company Ltd, both of 46 Brown Street, Manchester. By 1895, the novelty of a trip on the ship canal was wearing off, and the Passenger Steamer Company found a ready buyer for the "Fairy". Her new owners were The Western Australian Steam Packet & Transport Company Limited, of 24 Coleman St, London. The sale was registered on 31 December 1895. She was one of three vessels bought by Captain Webster for the Western Australian Company, the other two being the **Water Lily** and **St Mawes Castle**. David Heggie was appointed master of "the Fairy" on 2 March 1896, and all three vessels left on an incredible voyage for their new home on the far side of the globe. With limited coal capacity, she was not suited to the long oceanic passages, and made most of the voyage under sail. For a tiny coastal steamer used to a 16 mile run up the Manx coast, it was an astonishing change, but "the Fairy" was a stout little ship, and after a fraught voyage, arrived in Fremantle, Western Australia on 12 October 1896. The **Water Lily** suffered severe storm damage and was delayed for repairs, so did not arrive until 4 November 1897. Sadly, the **St Mawes Castle** vanished, and is presumed lost with all hands *en route*.

Perth, the principal city in Western Australia, is about 10 miles up the estuary of the Swan River, Fremantle being at the mouth of the river, where it enters the Pacific. A regular ferry service between Guildford, about 10 miles NE of Perth, and Fremantle commenced as early as 1831. Until the 1880s, the Swan was the most convenient means of communication,

but the advent of railways displaced it from its transport role. There was a period of decline, but from 1895 until the 1920s, cruising on the river was very popular, and it was for this traffic that **Manx Fairy** was sent out from the British Isles. In 1897, soon after the **Manx Fairy** arrived, the population of Western Australia was 157,819, of whom about 25,000 resided in Perth and 15,500 in Fremantle. By 1911, the population of the Perth metropolitan district, including Fremantle, had passed 100,000, so it was an era of boom, in which the river excursion enjoyed as much popularity as in home waters. She was under the command of Captain Webster from 10 February 1897, presumably working for the Western Australian company, but in May 1898 was sold to Zebina Lane and Frank Wilson of Perth, Western Australia. On 30 October 1900, "the Fairy" was sold once more, her new owner being Alexander Theodore Bernier, of Fremantle, WA., a marine engineer. He, in turn sold her to the Strelitz brothers, Paul and Richard, also of Fremantle. The brothers planned to operate her on excursions on the Swan River, but had an eye to the impending visit by the Duke and Duchess of Cornwall, later King George V and Queen Mary. The "Fairy" was borrowed by the government to act as tender to the royal yacht **Ophir**, and was hastily refitted for the visit in July 1901. The "Fairy", under the command of Captain C G F Wahl, carried the Royal couple from Perth to Fremantle to rejoin the royal yacht, but when she arrived alongside, consternation reigned. It had been planned that the royal couple would transfer from the upper deck of the "Fairy" to the royal yacht, but legend in Australia has it that she had never discharged passengers in this way before, and had no openings in her upper deck railings. The royal couple could hardly scramble over iron railings, so a workman was summoned from the royal yacht to cut away a portion of the offending railings! It is an entertaining story, but a photograph exists of the **Manx Fairy** discharging passengers at Ramsey at low tide, with a wooden gangway run from the quayside to the upper deck! It is hard to imagine the Australian story being made up, so the likely explanation is that when the **Manx Fairy** was sailing on the Ship Canal, that the upper deck opening was closed up. Had this work been done after she arrived in Australia, some-

body would have remembered the alteration.

In November 1902, Strelitz brothers transferred the "Fairy" to a company they had formed, Manx Fairy Ltd. She continued on the Swan River service until 1 July 1905, when her iron hull was found to be in poor condition, and she was hauled on to the bank of the Swan River for rebuilding. New plates were provided by the Hoskins foundry and the engines refitted and timber work renewed, and the reconstructed "Fairy" was launched broadside on and renamed **Westralian** by the Colonial secretary, Walter Kingsmill, (1864-1935) on 1 November 1905. The Colonial Secretary was one of the most important political offices in the colony, and Kingsmill, who had been born in Australia, served two spells in the post, in 1902-04, and 1905-06. The launch was in good time for the start of the new 1905/06 season. The owners, Manx Fairy Ltd decided to treat **Westralian** as a new ship, and on 24 April 1906 notified the Registrar of Shipping in England that the vessel had been broken up, the registry entry for **Manx Fairy** being closed on 30 April 1906.

By this time, the "new" **Westralian** was engaged in a deadly battle on the Swan River with a rival steamer, **Decoy**, owned by Miers, Sunman and Tasker. Both vessels carried bands on their excursions, and as **Westralian** was much faster, she would pass her rival playing derogatory tunes such as *"We shall meet in the sweet bye and bye"*. **Decoy** retaliated by arranging film shows on the open deck forward of the bridge in the evening, but **Westralian** was not to be outdone, and her Captain, C G F Wahl, played a powerful searchlight on the screen ! In 1906, **Westralian** was sold to Jack Olsen of Perth, another Swan river boat proprietor, but the venture proved too much for his finances, and tragically, Olsen committed suicide the following year. Apart from pleasure sailings on the Swan River, she was also used for towage work for timber ships outward bound from the Swan. Trading as Westralian Pleasure Steamers Ltd, the company was absorbed by a large Australian shipping line, McIllwraith, McEacharn Pty Ltd, who ran her until December 1921, when she was transferred to Sydney, and then shortly thereafter sold to a Tasmanian firm for use on the fruit trade, receiving a wooden wheelhouse, which must have made life bet-

The **Manx Fairy**, after her 1905 rebuild on the banks of the Swan River in Western Australia, became the **Westralian**. She is seen c1916 at Pt. Walker, which is on the south bank of the river, roughly midway between Fremantle and Perth. To the west of Pt. Walker, the river is quite narrow, but for most of the way up river to Perth it is between 1 and 2 miles wide until the Narrows just down river of Perth city centre.

ter for her master. Her last registered owner was A J Challenger, and she was registered at Hobart in Tasmania. I have not been able to trace when **Manx Fairy-Westralian** finally went out of use, but she was run ashore at East Risdon, on the soft mud of the banks of the River Derwent in Hobart, Tasmania in the 1940s, and stripped. Her hulk was to be seen for many years after World War II, but in December 1961, she was apparently towed by the tug **Misshin Maru** to Osaka to be broken up.

Most youngsters will recall blood-curdling stories of piratical characters such as Captain John Kidd, When the MSCo decided to sell **Fairy Queen** on 30 April 1901, her new owner was none other than a Captain John Kidd of 46 Leadenhall St London! He

appears to have been a shipping agent rather than a pirate, for the **Fairy Queen** also emigrated, heading for India, her owners later in 1901 being the Bombay & Persia SN Co. She was transferred to Bombay registry in 1902, being sold to Visram, Ebrahim & Co of Bombay. In 1905, she went to Shepherd & Co of Bombay, changing owners in 1906 to Hajee Ahmad Hajee Hassam, also of Bombay, and in 1907 to the Bombay SN Co. According to Lloyd's Register, **Fairy Queen** was dismantled in 1922/23, but what actually happened was that she became a floating workshop, being owned by Bombay Floating Workshop Ltd of Mallet Road, Wadi Bunder, Bombay. She was in the Bombay Merchant shipping list as recently as 1969 !

Although both Mona Steamship boats have long disappeared from Lloyd's register, two of the ships built by T B Seeth, the Australian **Coomonderry** and the Spanish owned **Gaviota**, were still active in Lloyd's seagoing register as late as 1962. Of these, the most interesting was the **Coomonderry**, Yard No 256, a 146 grt, auxiliary-engined schooner, which was registered at Adelaide, Australia. Sadly the end came for her in 1969, when she was driven ashore at Suva in the pacific. Four vessels, all now preserved survive in the British Isles, The **Esperance** and **Raven** on Lake Windermere, and the **Lady of the Lake** and another **Raven** on Ullswater. A fifth vessel, the **Nelcebee** is on static display in Australia.

CHAPTER FIVE
At Sea with the "Diamond King"

As you enter Kirk Michael from the north, an impressive house can be seen set back from the road. For decades, the owners have made the grounds available to race goers during the TT Races, but twenty years before the first bikes were to travel through the narrow streets of Kirk Michael on the celebrated Mountain Course, the house was owned by a legendary character, who might have stepped out of the pages of the most colourful novel. His name was Joseph Mylchreest, but he was universally known as "The Diamond King". He was the third son of John Mylchreest, a Peel fishing smack-owner, and Christian Moore, and was born in 1839. He was educated at Gawne's School in Peel, and on leaving, was apprenticed as a ship's carpenter in the town. At the age of 18, he married Catherine Skelly of Foxdale, but she died in childbirth a few months later. After this tragedy, feeling that the Island offered little prospect of advancement, and leaving his infant daughter in the care of her grandparents, Joe Mylchreest went out to the West Coast of Africa, working as a carpenter. News of gold discoveries in Australia prompted a further move in 1860. A few prospectors struck it rich, but for most, it was life of backbreaking toil, hardship, danger and no reward. Joe Mylchreest followed the prospectors' trail to New Zealand, California, British Columbia, Bolivia, Peru, Chile, and back again to Australia, working off and on in gold and silver mines. In this, he was typical of the itinerant nineteenth century prospectors who entered folklore in many countries, but are best recalled by the celebrated Forty-Niners in California or the Klondike gold rush fifty years later. Success eluded him, but in 1876, he went to the diamond mines at Kimberley, in South Africa. At first, panning in the Vaal River, he encountered his usual ill luck, and went back to work as a joiner, marrying Phoebe Bishop, a 21 year old miner's daughter from Oxfordshire in 1882. Joe heard that some claims in the Dutoitspan mine were not being worked, and leased them, using borrowed money,

Joe Mylchreest, (1839-1896), the "Diamond King", was a towering figure, physically, and in his impact on the Island in the few years between his return home in 1888 and his death at the end of 1896.

and the venture paid off. By 1885, he had 115 claims, all producing diamonds. In 1886, he revisited the Island, meeting his first child, Jamina, who, at 29, was a few years older than her stepmother. The mid-eighties were a period of consolidation in the diamond field, and on his return to South Africa, Joe agreed terms with Cecil J Rhodes, after whom the Country of Rhodesia was to be named. They were thrashed out across the kitchen table in Joe's bungalow at Kimberley, the agreement providing:

> *"Joseph Mylchreest agrees to sell and Cecil Rhodes agrees to buy the 115 claims in the Dutoitspan mine for the sum of £115,000 together with all equipment and horses. Completion to be made in six months from this date".*

Joe had six months to work his claims, and erected arc lights so they could be worked round the clock, extracting a fortune in that brief period, and making history with the 199 carat

Mylchreest Diamond, which was worth £100,000 in its own right. In 1888, with his fortune made, Joe Mylchreest made a fairy tale return to the Island, a classic case of a local boy from humble origins having made good. Known as "The Diamond King," Joe Mylchreest was a gigantic figure, weighing 20 stone, but of outstanding physical strength, a legacy of years of hard work prospecting. Black haired and with a thick moustache, he had a deep voice, but like many self made men in Victorian society, he also believed in putting back into the community. This Victorian ethic is often scorned today, but motivated men from disadvantaged backgrounds, including Joe Mylchreest, to rise to unparalleled distinction. Many who have accomplished that journey are glad to forget their origins and the friends of their youth, but that was not Joe's way. Contemporaries unanimously spoke of a rough exterior that concealed a kindly heart and great shrewdness. It was said of him that he never turned his back upon an old friend, however humble. Although he now lived at "The White House" in Kirk Michael, Mylchreest was keen to help his hometown of Peel. Perhaps the best account from those intimately associated with the birth of the Peel & North of Ireland Steamship Co came from Joseph Tatlow, an Englishman who had been appointed manager of the Belfast & County Down Railway in the 1880s. In his memoirs published in 1920, "Fifty Years of Railway Life in England, Scotland and Ireland", Tatlow recounted what happened.

> *Joseph Mylchreest was a Manxman, a rough diamond but a man of sterling worth. He left home when young and worked first as a ship's carpenter. An adventurous spirit led him to seek his fortune in various parts of the world, in the goldfields of California and Australia and in the silver mines of Peru and Chile. Later on he went to South Africa, where in the diamond mines he met with great success and made a large fortune. His property there*

he disposed of to Cecil Rhodes, and it now, I am told, forms part of the De Beers Consolidated Company's assets. In the late eighties he returned to his native island, settled at Peel, and became a magnate there.

One afternoon early in the year 1889 two gentlemen from the Isle of Man called upon me at my office. They were Mr. Mylchreest (the "Diamond King") and a lawyer friend whose name I forget, but I remember they informed me they were both members of the House of Keys. Mr. Mylchreest was anxious to do something to develop the little port of Peel, his native town, and a steamboat service between Peel and Belfast, Bangor or Donag-hadee, seemed to him and his friends a promising project. What did the County Down think? Would either Bangor or Donaghadee be better than Belfast? If so, would my company join in and to what extent? We had no power to expend money in steamboat enterprise, but I assured them we would do all we could to help in other ways, and that Bangor was the port to select. My directors heartily approved and other interviews followed. Once, I had hurriedly to go over to Peel to meet Mr. Mylchreest and his

The Company seal of the Peel & North of Ireland Steamship Co.

lawyer, on a certain day, as some hitch had arisen, and by this time I was desperately keen on getting the steamboat service started. The only way of reaching Peel in time was by a collier steamer, belonging to the East Downshire Coal Co., which plied between Dundrum on the Co. Down coast, and Whitehaven; the manager of the company was my friend, and would allow the steamer to drop me at Peel. It was a memorable crossing, the weather was "bad" and so was I. But my journey was successful, and soon the Peel and North of Ireland Steamship Company, Limited, in which the

"Diamond King" was much the largest shareholder, was estab-lished, and on the 26th June, 1889, the first voyage was made from Peel to Bangor. It was a great event for the quiet little town of Peel. Mr. Mylchreest had invited all his friends to the inaugural service, in addition a good number of the public travelled, and the steamer arrived at Bangor with nearly 300 passengers on board. On the return voyage from Bangor to Peel the same evening the "Diamond King" gave a great dinner, cham-pagne and speeches freely flowed, and music and dancing enlivened the proceedings. The service pros-pered for a time, but the traffic did not reach expectations. Ultimately it was taken over by the Isle of Man Steam Packet Coy, and after a few years discontinued.

Writing from memory thirty years later, Tatlow erred in a few details, for Joe Mylchreest had settled in Kirk Michael and not Peel, and did not become a member of Tynwald until 1891, but allowing for those trivial dis-crepancies, his account is a valuable first hand reminiscence. The only member of the P&NI board who was in the Keys in 1889 was John Joughin, although he was not a lawyer. As John Joughin was to manage the company in 1889, it is probable that he was the other visitor. Sadly, most of the records of the venture are long gone, but a few documents fill in some of the gaps. As the traffic from Peel to Bangor would be sparse, one might wonder at the viability of such a scheme, but Porter's Directory of 1889, which came out when the scheme was being devel-oped, provides an answer,

"... a still more practical effort is now being made, not only to make Peel more accessible to visi-tors, but to establish an overland route between the north of England and Ireland, whereby the voyager may break his Journey on the way by spending a pleasant hour or two on the way in Mona's Isle, and yet perform the journey quicker and at less expense than any other way now open to the public, viz., the institution of a daily service of boats to and from Belfast. Manxmen, by this quiet and thoughtful endeavour, have rendered a signal service to England and Ireland, which it is hoped may be appreciated in the

The brief lifespan of the Peel & North of Ireland Steamship Co and the passage of more than a century have eliminated most of the paper trail that historians welcome, making the survival of this indemnity doubly welcome.

*Until the traumatic events of 1887, when the whole of the Steam Packet fleet was outperformed by the Fairfield twins, the **Queen Victoria** and **Prince of Wales**, the **Mona's Isle III** of 1882 came second in the Steam Packet hierarchy after the slightly newer **Mona's Queen** of 1885. It says much for Joe Mylchreest's standing on the Island that he was able to extract such a prestigious vessel from the Steam Packet for the inaugural sailing of the Peel-Belfast route on 26 June 1889. It must have been a proud moment for the people of Peel when she came alongside the breakwater for the start of their own direct service to Ireland.*

immediate future. The journey from Liverpool to Douglas may be, and is frequently, accomplished in three and a-quarter hours from thence to Peel in half-an-hour, and from Peel to Belfast in three hours, making the complete journey from England to Ireland, via Mona, in 6½ hours, or little more than the time required to go from Liverpool direct to Belfast by steamboat, or by rail to Holyhead, and steamer to Greenore".

If the P&NI were to function as a link in such a chain, then the company was dependent on the goodwill of the railway companies at each end. Conscious that the risks on steamships were much higher than on rail, the Isle of Man Railway Company demanded adequate safeguards, as a two-page hand written document reveals. On 24 June 1889, just two days before the inaugural voyage, the directors of the shipping company agreed to an indemnity.

"In consideration of your agreeing to further the interests and facilitate the business of the Company known as the Peel and North of Ireland Steamship Company Limited, hereinafter known as the said steamship Company, by booking passengers at any of the stations on your lines through to Bangor or elsewhere in Ireland to travel by the steamers of the said Company, we undertake and guar-

antee to indemnity and keep you harmless from and against all actions, claims, demands, costs, damages and expenses of any kind which may at any time hereafter be made or incurred or recovered against you in respect of any loss, damage or injury sustained or alleged to be sustained by any passenger or by reason of any loss or alleged loss or damage to goods or luggage of any passenger whilst travelling on the said steamers between Bangor in the County of Down and Peel in the Isle of Man aforesaid whether on the outward or return journey. This guarantee shall apply also to loss of, delay or injury to any goods or luggage not in charge of a passenger and which may have been booked by you."

In the actual deed, the phrase "to Bangor or elsewhere in Ireland" is a correction of the original wording which reads "to Peel or elsewhere in the Isle of Man" which suggests that the guarantee to the IMR is a clone of an earlier guarantee to the BCDR. The signatories were J Mylchreest as chairman, H T Graves, Robert Corrin, John Joughin, Wm Moore, and Edward Ewan Christian. Apart from "The Diamond King" himself, who was chairman of the company and had contributed much of the £10,000 capital, the other signatories were a "Who's Who" of Peel life. Henry Thomas Graves (1845-1900) was a shipyard owner in Peel, supplying fish-

ing boats and also a JP. John Joughin, MHK, (1831-1901) was the son of John Joughin, Senior (1803-1868), who had been a shopkeeper and master mariner. John inherited his father's fishing boat and grocery business, and ran a fishing net factory in Peel that he expanded to employ over 100 people. He was a member of the Peel Town Commissioners, and was MHK for Glenfaba from 1876 until his death. He was also my Mother's great uncle. Robert Corrin (1823-1899) was a former member of the Keys and a JP. He was a business rival of John Joughin, operating a major fishing net manufactory and a grocery business, and had an interest in the boats as well, instituting the sending of Manx boats to Kinsale. Edward Ewan Christian of Athol House, Peel, and William Moore were both leading merchants. The only director missing from the indemnity was Thomas C S Moore, Captain of the Parish of German, and another past member of the House of Keys.

Although the service might appear to be competitive with the IOMSPCo, and hostility might have been expected, the inaugural voyage in June 1889 was taken by the IOMSPCo **Mona's Isle**. The service was advertised as leaving Peel at 9.15am for a 3½ hour sailing to Bangor, the connecting train leaving Douglas at 8.15am. In the return direction, the train left Belfast Queens Quay station at 3.05pm, and the steamer departed from Bangor at 4.05pm. Because steerage accommodation on board was much poorer

The **PS Paris**, which handled most sailings in 1889, including the final 4.05pm departure from Bangor on Saturday 31 August 1889, was an iron paddle steamer, launched by J Elder & Co of Govan in 1875. Despite her reboilering by Fairfields in 1888, and transfer to Richard Barnwell, she was not of the same calibre as the **Queen Victoria** or **Prince of Wales**, but the Packet Board must have been relieved that Barnwell was now "on board" as a director of the IOMSPCo rather than as a rival, as had been the case in 1887-1888 with "Manx Line". From 1892 to 1895 she sailed as the **Flamingo** for Albert Ballin, a well-known German ship owner, working between Hamburg and Heligoland, but was thereafter returned to Barnwell. From 1896 to 1902 she was owned by W Rhodes, who also had close connections with Fairfield, and became **La Belgique**, working on the competitive Tilbury-Ostend service. From 1902, she ran for MacBrayne's as the **Glendale** until she ran aground and was wrecked off Kintyre in July 1905.

than 3rd class on rail, three types of through rail/sea tickets were usually issued, 1st class and saloon; 3rd class and saloon and 3rd class and steerage. The fares were as follows:

	Single	Return
1st/saloon	6/-	10/-
3rd/saloon	5/-	8/6d
3rd/steerage	3/6d	5/-

The use of the **Mona's Isle** was a temporary measure, probably facilitated by the influential figures on the P&NI board, but for most of the season, sailings were entrusted to the **PS Paris**, the final sailing being the 4.05pm departure from Bangor on Saturday 31 August 1889. The **Paris** was an iron paddle steamer, launched by J Elder & Co of Govan in 1875. She was 220 feet in length, and had cost £25,796 when new. The yard had been laid out on the south bank of the Clyde in 1864 by John Elder, and after his death in 1869, the company continued to bear his name until 1886, when it became the Fairfield Shipbuilding & Engineering Co. The **PS Paris** had been built for the Newhaven-Dieppe service of the London, Brighton & South Coast Railway. She was driven by compound oscillating engines with a 41" diameter HP cylinder and a 72" LP cylinder, taking steam at 60 psi from a pair of boilers. She was a splendid sea boat, but with a speed of 13 knots, was rather slow for the route. The orig-

inal flat floats to the paddle wheels were replaced with curved steel floats but with little effect. On 3 March 1888, after thirteen years on the route, she made her first crossing in under

Although the Diamond King was the main financial backer, he was not yet in Tynwald, so the company relied on John Joughin MHK, for political backing. He had been born in 1831, and was a net manufacturer, fishing boat owner and merchant in Peel, and in 1881 had employed 105 men, 15 boys and 30 women in his businesses, making him the major employer in the town. Despite his busy workload, Joughin, who was an MHK from 1876 to 1900, wrote the more important Peel & North of Ireland correspondence in his own slightly spiky hand. His father, John Joughin Snr, had been born in Peel in 1804, and by the time of his death, owned two houses, a fishing lugger and a shop. John (MHK) inherited his father's flair for business, a skill he shared with his sister, Mary Ann Corrin (nee Joughin) who set up a successful and profitable restaurant in Victoria St in Douglas in the 1880s at a time when women in business were a rarity. Mary Ann's husband, Henry William Corrin, was descended from old Hal Corrin, and we met his daughter Sukie in Chapter 1. John Joughin was buried at Peel on 15 March 1901.

five hours, taking just 4 hours and 50 minutes, but this spurt did not ensure her future as she was sold later that year to Fairfields, who re-boilered her, the new boilers working at 80 psi. She was transferred to Richard Barnwell, managing director of Fairfields, and appeared on the Peel service, and was also operated along the North Wales coast in competition with the Liverpool, Llandudno & Welsh Coast Steamboat Co. Barnwell, who was the powerhouse behind the Fairfield backed Manx Line of 1887-88, which had offered such ferocious competition to the Steam Packet, had joined the IOMSPCo board following the

John Joughin, MHK, had married Emily Jane Fenton, and their son, John Joseph Joughin, who was christened on 3 October 1862 at Kirk German, worked in the family businesses in Peel, so it was natural that he dealt with routine correspondence for the Peel & North of Ireland Steamship Co as well. His older brother, William J Clucas Joughin was a celebrated writer, whose novel "Gorry, Son of Orry" was a splendid adventure story set in and around Peel, Castle Rushen, and the Calf of Mann. J J Joughin, aged 69, was buried at German on 13 January 1932.

merger of the 1887 Manx Line and the Packet, and was to repeat that coup on the North Wales service, the LL&WCSCo being merged with the Barnwell interests to form the celebrated Liverpool & North Wales Steamship Co, with Barnwell on the board.

The results of the first season of the Peel route were disappointing, as few people seem to have used it as a way of travelling from England to Ireland. Had the railway extended to the quayside at both ends, it might have been a different matter, but the effort and loss of time in transfer between the stations and steamers made it unattractive as a through route. Over the winter, the Diamond King and his colleagues must have lobbied the Steam Packet. When the service was resumed on 1 July 1890, it was under the auspices of the IOMSPCo, and was to run until 31 August 1890. In 1891, Joe Mylchreest was elected to the House of Keys, but died shortly after Christmas 1896, following a chill with complications developing later. His widow, Phoebe, survived until 1942. His descendants included Lt-Col J B Mylchreest, who ran Mylchreest's garage, and was ADC to the Governor for many years after the war. Relations benefited from his kindness, including the orphaned T M Sheard, the first Manxman to win a TT race, and A M Sheard, whose outstanding management of the Steam Railway from 1927 to 1965 ensured the survival of the Port Erin line.

At first a daily service frequency was reduced, but the route limped into the twentieth century, although Bangor was replaced by Belfast as the destination. Traffic remained light and the service was marginal at best. In 1902, the Steam Packet decided not to run the service. G H Wood, the manager of the Steam Railway, noted ruefully at the end of the summer, "The Belfast traffic was missed this year". Surprisingly, the route was re-opened in 1908, running on Thursdays only from June 24th to September 2nd, with a 9.10am sailing from Peel, and a 4.30pm sailing from Belfast. It was one of the last decisions taken by Thomas P Ellison, the long serving IOMSPCo General Manager prior to his retirement in August 1908. Round trip Tourist Tickets in conjunction with the Belfast Steam Ship Co direct Belfast Liverpool sailings permitted passengers to travel by the Steam Packet from Liverpool to Douglas, and subsequently from Peel or Douglas to

Isle of Man Steam Packet Company, Ltd.
(Incorporated in the Isle of Man.)

Coronation Day.

DELIGHTFUL
SEA EXCURSIONS

DOUGLAS to LIVERPOOL,

WEDNESDAY, 21st June, at 12 night (Douglas),
THURSDAY, 22nd, 9 a.m. (Tynwald).
Returning from Liverpool, Thursday, at 2-45 p.m. (Tynwald), or 12-50 night (Snaefell).

DAY FARES—Steerage, 4/-; Saloon, 6/-.

DOUGLAS to BELFAST (via PEEL).
by large and fast steamer MONA'S QUEEN

To BELFAST.	From BELFAST.
Douglas ... Train dep. at 8-10 a.m.	Belfast ... Steamer dep. at 4-30 p.m. (a)
Ramsey ... ,, ,, at 7 50 a.m.	Peel ... ,, due about 8-30 p.m.
Peel ... Steamer dep. at 9-10 a.m.	Peel ... ... Train dep. at 9-15 p.m.
Belfast Steamer due about 12-15 p.m. (a)	Douglas... ... Train due at 9-53 p.m.
(a) Irish Time.	Ramsey ... ...Train due at 10-18 p.m.

Open Sea Passage 2¼ hours, and Belfast Lough 1 hour.

SPECIAL DAY FARES—From Douglas and Ramsey : Steerage and 3rd Rail, 4/6 ; Saloon and 3rd Rail, 6/9 ; Saloon and 1st Rail, 7/6.

From Peel—Steerage, 4/-; Saloon, 6/-.

CARRIAGE DRIVE TICKETS, 2/6 Each, which must be purchased at Douglas or Ramsey when booking, as seats are reserved for Ticket-Holders only.

Afternoon Cruise
(For 2 Hours)
To Ramsey Bay and round Bahama Lightship.
By the Magnificent New R.M.S. SNAEFELL,
Leaving Douglas at 2 p.m. Due back about 4 p.m.

FARE—ONE SHILLING.

Breakfasts, Luncheons, Dinners, Teas, and Refreshments, can be obtained on board all Steamers.

Passengers, their Luggage, Live Stock and Goods, conveyed subject only to the conditions of carriage of the Company as exhibited in their offices and on board their Steamers.
WM. M. CORKILL, Secretary and Manager.
Douglas, June, 1911.

Broadbent & Co. Ltd., Printers, "Examiner" Office.

Nowadays, major events such as Royal Jubilees, Coronations or Presidential Inaugurations, attract a TV audience of millions, but in the far-off days before World War One, it was different, as no instant media existed. However people were as keen to celebrate then as now. If you lived on the Island or were a visitor, one way to do so was a sea trip, as there were special excursions from Douglas to Liverpool, from Belfast to Peel, and an afternoon cruise to Ramsey Bay and round the Bahama Bank lightship. The afternoon cruise, which was often a way of obtaining useful employment for a vessel that would otherwise be tied up in port, was particularly good value and although two class travel prevailed on normal sailings, were commonly one class sailings, allowing all to savour the delights of saloon accommodation.

Belfast and to make the return leg by direct BSS boat, or vice versa. The saloon fare in 1908 was 21/- and the steerage fare was 10/6d. Sadly, results were disappointing. Startling confirmation of this comes from letters exchanged between William Corkill, the Manager of the IOMSPCo and Thomas Stowell, his counterpart on the IOMR. On 19 June 1911, three days before the summer service was due to start, Corkill suggested a remarkable change in through ticket arrangements. Railway and shipping companies were ordinarily punctilious in the types of tickets they issued on their own system and even more so in the case of through tickets, but he proposed that the IOMSPCo Belfast agent and the purser on the steamer would issue single or return tickets to Douglas when asked for tickets to Ramsey, and that IMR ticket collectors would accept them as valid despite the "wrong" destination. Astonishingly, Stowell agreed the following day. As the distance from Peel to Ramsey was greater than to Douglas, and the fare proportionately higher, this was a remarkable concession, and required a special instruction to ticket collectors to do what would otherwise have led to their dismissal, viz. to accept a ticket as valid, although it was to a wrong, and cheaper, destination. The first day of

the 1911 season, on 22 June, coincided with the Coronation of King George V. With 3 million people thronging to London for the event, steamer companies feared a quiet day, and offered special services to celebrate the event and to bolster up their own traffic, the IOMSPCo providing cheap fares from Douglas to Liverpool, from Peel to Belfast, and a two-hour afternoon cruise from Douglas to Ramsey bay. The Peel sailings limped on from year to year, but the disruptions of World War One brought them to an end. The fortuitous survival of records from 1911 means we know what vessels were used for every sailing that year, and given the rarity of such data, I feel it is worth recording:

22 June	*Mona's Queen*
29 June	*Tynwald*
6 July	*Mona's Queen*
13 July	*King Orry*
20 July	*Mona's Queen*
27 July	*King Orry*
3 Aug	*King Orry*
10 Aug	*Tynwald*
17 Aug	*Tynwald*
24 Aug	*Tynwald*
31 Aug	*King Orry*

What of these three vessels? Out of the eleven sailings during the season, the *King Orry* and the *Tynwald* each took four, the *Mona's Queen* handling the other three. The *PS King Orry* was a predictable choice. Dating from 1871, she was the oldest vessel in the fleet, and was broken up the following year, so was a logical selection for a minor route with limited traffic. The *Tynwald* of 1891 was twenty years old, and although a good ship in her day, was slower than the celebrated Fairfield twins of 1887, the *Prince of Wales* and *Queen Victoria,* or the modern turbine ships acquired after 1905. In contrast to the other two vessels, one a little over 1000 gross tons, the other a little below, the *Mona's Queen* was half as big again, at 1.559grt, and with a length of 320 ft 1 ins, was not much different in length to the 322 ft of the second *Lady of Mann* of 1976. She was a big ship, and at 19 knots, fast for her day. Until the turbine steamers delivered from 1905 on, she was one of the premier vessels in the fleet, but her appearance on the Peel run shows how fast she was slipping down the order. The surprising omission is the *SS Fenella* of 1881, as she is known to have operated on the Peel route, but the records for 1911 reveal she did not make an appearance that year.

*One of the regular vessels on the Peel-Belfast route in 1911 was the **SS Tynwald** of 1891. Smaller than the superb Fairfield twins of 1887, the **Empress Queen** of 1897 and the turbine steamers delivered in the early 1900s, the **Tynwald** was used on secondary services and winter sailings. She was not particularly fast, her 3,800 indicated horsepower reciprocating engines delivering a top speed of 18 knots. We see her departing from Douglas at the turn of the century in this enchanting study by my great-grandfather, Robert Applegarth Hendry 1st. She was laid up at Barrow from 1930 to 1933, due to the depression and then sold. She passed to R A Colby Cubbin, for conversion to a private yacht, **Western Isles**, but was requisitioned by the Admiralty in 1940.*

Except where man-made barriers intervene, ships may ply the waters of the world freely, so no study of "Manx" Shipping would be complete without looking at the vessels from afar that visit our shores. Initially I had hoped to explore many different operators, but as data was amassed, the numbers that could be covered fell, so we are left with two very different shipping lines that were contemporaries of one another at the close of the Nineteenth century. Fascinating though the passenger boats are, I realised that cargo services, especially where the vessels were not registered on the Island, had left little trace, so a file containing a dozen letters and telegrams that were exchanged in 1898 between the Isle of Man Mining Co at Foxdale, the Manx Northern Railway in Ramsey, a Glasgow steam coasting company, and granite quarry owners with an office in Liverpool, shed important light on cargo services. They also highlighted a problem that I recall Bernie Swales, the manager of the Ramsey Steamship Co, mentioning to me, which was the imbalance between substantial inbound cargoes, and limited shipments outwards. If most outbound voyages are light ship, it is less profitable than if a reasonable number of outward cargoes can be secured. The correspondence introduces us to "The Glasgow Steam Coasters Ltd", the managing agents being John Paton & Peter Hendry of 50 St Enoch Square,

Glasgow. It was fun to discover that ships bearing my own family name had actually sailed to and from the island. Paton & Hendry had joined forces in the 1890s to build up a large fleet of Clyde "puffers" as the small Scottish coasters were known, moving to larger steam coasters later on, cargoes of coal from the Ayrshire and Lanarkshire coalfields to the Isle of Man and the Western Isles being frequent. By 1898, their letter head listed no fewer than 29 vessels, ranging in size from the 470 ton **Ferguslie** to the 85 ton **Ashdale Glen**, and at the close

of the Victorian era, they had become an important force in coastal shipping on the West Coast of Scotland.

The story opens with a message that at first sight has little to do with the sea. Captain Kitto, the manager of the Isle of Man Mining Co sent a telegram to David McDowall, the manager of the Manx Northern Railway Co, "We are out of fine sand at present". Why had he done so ? Lead mining was in decline in the latter quarter of the nineteenth century, due to low cost foreign ores, and Kitto was desperate to develop any source of revenue he could

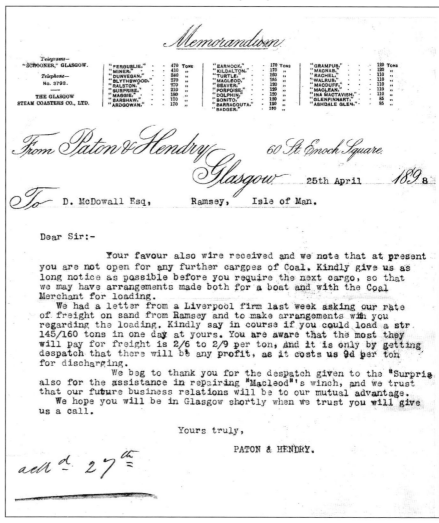

The House flag of Glasgow Steam Coasters has not been seen in Manx waters for best part of a century. Lloyd's Book of House Flags & Funnels records that it was a red flag with a blue triangle bearing a white spot.

*Nowadays shipping lines often use themed house names, which can become stereotyped. Paton & Hendry were more varied in their tastes, with places, girls, Scottish Clans, marine creatures and the amusingly named **Surprise**, being included in their 29-strong fleet. This letter includes a reference to **Surprise**, which was one of the boats bringing coal to the Island at the time. The variation in size, from 85 to 470 tons is remarkable, and in the decade or so up to the break up of the company, the trend was to increase the size of individual vessels.*

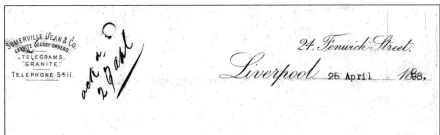

Somerville Dean & Co.
GRANITE QUARRY OWNERS.
TELEGRAMS,
"GRANITE"
TELEPHONE 5411.

24, Fenwick Street,
Liverpool 25 April 1888.

Mr. McDowall
Manager
Manx Northern Railway
Ramsey.

Dear Sir,

Ramsey / Birkenhead.

Referring to your recent conversation with our Mr. Somerville regarding time required for loading vessels with Foxdale Sand viz 48 hrs. We hope you can now see your way to shorten this period. We find it so difficult to engage steamers with this 48 hours loading condition that the trade promises to be quite limited if not altogether killed. We want to fix a steamer /200 tons for about Friday next and if we had your assurance that she could be loaded within a reasonable time it would help us considerably in engaging a steamer at a rate of freight which would let us out whole.

Hoping to hear from you.

We are,

Yours faithfully
Somerville, Dean & Co

Could not engage to do 200 tons than 2 Days and to ensure that Capt Kitto would have to meet us in quick supply

David McDowall has roughed out a reply in pencil at the foot of this letter from "Granite" for his clerk, who was his son James, to write. It was a common business practice amongst small businesses, and can be useful for the historian if the inward letter survives, but the copy of the reply has been lost, which is not uncommon, as many companies still used letter books of 500 or 1000 sheets of thin almost translucent paper. The reply was written in a special copying ink, and then placed next to a blank sheet in the letter book. This was dampened, the book closed and squeezed in a letter press transferring a mirror image to the blank sheet, which was then read from the other side. By the early 1900s, carbon paper was replacing this early business technology.

find, and with sand as a by-product of mining operations, he was keen to export it. David McDowall, the railway manager was happy to carry the sand from Foxdale to Ramsey where sidings extended on to the quay. The day after Kitto's warning, Somerville Dean & Co, who were quarry owners with the appropriate telegraph code name "Granite", contacted McDowall. To meet their customer's needs they were keen to widen the range of materials they could supply, and in the abrupt telegraph language where every word costs the sender, their wire read,

"Book order about 200 tons delivered fob Ramsey at 1/6 per ton including everything shipment Wednesday shipping instructions following wire Confirmation today Granite".

"Fob" means "free on board" or that the price quoted must include loading. Clearly Somerville & Dean did not believe in spending on punctuation, which was given in word form, "Stop", in a telegram. McDowall immediately telegraphed Kitto to see if sand could be supplied, and received a plaintive reply,

"Capt Kitto not at home today".

By 18 April, with a coal boat dis-

charging in Ramsey and in need of sand, "Granite" wired in desperation,

"Any Quantity Foxdale sand obtainable vessel ready load tomorrow wire quickly Granite".

Sadly, Kitto could not supply, so the vessel had to sail empty.

However a new problem was already dawning. We hear of crude oil cargoes being loaded on to tankers and the ships sailing before a destination or buyer is known, and assume it is a modern phenomenon, but with a steady flow of coal coming out of the Ayrshire and Lanark coalfields, and in order to keep their boats moving, Paton & Hendry were doing the same thing more than a century ago, and loading cargoes "on spec". They then needed to find customers, and on 21 April, David McDowall received a wire,

"We are informed by Messrs Wood that they could give you another cargo of coal next week – subject to reply by wire to-morrow. Kindly telegraph on receipt if you can take the cargo, and we shall arrange accordingly".

Apart from using coal for the railway, David McDowall, the MNR manager was happy to seek customers for coal, as it brought traffic to the line, but he had to wire,

"Sorry cannot take coal just now and cannot find buyer".

A telegram to Kitto at Foxdale to see if he was interested revealed that the Mines had ample stocks of coal. "Wood" probably referred to Wood's Shieldmuir Colliery No 6 at Flemington, Lanarkshire, on the Caledonian Railway. Four days later, Paton & Hendry wrote to McDowall over inward and outward freight, their letter covering such a wide variety of issues that I have illustrated it, together with a letter from "Granite".

The correspondence revealed just how keen the shipping lines were to obtain a paying return load, and how much the Isle of Man Mining Co and the Manx Northern Railway wanted the business it would bring, but the limited sand output from the mines made supplies erratic, whilst the small workforce available at the mines, the lack of railway wagons and absence of mechanised loading facilities at Ramsey meant that the insular companies needed up to 48 hours to load, whereas the shipping lines expected a 12 hour turn round. "Granite" summed things up in a subsequent letter,

"Whilst there is every disposition with each party concerned, to supply us with the sand there are so many difficulties in the way as well as costs that we see little hope of getting a supply. For instance ship brokers will not agree to more than 12 hours for loading which you say you cannot agree to; then again 1/6d per ton for carriage on sand is enough to kill the trade".

The low level of production meant that it was not economic to invest in the plant that would make a fast turn round possible, and without it, it was uneconomic to ship the volume that was available. Similar factors have mitigated against outbound freight from the Island to this day. What of the parties? In 1911, the Foxdale Mines closed whilst J M Paton went his own way about the same time, being one of the first ship owners to see the benefits of motor ships. He formed the Coasting Motor Shipping Co. Sadly, the early promise that the pioneer motor ships had displayed was not fulfilled in everyday service, due to mounting reliability problems, and the CMS fleet declined from a maximum of 16 motor ships to just one within a few years, Peter Hendry remained in steam, trading as Hendry, McCallum & Co from 1911, and retiring a few years later. David McDowall, a former Caledonian Railway officer, who had only become manager of the MNR in April 1898, died in 1900, but his railway survived until 1968, though the quay tramway had vanished in the early 1950s.

In 1887-88, the Steam Packet faced severe competition from the Fairfield backed Manx Line, the two companies being merged after the second season of racing. There was an interval and then a spate of rivals in the

1890s. The first was the Workington & Isle of Man Steam Ship Co Ltd (also called Steam Packet Co), which operated a former Barrow Steam Navigation vessel, the **PS Herald** for a single season in 1892. In 1894, the "Douglas, Llandudno and Liverpool Line," with T. & H. Aspinall as managers, was registered. Three fast steamers were alleged to be under construction at the Naval and Armament Construction Company, of Barrow, but the scheme collapsed without services commencing. In 1894, the Mutual Line of Manx Steamers, Ltd chartered the **Lady Tyler**,

*The Ship that never was! In Victorian days, the City of Dublin Steam Packet enjoyed much greater acclaim then the IOMSPCo. Its vessels were always amongst the fastest afloat, and it held the prestigious Holyhead-Dublin mail route from the 1850s to the start of the 1920s, and was the preferred route for Anglo-Irish gentry travelling between their estates in Ireland and England. Its four most legendary vessels were the **Ulster, Munster, Leinster** and **Connaught** of 1860. In 1897, four new twin-screw steamers bearing the same names, which are the ancient provinces into which Ireland was divided, replaced them. Sam Higginbottom, aware of the high reputation of the quartet, bought the **Munster** when she became available in 1897 for the rival service he was planning between Liverpool and Douglas. With her acquisition on 19 March 1897, Sam Higginbottom must have felt that his plans to establish a steamer service between Liverpool and Douglas were well under way, but would need a running mate as soon as the City of Dublin Steam Packet were prepared to release another of the four 1860 paddle steamers that had performed so well on the Holyhead-Dublin service. To Higginbottom's undoubted surprise, the Steam Packet reacted fast and ruthlessly, buying the **PS Ulster** and the **PS Leinster**, not to run, but to eliminate them as potential rivals. Left with just one boat for 1897, Higginbottom's venture collapsed and the **Munster** was sold a few weeks later. The four steamers were similar but not identical and some of them were fitted with four funnels when new, two grouped ahead of the engine room, and two abaft the engine room. This illustration is said to be of the **PS Ulster**, which briefly entered IOMSPCo ownership in 1897, before being sold on for scrap.*

Engraving from the Tom Lee collection

which had been built for the Great Eastern Railway. At 13.25 knots, she was so slow that she took six hours on the passage, and the service lasted for just two months.

Samuel Wasse Higginbottom now came on to the scene. He had been christened at St Paul's church, Stalybridge, on 21 August 1853. His parents were Thomas Robert Higginbottom, (1822-1880), "gentleman" in the census records, who had been born in Dukinfield, Cheshire, and Eliza Hurst, who had been born in Hayfield, which is a short distance south of Glossop, Derbyshire. Census records suggest 1831, but were notoriously inaccurate, and it is likely that she was born to William and Harriett Hurst, on 18 July 1828. Thomas Higginbottom and Eliza Hurst married in 1849, their daughter, Harriet Hannah being christened at St John's Church in Dukinfield in March 1852, followed by Sam in 1853, and another son, John Owen, in 1857. Samuel may have taken his first name from his grandfather, Samuel Higginbottom Snr, but his middle name seems to have been in honour of the Revd Samuel Wasse, MA, the curate of Hayfield Parish church. It was an unusual curacy, as freeholders of the parish had the right to nominate the minister under a charter granted by Richard II in 1386. Samuel, who was living at 36 Sussex Rd, Southport at the time, married 21 year old Ann Sharrock at the United Methodist Free Church in the Ormskirk registration district on 20 June 1877, by which date he was a colliery secretary. Unless Sam's father, T R Higginbottom, was engaged in the coal business as a mine owner, this would have been remarkable progress for a 23 years old. T R Higginbottom died in 1880, and within a few years, Samuel had become a a highly successful colliery owner. His Norley Coal & Cannel Co operated four pits, Norley No's 2, 3, 4 and 5 in the vicinity of Pemberton, Wigan, whilst Higginbottom was jointly

*In the 1880s, the CDSPCo four stackers had been rebuilt with new boilers and with just two funnels, altering their appearance considerably, as we see in this view of two of the "Provinces" at the Carlisle Pier at Kingstown Harbour in the 1890s. After the partition of Ireland, Kingstown became Dun Laoghaire. Handsome boats with good passenger accommodation, their 18 knot speed placed them at the forefront of cross channel passenger ships when new, but by 1897 they would have been outclassed by the **Queen Victoria**, the **Princess of Wales** and the **Empress Queen**. None of the quartet ever operated out of Douglas, but with three of them owned briefly by the IOMSPCo or its would-be rival, they merit coverage.*

---

*Looking at this superb engraving of the **PS Ireland** of 1885, with her clipper bow, and elegantly raked masts and funnels, I can see why Frank Burtt called her "the fastest and most beautiful cross channel steamer afloat". Tubular boilers, working under forced draught, provided the steam to develop 6000 i.h.p. She could accommodate 412 first class and 328 second class passengers.* Illustration from the Tom Lee collection.

interested with Horace Mayhew of Broughton Hall in a colliery at Lostock, and was the proprietor of New Broughton Collieries, Wrexham. Other collieries at Bettisfield, Holywell, Huyton, and Prescot were included in his portfolio.

Sam's wife, Ann Sharrock, was the eldest child of Henry Sharrock (1831-1858) and Isabella Wright (b1834). The couple married in 1856, the same year that Ann was born. A younger sister, Elizabeth Ellen was born in the summer of 1858, but sadly Henry Sharrock had passed away, aged 27, on 22 May 1858, so did not live to see the younger girl. He was buried at Scarisbrick, Lancs. By the time of her marriage in 1877, Ann was living at 49 Linaker St, Southport. Their first son, Henry Sharrock Higginbottom, was born on 11 April 1880 in Southport, a popular residential area for wealthy businessmen from the North West. By 1881, Sam was living at 47 Linaker Rd, North Meols, just outside Southport, his mother in law, Isabella Sharrock, and the unmarried Elizabeth Ellen residing next door at No 49, so it may be a case that Sam had married the girl next door ! Sam and Ann had three further children, all girls, Ella Maud in 1884, Winifred M in 1890 and Harriet Rose (Rosie) in 1894. At the time of the 1881 census, Ann was staying with Richard & Elisabeth Waring in St Asaph in North Wales, Mrs Waring seemingly

being her aunt. The Welsh connection is interesting, as one branch of the Sharrock family, which was probably related to Ann, shared coal mining interests in North Wales and Lancashire with Higginbottom. In 1891, Sam and Ann were still living in North Meols, Southport, but had moved to 64 Sefton St. Ella and Winifred had been born, and Sam's mother, who had remarried in 1884, after the death of T R Higginbottom was living with them. Her second husband, John Kenyon has also passed away, and Eliza was shown as "of independent means".

Sam was ambitious, and Liverpool came to dominate family life, with Sam having offices controlling his colliery interests in Liverpool. In 1895, he had become a member of Liverpool City Council, and when the chairman of the Tramways Committee, Alderman Petrie, was appointed Lord Mayor in 1901, Sam took his place on the Tramways Committee, relinquishing the post on his own initiative in favour of Petrie when the period of his Mayoralty was concluded in 1902. He became the Conservative MP for the West Derby constituency in the then affluent Northern suburbs of Liverpool on 29 September 1900. Today it is a safe Labour seat, but in his day it was true blue territory, and many of the Liverpool shipping magnates were his constituents. More interested in committee work, and getting things done than in "gab", Sam only made one speech in parliament, so far as is known, which was to oppose the 8-hour day proposals advanced by the legendary Labour leader, Keir Hardie. In opposing the measure he said "I am sent here by a very large constituency to oppose this measure, as I am sure it is against their interests. I represent one of the divisions of Liverpool, and if this Bill passes I look upon it as a most serious matter for the shipping industry of Liverpool. I look upon it as a most serious matter for the various trades in the county of Lancaster, particularly the cotton, chemical, and iron industries."

Apart from coal and politics, Higginbottom had maritime interests, and one of his descendants recalled a picture in the family home of a vessel thought to have been named the **SS Higginbottom**, which was presumably a collier. Sam had wider ambitions, however, and was keen to set up a shipping line between Liverpool and Douglas, where he had established a branch coal office in Athol St.

ISLE OF MAN.

FIRST-CLASS SALOON RETURN FARE TO DOUGLAS.

SECOND SALOON
3/-
RETURN.

5/-

SECOND SALOON
3/-
RETURN.

THE NEW LIVERPOOL & DOUGLAS STEAMERS, LTD.

The ex-Royal Mail Steamer IRELAND

Will leave LIVERPOOL, Prince's Stage, Daily at 10 o'clock; Return the same day from DOUGLAS at 3.15. 4.15.

For Ease and Comfort—THE IRELAND;

First Class Return Fare, 5/-, Second Class Return Fare, 3/-, First Class Season Tickets, 21/- each.

This magnificent Steamer, built by Messrs. LAIRD BROS., Birkenhead, at a cost of over £100,000, is furnished throughout in the most elegant style. Drawing Rooms, Dining Rooms, beautiful Private Cabins, fitted with Electric Bells and Lights; Grand Promenade Deck; also Private Cabins, fitted with every convenience for Ladies. This lovely Steamer, **THE IRELAND** will sail to Douglas in about three hours and twenty minutes.

THE IRELAND will Sail Daily from JULY 1st, 1899.

For Ease and Comfort—THE IRELAND.

First Class Saloon Return Fare, 5/-, Second Class Saloon Return Fare, 3/-, First Class Season Tickets, 21/- each.

Passengers need not fear sea-sickness. THE IRELAND sails in all weathers smoothly and beautifully. No better paddle steamer in the world.

Tickets and Handbills can be had at WALKER's Tobacco Market, 53, Whitechapel. Tramcars pass WALKER'S every few minutes to the Pierhead. Fare, One Penny.

*Unless this was a proof copy of the handbill Sam Higginbottom was planning to issue to promote the **PS Ireland**, which is possible though unlikely, it seems that the literature was produced before the company title or times were finalised, and these had to be altered by hand. Sam was quite right in his description of the **Ireland**. She was magnificent, and had cost a fortune to build. Her drawing rooms and dining rooms had attracted lavish praise from the day she was built, and she was justly popular with passengers, but she was mechanically archaic when she was built, and hopelessly uneconomic to run, which is why the City of Dublin Steam Packet were happy to sell her.*

When the Mail contract between Dublin and Holyhead for the City of Dublin Steam Packet Co came up for renewal in 1897, one of the terms in the new agreement was that they would replace the four paddle steamers, **Ulster**, **Munster**, **Leinster** and **Connaught**, that had dominated the route ever since they had been built in 1860, with four new twin screw steamers. Initially working at 25 psi, with 2 cylinder oscillating engines, the paddle steamers were advanced for their day and at 18 knots, were the fastest vessels afloat. With nine trans-

verse bulkheads and a turtle back forecastle, they were soundly designed. The adoption of forced draught in 1885 enhanced their performance. Higginbottom, with offices at 19 Old Hall St, Liverpool, which was a short distance inland from Princes Dock, bought the **Munster** on 19 March 1897, with the intention of adding further CDSPCo boats in due course. She had been built by John Laird at Birkenhead in 1860, with engines by Boulton & Watt. She was 326′ 6″ x 35′ 2″ and 1750 grt. Charles Parks was appointed master on 6 April

The PS *Violet* and PS *Lily* were sisters, and had been built for the London & North Western Railway in 1880. This is the PS *Violet* at Holyhead whilst in LNWR service. Of 1175 grt, both steamers passed to Higginbottom, the *Lily* in 1900 and the *Violet* two years later. Both were sold to T W Ward for breaking up. I am indebted to Tom Lee for this interesting view.

Tom Lee

1897, and a service between Douglas and Liverpool, which was to commence at Easter 1897, and which fell in mid-April, was advertised, but before Higginbottom could acquire any more of the CDSPCo boats, the Steam Packet stepped in, and bought the *Ulster* and the *Leinster*, selling them on for scrap, to make sure that they were not available to him. It was a ruthless policy, but the Steam Packet did not relish another price cutting war as in 1887 against Manx Line. Although they would not have been of the same calibre as the Fairfield twins, their 18 knots, good accommodation, and an 1880s refit meant that they were serious challengers, and not junk as has sometimes been alleged. As *Connaught* was sold to H E Moss & Co. there was just the one boat available, so Higginbottom reluctantly gave up for 1897. *Munster* was sold on 10 May 1897 to Edward Thirkell, ship breaker of 28 Brunswick St, Liverpool.

With such prompt and ruthless opposition, that would have been more than enough for most men, but Higginbottom bounced back in 1899 with another former City of Dublin boat. She was the PS *Ireland*, and at 366' 3", was some twenty feet longer than the 1860 quads. To see her in a Manx context, she was six feet longer than the magnificent new PS *Empress Queen* delivered to the Packet in 1897. At 2095 grt she was exactly 100 tons bigger that the Steam Packet's biggest ship, and her 21 knots speed

made her comparable to the best the Packet had. Higginbottom must have been pleased that he had gone from the *Munster*, to one of the biggest and fastest cross channel steamers afloat. Frank Burtt, secretary & treasurer of the Institution of Locomotive Engineers, knew her, and described her as "the fastest and most beautiful cross channel steamer afloat", and her passenger facilities were outstanding. She was just fourteen years old, having come from Laird Bros of Birkenhead in 1885, and that might have given Higginbottom food for thought. Why had the City of Dublin Steam Packet kept the 1860 boats for almost forty years, yet decided to discard this magnificent steamer so quickly? To understand the answer we need to know a little of marine engineering. Low-pressure simple engines drove the early paddle steamers, but as the years passed, high pressure compound engines came into favour, with the steam used twice, initially at high pressure in a moderate sized cylinder, and then at a lower pressure in a much bigger cylinder. Triple expansion engines followed, using the steam three times, and were more compact, making more space available for cargo or passenger accommodation, and were much more efficient, burning less fuel. One contemporary writer estimated that in a full year, compound engines would save some 4000 tons of coal ! By 1885, when the PS *Ireland* was built, compounding was well established and the IOMSPCo

Mona's Isle of 1882 was an example of up to date engineering. However the CDSPCo had opted for low-pressure simple propulsion at 30 psi, and to drive her at 21 knots, this required a pair of incredible 102 inch diameter oscillating cylinders. That is 8 ft 6 ins, or 2.59 metres! Even when she was delivered, the maritime technical press were scathing, as she was cumbersome and her vast low-pressure engines were hungry on fuel, the engine room occupying no less than 116 feet. Although the principle of oscillating cylinders was well proven, the sheer size and mass of the cylinders on the *Ireland* placed immense strains on the trunnions, and she suffered several mishaps as a result. She was a dinosaur when she was built and the years had only emphasised the mistakes in her design. She was sold by the CDSPCo to Higginbottom himself, and her registration changed from Dublin to Liverpool, but she was transferred to a new company set up by Higginbottom, called Liverpool & Douglas Steamers Ltd, on 24 June 1899, William McShea having been appointed master just over a week previously. Publicity material stressed her good points, including her size and speed, and that the service was to start on 1 July 1899. They also revealed that the name of the company, "The New Liverpool & Douglas Steamers, Ltd", but the word new was crossed out in ink, suggesting a change of plan over the title, for the word "new" did not appear in the registered title of Higginbottom's latest venture. Had Higginbottom only been a coal master, he might have relished the amount of fuel that the *Ireland* consumed every trip, but as a ship owner, it was another matter, and she was sold to T W Ward, ship breakers on 21 August 1900.

Undaunted by this further reverse, Sam Higginbottom re-thought his strategy during the winter, and came back for his next attempt in 1900. The London & North Western Railway operated a Holyhead-Dublin service in direct competition with the City of Dublin Steam Packet, and in 1880, Laird's had provided two handsome paddle steamers for a new overnight service, the PS *Lily* and PS *Violet*. They had simple oscillating engines, but in 1890-91 both were rebuilt to increase their speed from 17¾ knots to 19½ knots, a rebuild that was complicated by the LNWR insisting that no passenger or cargo space should be sacrificed. They were fitted with triple expansion steeple engines. Steam was supplied by six locomotive type boilers at 150 psi, with forced draft, offering much greater power output for the space and weight. It was from the then new **PS Lily** that the Prince of Wales, later King Edward VII, opened the new harbour at Holyhead in June 1880. **Lily** was taken out of service in April 1900, so was available for Higginbottom. He would have liked to buy her sister, **Violet**, as well but the LNWR were not prepared to release her until April 1902, when she travelled north from Holyhead to join Higginbottom's growing fleet at Liverpool.

To provide a running mate for **Lily**, Higginbottom selected the **Calais-Douvres** of 1889. She had come from Fairfield's yard at Govan, which suggested she would be good. She was, and she had been built for the London, Chatham & Dover Railway to cope with the rush of traffic for the great Paris exhibition of 1889. It is worth emphasising that the boat purchased by Higginbottom was entirely normal, as she is sometimes confused with her predecessor in the LCDR fleet, which was a bizarre 1877 attempt to combat seasickness by having two hulls side by side, each with its own superstructure and funnels. A freak vessel, she could barely manage 13 knots and ended her days as a hulk on the Thames. The boat Higginbottom acquired in 1900 was very different. She had a 2 cylinder compound diagonal engine, with a 59" HP cylinder and a 106" low pressure cylinder that could drive her at 21¼ knots, making her a match for the best of the Steam Packet boats. She was electrically lit, and was a great deal better than the **Lily**. A contemporary colour portrait of the **Calais-Douvres**, from as late as the winter of 1898-99, which was used by the LCDR to promote their cross-channel services appears on the inside rear cover. At this time, she was still used on the important 1.00pm sailing from Dover (Admiralty Pier) to Calais, arriving at 2.20pm, with a return sailing ex Calais at 3.45pm, with an official arrival time of 5.05pm, but LCDR literature proudly proclaimed that she had made many passages in "under 63 minutes from Pier Head to Pier Head". The main reason she was disposed of was the creation of a Joint Managing Committee in 1899 to co-ordinate the previous rival companies, the LC&DR and the South Eastern Railway.

Although they were both second-hand, Higginbottom finally had one good boat and one excellent boat, and was in a position to offer serious com-

TELEPHONE No. 6299.

Liverpool & Douglas Steamers Ld.

☞ **NEW DAILY EXPRESS STEAMERS.**
(SUNDAYS EXCEPTED.)

— THE —

'CALAIS DOUVRES' and 'LILY'

Are two of the Finest and Fastest Paddle Steamers.

Sailing Daily from Prince's Landing Stage.

From LIVERPOOL 10-45 a.m.   From DOUGLAS 4-5 p.m.

5/6 First Return. | **3/6** Second Return.

3/- Single Fare.   **2/-** Single Return FARE.

Children under 12, Half-Price.

WEATHER AND CIRCUMSTANCES PERMITTING.

SEASON TICKETS, Now Ready, 25/- Each

NOTICE.

Parties living in the Country will do well to Book only to Liverpool per Rail. and then take return ticket per "Calais Douvres" or "Lily" on Prince's Stage, and save many shillings. The Steamers' Funnels are painted White with Black Band round top.

For Extra Sailings See Liverpool Daily Papers or Handbills at WALKER'S, 53, Whitechapel, Liverpool.

Return Tickets are available up to the 1st September.

Tickets and Handbills at WALKER'S, 53, Whitechapel.
Booking Office Prince's Landing Stage.
Douglas Office, 2, Victoria Pier Buildings.

Bicycles conveyed at Owners' Risk—1/- each way.

Matthews Brothers, Printers, Thomas Street, Liverpool.

*Following the costly mistake of running the **PS Ireland**, Higginbottom was much better placed to cope the following year with the **Calais-Douvres** from the London Chatham & Dover Railway, and the **Lily** from the LNWR. Both boats had to go head-to-head against the IOMSPCo, but if boats have souls, they would not have found that surprising, for the LCDR had spent its entire existence in murderous competition with the South Eastern Railway, whilst the LNWR boats on the Holyhead station were in direct competition with the City of Dublin Steam Packet Co. A contemporary colour impression of the **Calais-Douvres** appears on the rear inside cover.*

*This dramatic portrait from the Fairfield Ship Building & Engineering Co, of the **PS Calais-Douvres**, shows her on her acceptance trials in 1889 at full power off Skelmorlie, the location of the celebrated "measured mile" on the Clyde, where ships showed their paces. Her maximum speed was 21.25 knots, but as with many boats, once her machinery had settled in, she exceeded her acceptance speed, her best performance between Calais and Dover giving an overall speed of 22.63 knots! Her two diagonal direct-acting compound engines could develop 6,450 i.h.p, when she was worked under forced draught. "Forced Draught" means that the boiler room was sealed off and operating under slightly higher than normal atmospheric pressure. This created an added air current through the boilers, enhancing combustion rates and steam production. I have no doubt that one of those on board on this important occasion was Richard Barnwell, the forceful managing director of Fairfield whom we encounter elsewhere in these pages.*

petition to the Packet. He looked around for more to strengthen his fleet, and now aware of the need for efficient compound engines, settled on a pair of boats that had come from John Elder's yard on the Clyde for the Newhaven-Dieppe service of the London, Brighton & South Coast Railway in 1882. They were the **PS Brittany** and **PS Normandy**. The LB&SCR locomotive engineer, William Stroudley was one of the foremost locomotive engineers of his day, and he had developed and patented feathering paddle wheels, which improved efficiency and offered a 1.5 knot advantage in speed without any increase in engine power. This permitted **Normandy** to cross from Newhaven to Dieppe in under three and a half hours. As with the LNWR, the Brighton would only release one boat in 1901, the **Brittany**, so Higginbottom had to wait until March 1902 to add **Normandy** to his fleet. Although adequate in their day, the Brighton boats were not good enough to compete against the Steam Packet fleet, and their purchase was a mistake. As it happened the **Violet** was also available in April 1902. Although Higginbottom had built up an impressive fleet on paper, with the exception of the **PS Ireland**, which had been fast but horrendously costly to run, the only one that was a match for the Steam Packet was the **Calais-Douvres**.

By 1901, life was going well for Sam Higginbottom, who was still under fifty. It was largely through his own restless energy. The family were now living at "Elsinore", 36, Devonshire Rd, Claughton, Birkenhead, on the Wirral, and apart from Samuel and Annie themselves, all four children were still at home. Henry was 21 and studying for the Bar, whilst their youngest daughter, Harriet, who had been born in Birkenhead, was just seven. Membership of Liverpool City Council, a seat in parliament, recognition by many bodies, and a highly profitable coal business were things to be satisfied with. A keen horseman, jovial and good natured, and seemingly impervious to the taunts of others, Sam Higginbottom had marked his assuming charge of the Tramways Committee of the City Council by offering all the employees of the tramways undertaking a free trip to the Isle of Man on his Liverpool & Douglas Steamers. It was a move that stood him well on the Island where it generated a large number of extra visitors, and with the tramway men as well, but Sam made a genuine effort to get to know as many key workers in the Tramways as he could. Although he had opposed Keir Hardie, so might be seen by modern writers as against the working man, Sam was well aware of the awkward hours worked by the tram men, and had encouraged the establishment of a non profit making coffee stall run by tramway "wives" at Walton depot in 1902. With many workers still dubious about unions, Sam's good nature and hands on approach made him popular with the workforce, who saw his Conservative principles as no problem.

Even the shipping side was looking up. 1902 opened on a high note, for traffic was building up to a reasonable level at weekends, and through ticketing arrangements were working with the UK and IOM railways. This had been a weakness at first, as the earlier advice to prospective travellers in the **Calais-Douvres** handbill revealed, and was vital if the venture was to prosper. Much of the traffic came from the North of England, and rather than the 9.00am morning sailing from Douglas, Higginbottom sailed at 10.30am, which was convenient for the northern towns, with their shorter mainland journeys, but not so good for the Midlands or the south, but traffic from that direction was limited. On Fridays and Saturdays, the IOM Railway agreed to run a special boat train to Port Erin in connection with the morning sailing from Liverpool, which arrived in Douglas around 3.30pm. On Saturday 9 August, to

*The LB&SCR **Normandy** is seen at Newhaven in 1893. This view is from the Brian Fisher collection and comes via Tom Lee. After the Higginbottom venture collapsed, Mr Constant of London purchased **Normandy**. In 1905, she was sold to a Mr Richards, for The Normandy Steamship Co, and worked out of Swansea in competition with the **PS Brighton**, whom she regularly raced across the Bristol Channel. The Normandy Steamship Co survived until 1907 and **Normandy** was broken up at Rhyl in 1909.* Tom Lee

give one example, 14 passengers had pre-booked, out of a total of 85 steamer passengers who travelled to the south of the Island on the special. It is commendable that although Dalrymple Maitland was chairman of the Steam Packet as well as the IOM Railway, he did not use his powers as railway chairman to block through ticketing with his rival. On 4 September 1902, Higginbottom opened a new route, from Liverpool along the North Wales coast to Llandudno, in competition with the Liverpool & North Wales Steamship Co, the service running until the end of September. Despite all his efforts, the company was still losing money, and the end came when Samuel Wasse Higginbottom died of heart failure brought on by pneumonia at his home in the early hours of 28 December 1902 at the early age of 49. (The date often given, of 27 Dec, is incorrect). He was buried at Flaybrick Cemetery on 1 January 1903. Apart from his immediate family, the funeral was attended by representatives of Liverpool City Council, the Tramways Department, of which he had been chairman, and which was represented by the general manager, C R Bellamy, and his deputy C W Mallins. The Gallimores from the L&D steamer offices were present, as were Captains Hudson and Mylchreest of the **PS Calais-Douvres** and **PS Violet**, and officials from Whiston, New Broughton, Norley, Sutton Heath and Hulton Collieries. Sam Higginbottom's opposition to Keir Hardie had not harmed his popularity with the working man, and in a space of two hours, over 1000 Liverpool Tramway Men had signed a memorial of sympathy, and there were similar sentiments from seafarers and miners. Sam had the rare gift of being respected and liked by his fellow businessmen and by his workers.

By the date of his death, only the **Calais-Douvres**, **Violet** and **Lily** were left, and all three were disposed of in 1903, the IOMSPCo recognising the worth of the **Calais-Douvres**, and buying her. She was renamed **Mona**, and ran until 1909. After his abortive attempt in 1897, when the boats he wanted were bought from under his nose, Higginbottom had come back with a new fleet each year from 1899 to 1902. For a down-to-earth and successful coal master, it did not make obvious commercial sense, but Higginbottom may have sensed that the holiday market was developing

rapidly, and the Island was one of the premier resorts for Lancashire, an area he knew intimately. Seasonal arrivals rocketed from 351,238 in 1900 to 634,512 in 1913, the last full peacetime year. That may have been the market he was looking to, but by then, he was long dead. What makes the whole episode so fascinating is his dogged persistence. Despite the losses on Liverpool & Douglas Steamers Ltd, Sam Higginbottom left an estate of £44,456. Inflation indices vary greatly, but a 200-fold increase would not be unreasonable, which would mean an estate worth over £8m in modern terms. Wealthy though he was, the figures reveal that Higginbottom had no choice but to look for second-hand tonnage, as a new vessel comparable to the latest ship in the Steam Packet

fleet, the **PS Empress Queen** would have cost over £100,000. After Sam died in 1902, the colliery business passed to his son Henry Sharrock Higginbottom, although he was only in his early twenties. Within a few weeks of his father's death, Henry married Martha Hartley of West Derby, and abandoned the loss making shipping service to concentrate on the Norley Pits at Garswood, which continued to bear the family name for many years, and the other coal businesses, although his interest in the mines at Lostock was sold in 1908. For some years, he remained sole proprietor of the mines at New Broughton near Wrexham, whilst the coal office in the IOM was also kept on. Henry died at St Pancras, London on 5 April 1929.

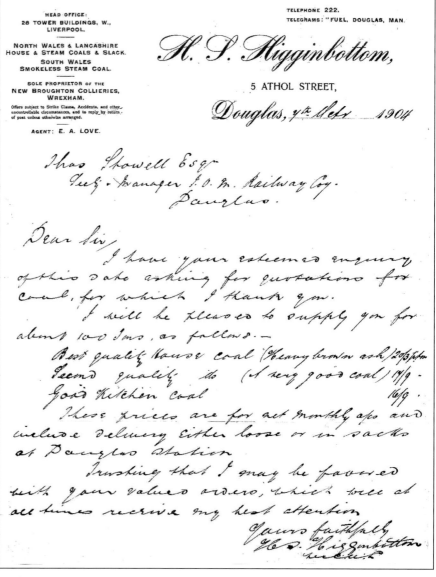

By the autumn of 1904, two years after Sam Higginbottom's death, the only trace of the Higginbottom empire in the Isle of Man was the coal office at 5 Athol St, Douglas, which was managed by the local agent, E A Love. At that time, coal cost £1 a ton or less. Shortly after his father's death in December 1902, Henry had married Martha Hartley in West Derby, which had been his father's parliamentary constituency.

CHAPTER SEVEN
"The Li'l Daisy"

The little girl was not quite three years old. She had been born in November 1906, and in later years, was delighted to relate that it was on Lord Mayor's Day, when the Lord Mayor of London went in solemn procession through the city. She lived in Ramsey, where her father was a successful draper with his own business. She was now old enough to walk steadily, and whilst she was fond of her mother, she idolised her father, and whenever he went out, Elaine wanted to go with him. When he went to work in the morning, she protested long and loudly if she was not allowed to accompany him. Sometimes she was, and would play contentedly on the floor behind the counter of the shop. If he went for a walk about town wearing the immaculate light grey morning suit, top hat, gloves and buttonhole that he wore to work, and she was left behind, her protests were even louder. The only drawback to these walks was that her father had the common failing of grown-ups, that when he met an acquaintance, and as a leading businessman and member of the town commissioners, that was frequent, he would stop to pass the time of day. Despite such distractions, walks were fun, and if you asked what her favourite walk was, she would give two answers. The Queens Pier came first, but it had a close rival. If her daddy turned north, she knew they were going to the harbour, and even though the shop was in sight of the harbour, a walk along the quay was thrilling, due to the ceaseless bustle. In those far off days, Ramsey had its own steamer. In truth, she was not owned by the town, but by the Isle of Man Steam Packet Company; however she was based in Ramsey for the direct Liverpool service, so to the towns-people, she was their boat. She was an old boat, for she had been built as far back as 1860, so was not far off celebrating a half-century of service by the summer of 1909. Probably she would go for scrap within a year or two, an eventuality the people of Ramsey preferred not to dwell upon, as "The Lil Daisy" was their boat, and they loved her. That was not her real name, of course, for she had been launched as the **Mona's Isle**, but after a rebuild, became the **Ellan Vannin**. More than three score years had passed after those trips to the harbour with her daddy, but Elaine still loved to walk along the quay, and reminisce about the sights and sounds of her childhood. One day as my mother and I stood near the base of the southernmost of the two piers that protect the entrance to Ramsey harbour, she said quietly, "This is where the **Ellan Vannin** used to be". There were tears in her eyes as she gave a vivid description of fishermen in their thick jerseys and seaboots, of fishing tackle littering the quay, and of the **Ellan Vannin**, her tall thin red funnel an indication of her age, surrounded by cargo, passengers, crew, and on-lookers. She recalled T H Midwood, a leading photographer in the town, and how he was a familiar sight around the quays with his plate camera and tripod. Until I began to study this Midwood view for this book, I had not realised that he had captured on film what my mother spoke of, for this is the **Ellan Vannin**, and this is where my mother remembered seeing her.

T H Midwood

74

Compared to the new steamers sailing out of Douglas, and in particular the magnificent **Ben-my-Chree** of 1908, which was so fast that only the Cunard greyhounds, the **Lusitania** and **Mauretania** on the Atlantic could show her a clean pair of heels, "The Lil Daisy" was slow and decidedly old fashioned. Built as a paddle steamer in 1860, she had been rebuilt with screw propulsion in 1888 by Westray, Copeland & Co of Barrow, and was a graceful ship. A high forecastle and stern, wells for cargo and a raised centre section, topped by an open bridge, conformed to the pattern of many of the company's ships, and despite her age, she was a stout vessel. On days when the Atlantic liners that thronged the Landing Stage at Liverpool remained in port storm bound, "The Lil Daisy" would cast off from the section of the Landing Stage reserved for the Packet boats, and head down river to fight her way through the storms to her home in Ramsey. Later on, she would make the return voyage, and she became an institution on Merseyside and amongst the liners that she rubbed shoulders with. When the gales of winter lashed the Mersey, it was common for them to herald her return with their sirens. At the start of December 1909, the Island was wracked with storms. Elaine was snug in the family home at Seamount, glad that she was not out in the dreadful weather, when her brother Greetham got in. He was a lively lad, seven years older than his sister, and a great practical joker. His face was pale and he looked shocked. His mother asked what was the matter. He replied hesitantly that there was a poster in the window of the "Ramsey Courier" office that the **Ellan Vannin** had been lost. Christiana, knowing her son's penchant for jokes, said it was in bad taste to joke about something like that, but when Greetham persisted, Arthur Brown was dispatched to the "Courier" office to find out, and there was the poster, with a knot of frightened and worried townsfolk. "The Lil Daisy" had sailed from the harbour on 3 December with 21 crew and 15 passengers, many of them Ramsey folk. It would be fair to say that even if they were not related, everybody in the town at least knew someone who had sailed on the **Ellan Vannin** a few hours earlier. In Douglas, the loss, if not so personal, was deeply felt, and at Imperial Buildings, the IOMSPCo head offices, directors and officers remained hour after hour, hoping against hope that there would be survivors. News filtered through of lifebuoys and wreckage floating in the Mersey near Formby, and then five days later, the first bodies were recovered. The official enquiry concluded that the ship had been fully seaworthy and no criticism was offered against the company, the officers or crew of the **Ellan Vannin**. From a study of the wreckage, it appeared that she had been overwhelmed by a severe Force 12 storm as she was approaching the Mersey and safety. Force 12 is the highest measure on the Beaufort scale that is used by mariners, and is the equivalent of a hurricane. Such conditions are seldom encountered in the coastal waters of the British Isles.

T H Midwood

Some events stay in our minds forever, such as the assassination of President John F Kennedy, or the death of Princess Diana. To the Manx people, the loss of the **Ellan Vannin** was one of those moments. I discovered that every one of my elderly relatives who was alive at that time, could say what they were doing when they heard the news. The Steam Packet Company, and the Manx community on the Island and further afield, joined ranks to raise funds for the dependents of the crew and passengers who were lost. Just over a month later, on 12 January 1910, the prestigious Manchester Manx Society held a tribute concert to raise funds for the bereaved. The concert opened with "God Save the King", but as soon as the echoes of the National Anthem had died away, the strains of Ellan Vannin, that most beautiful and haunting Manx air rang out. It is a piece of music that can bring tears to the eyes of Manxmen far from their native land on an ordinary occasion, and must have been a hundred times more powerful, as it symbolised the loss of a much loved ship bearing that name, and all aboard her. A programme of music with a predominantly maritime theme, much of it moving, including the haunting "Sands of the Dee" and "Anchored" was concluded with another majestic air, "The Manx Fisherman's Evening Hymn". The second verse was particularly fitting,

> Thou, Lord, doth rule the raging of the sea,
> When loud the storm and furious is the gale;
> Strong is Thine arm, our little barques are frail;
> Send us thy help; remember Galilee;

The late J. CRAINE (1st Mate).

The late J. KINLEY (2nd Mate).

A CONCERT, Organised by the Manchester Manx Society.

To raise funds for the relief of those left Destitute by the Disaster to the

ISLE-OF-MAN .. STEAM PACKET **ELLAN VANNIN**

Held in the FREE TRADE HALL, MANCHESTER,

On WEDNESDAY, JANUARY 12th, 1910.

Commencing at 7.30 p.m.

Artistes :

Miss MABEL CORRAN - - Contralto
Of the London and Provincial Concerts.

Mr. HORACE GRAY } Tenor
Mr. PERCY MOORE } Duettists { Baritone

Mr. FRED MINAY - - Baritone

Mr. HAYDN WOOD - - Violinist
Of the London and Provincial Concerts.

—AND—

The Douglas Male Choristers
Hon. Conductor—Mr. NOAH MOORE.
At the Piano - Mrs. H. RUSHWORTH.

The late JAMES TEARE (Captain).

The Manchester Manx Society gratefully thank—

The Douglas Male Choristers, who travel from Douglas for this Concert and who give their services free ;
The Soloists, who have given up other engagements, and who give their services free ;
The Isle-of-Man Steam Packet Co., who convey the Choir from Douglas to Liverpool free of cost ;
Messrs. Forsyth Bros., who rendered valuable assistance and advice ;
Those who entertain the Members of the Choir while in Manchester ;
Mr. Frank Graves for the design of the Cover of this Programme ;
Isle-of-Man "Times" and others who have lent blocks.

CHAPTER EIGHT

The Roaring Twenties

The 1920s were one of the most extraordinary decades in history. At the start of 1919, which is better considered with the Twenties, the world had just come out of "The War to End Wars". Servicemen coming back from the trenches were marked by what they had been through, and a significant part of a generation of young men were dead. Amongst the survivors, there was an almost hysterical need to enjoy life. Homes were mostly lit by gas or oil lamps and a national electricity supply was a dream of the future. Homes looked essentially Edwardian, and women wore long skirts that were not much different to Victorian or Edwardian days. Over the next decade, women in England gained the right to vote, although Manx women had enjoyed it for forty years. Hemlines rose with almost unseemly haste to produce skirts that were as short or shorter than the tiniest "minis" of the late 1960s, although the term miniskirt had not then been coined. The desire for pleasure led to the term, "The Roaring Twenties", the image of "the flapper" and the writings of Scott Fitzgerald. The Americans dabbled with prohibition, the banning of alcohol, with catastrophic results, and there was boom, a modest but persistent recession, strikes and industrial unrest, and at the end of the decade, the Great Depression. Life in 1929 was totally different to 1919, and it is against this extraordinary and restless background that we will chart the course followed by the Isle of Man Steam Packet. It was Cole Porter who summed up this era best in his hit musical, "Anything Goes", and for those brought up in staid Victorian or Edwardian times, it must have seemed to be so, but many of those who were young, such as my mother, looked back on it as an exciting era when the world also seemed young. It is a measure of the abilities of the Steam Packet board and management that Dalrymple Maitland, John Donald Clucas,

Dalrymple Maitland was born in Liverpool on 22 March 1848, and was the son of John Maitland, proprietor and editor of the "Liverpool Mercury", and Agnes Dalrymple, the Scottish born daughter of James Dalrymple, the manager of the mills at Union Mills. Maitland came to the Island as a young man, and later took over the mills from his uncle, before entering Tynwald and becoming a director of the Steam Packet, the IOM Bank and the IOM Railway. He married Frances Caley in 1879. Sadly she died in 1891, soon after giving birth to their only child, Jack Dalrymple Maitland, who was killed in Flanders in 1916. A pipe and a good book by the fireside was his preferred way to pass his spare time, but the calls of duty in his many public offices left little time for such pursuits. On hearing of the death of their late speaker on 25 March 1919, the House of Keys adjourned, as did the Legislative Council as a mark of respect, and his coffin was carried by relays of pall bearers from his home, Brook Mooar, in Union Mills, to Braddan cemetery.

Dalrymple Maitland's characteristic but unusual signature with the horizontal stroke of the letter "t" crossing the entire signature. When I first encountered this, I thought it might be an accident, but I have seen sufficient examples to know it was intentional. This signature dates from 1901 soon after he became chairman of the Packet. As his health deteriorated in later years, the curve of the D became more angular and unsteady.

Hugo Teare, William Corkill and Thomas Craine, all of whom had grown to maturity in Victorian days, guided the company so well in these choppy waters.

The quotation from the testimonial dinner to Robert Napier a few days after the **Mona's Isle** entered service in 1830, about "The usurpation of a gang of Strangers and Adventurers" recalls the spirit behind the formation of the Packet, the feeling that the Island deserved more than to be exploited by outsiders who had no regard for its interests. By 1914, the Steam Packet fleet had grown from the one vessel it had when the company was founded to fifteen of the finest short sea ships anywhere in the world. First and foremost was the **Ben-my-Chree** of 1908, the third fastest merchant ship afloat. Only the legendary Cunarders, the **Mauretania** and **Lusitania** could show her a clean pair of heels, but the **Viking**, the **Snaefell** and the **King Orry** were magnificent turbine steamers less than a decade old. Although old fashioned by the ideas of 1914, the **Empress Queen**, the **Queen Victoria** and the **Prince of Wales** were amongst the finest paddle steamers afloat. By 1918, wartime requisitions by the Admiralty had reduced that proud fleet to just four ships. That in itself was a blow, but the ships that had gone were the fastest and the finest. By November 1918 when the Armistice finally came, all that was left was the **Tyrconnel**, a small freighter, the **Fenella**, the **Tynwald** and the **Douglas**. Not one of them grossed 1,000 tons. From time to time, the company received news of losses, and these were passed on to stockholders in the annual reports. The last loss to be recorded was of the **SS Snaefell**, which was torpedoed in the Mediterranean on 5 June 1918. The Annual Report for 1918 recorded,

'The Directors regret having to report the loss of the **s.s. "Snaefell"** in June last year, whilst in Government service, and *deeply deplore the loss of life involved.'*

Who were the people running the Packet at the time? Heading the company was Dalrymple Maitland, JP, Speaker of the House of Keys, a leading Manx businessman, who was also chairman of the Isle of Man Railway Company. He had been chairman of the Isle of Man Bank ever since 1894, and that role, leading the Island's three most important institutions, and playing a key role in its political life, indicates his unique status in the community. W A Waid, R T Curphey, C T W Hughes-Games, W H Kitto, F M LaMothe and J B Waddington completed the board. W A Waid was the son of William Waid, a Grocer from Manchester, who had married Margaret Collier at the Sacred Trinity Church, Salford in 1843, but within a few years was suffering from severe rheumatism and came to the Island to recuperate. The Island must have suited him, as he opened a Tea and grocery business in Douglas in 1851 and lived until 1909, when he was reputed to be a centenarian, although there is some evidence he was actually born c1817. William Albert Waid, was born at Lezayre in 1861, working at first on his fathers farm. In the 1880s, he became joint proprietor with Joseph Sharp of J Sharp & Co, coal merchants, which was established about 1880. In 1887, he married Blanche Roberts. From c1886, the company had the contract for supplying the IOMSPCo with coal, ordering the **SS Sarah Blanche** from John Fullerton & Co of Paisley in 1891. The vessel was named after the two proprietor's respective wives, Sarah Sharp and Blanche Waid. Although Sarah took precedence as the wife of the senior member in the firm, it was Blanche whose name was to survive, after the boat was purchased by the Ramsey Steamship Co in 1923, becoming the SS Ben Blanche, retaining that name until she was lost off S Wales in 1933. Coal offices were erected at the turn of the century on part of the original Noble's Hospital site in Fort Street, which was later to pass into Steam Packet ownership. With his business dealing with the Packet, Waid was appointed a director in the early 1900s.

Cyril Tomlinson Wynne Hughes-Games, M.A., J.P., of Homefield, Laureston Rd, Douglas, was born at

John Donald Clucas was born on 3 April 1869, his parents being John Thomas Clucas and Margaret Callister. His father was an MHK, secretary to Governor Loch, Treasurer of the Isle of Man, and a director of the Isle of Man and Manx Northern Railways. J D Clucas was admitted to the Manx bar in 1894 at the start of a public career that covered more than thirty years, and included membership of the House of Keys and various directorships including the Manx Northern Railway and the Isle of Man Bank. His defence of the Steam Packet in 1919 was his greatest achievement, and saw him appointed to the board. A keen collector of early Manx coins, his collection is now in the Manx Museum. At times quick tempered and irascible, he respected someone who would stand up to him. On one occasion he suffered an abscess on his nose, and complained bitterly to the doctor treating him, forcefully demanding an instant cure. Told it would be painful, he demanded, "Dammit Man get on with it". A resounding punch to his nose burst the abscess, and after a momentary flare of anger, and a copious flow of blood and bad language, he realised the pain had gone, and remained friends with the doctor whose cure, albeit unconventional, was what he had demanded in no uncertain terms.

King William's College, on 4th January 1868, and educated at King Williams and Cambridge. He became a member of the Manx Bar, and was appointed Vicar-General in 1906, and was an ex-officio member of the Legislative Council until 1919. He was Chairman of the Isle of Man Highway Board and a member of the Asylums and Assessment Board, and the Local Government Board. Kitto was a member of the family that had been associated with the Foxdale mines for as long as anyone could recall, and although the mines had closed back in 1911, this was the result of falling ore prices throughout the world and no reflection on the Kitto family. F M LaMothe, a descendant of Dominique and Sukie, appears earlier in this book, along with his signature. The manager & secretary was William M Corkill, grey haired and with a beard that resembled King George V. He had been manager ever since 1908. At the AGM early in 1918, Dalrymple Maitland, aware that the situation was very different to what it had been in 1914, and that with substantial cash reserves arising out of the compulsory acquisition of much of the fleet for war service, there were some in the company who favoured treating the cash as a windfall. Maitland had expressed his own belief in what he called the "Carry On" policy when peace was restored. Today that phrase, "Carry On" is associated with a celebrated and brilliant series of comedies, but in 1918 it had no such connotations. As 1918 progressed, the rift within the Steam Packet deepened, and it was clear that 1919 would be decisive.

The annual report for 1918 appeared early in 1919, and revealed that the company had earned a gross profit of £73,313. At first sight this was surprising, as the collapse of tourism for four long years had been catastrophic to many businesses and families on the Island, but the establishment of the Knockaloe Alien internment camp just outside Peel, which was to house some 25,000 detainees increased the Island's all year population by a half, and brought traffic to the Steam Packet and the railway. After setting aside £25,000 for the future, the profit was sufficient to pay a dividend of 10% and a bonus of 10%.

Overshadowed in popular esteem by a truly outstanding father, John Donald Clucas made an immense contribution to Manx life, defending the Steam Packet successfully when it was under threat, and devoting his analytical skills to conserving aspects of the Island's heritage. He was a great Manxman.

(turn to page 79)

The Steam Packet customarily issued sailing arrangements handbills that were printed in black on white or off white paper. They measured approx 10" x 12.5" and in summer might cover a single month but in winter would cover two or three months. November and December were customarily covered in the same issue, so the first post war Sailings handbill to be produced after hostilities ended covered January to March 1919. With Manx ancestry that I can trace back to 1400AD, I can say that the Manx people can be very "clannish", and suspicious of outsiders, or "Comeovers" to use a derisory term. Some "Comeovers" deserve that; others, such as Maitland, have served their adopted land better than its own sons and daughters. For those who settled on the island, but failed to accept its customs and traditions, there was a devastating put down, "There's always the Nine of Clock Boat". With changes in the timetable in the 1980s to an 8.45am departure, the old jibe has faded away, but this 1919 handbill recalls the days of the "nine of clock" sailing from Douglas to Liverpool. The inbound sailing was at 11.30am from the Landing Stage in winter, and 10.30am in summer when the double daily sailing operated, the inbound and outbound boats crossing somewhere near the Bar Lightship at the mouth of the Mersey. The 11.30 winter sailing gave people a chance to catch an early train from London or the Midlands to Liverpool and to connect with the steamer. The Ramsey service did not operate in winter, but a freighter, the **SS Tyrconnel** provided weekly sailings to Castletown and Peel and fortnightly to Port St Mary, whilst there was also a weekly freight sailing to Ramsey and several sailings to Douglas. Freight sailings from Douglas to Belfast and Glasgow were arranged whenever sufficient cargo was on hand, and a freight only run from Ramsey to Whitehaven was provided on the same terms.

William Mathias Corkill was the son of Edward and Jane Corkill, and was christened at St Matthews Church in Douglas on 17 July 1859. Given the career he was to follow, it was perhaps appropriate that the church was located on the North Quay, within sight and sound of the ships that he was to get to know so well. He joined the company in the mid 1870s, and when he was in his early twenties, became chief clerk to Thomas P Ellison, who was general manager from 1879 to 1908. By 1881, he was lodging at 1 Bath Place, again within a stone's throw of the harbour. The post of "chief clerk" does not sound very significant today, but was in effect Assistant General Manager. When Ellison stood down on health grounds, William Corkill was appointed General Manager & Secretary on 27 August 1908. He is remembered as a shrewd manager and a tactful and kindly man. TV programmes today eulogise ill mannered and domineering bosses. Corkill was neither, but was an outstanding and highly successful manager.

Struggling with ill health in his latter years, William Corkill continued to discharge the arduous duties of General Manager & Secretary until 31 December 1927, although his signature latterly revealed the strain he was under. Sadly, he did not enjoy a long retirement, passing away on 13 December 1930 at "Eastbourne", Woodbourne Road, Douglas. Most surprisingly, he had amassed an estate of £12,500.

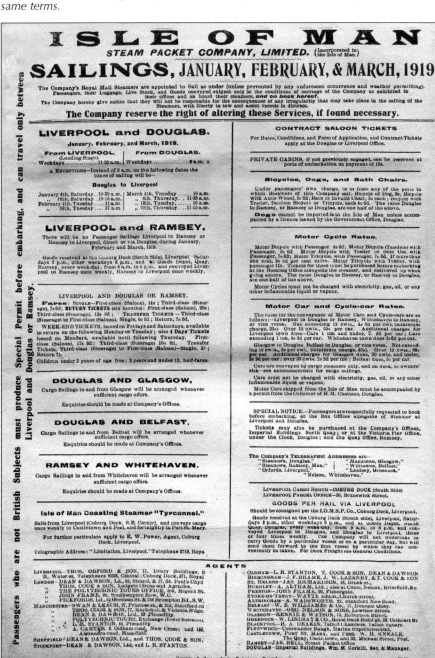

*"She could roll on damp grass, that boat". An elderly Steam Packet employee was regaling me with tales of the Packet boats of his youth, and the **Mona** came in for some caustic remarks. Because she had been built as the **TSS Hazel** for G & J Burns to negotiate the shallow bar at the mouth of Coleraine harbour, she was of shallow draught with a flat bottom, a combination that in the more measured terms of the marine architect would make her "lively" at sea. This portrait of **Mona** alongside the south pier at Ramsey shows her underwater lines to good effect and the fairings for her screw shafts. My father had many passages on her and could attest to the liveliness. Nevertheless she was a welcome acquisition in May 1919 when shipping was in short supply. Her first appearance in the public sailings handbills seems to have been July 1919, and she was one of the winter boats for some years. In 1923, for example, she worked with the **Tynwald** over the Christmas period, her busiest day being Monday 24 December 1923, when she took the 10.30am Liverpool to Douglas, the 4.00pm from Douglas to Liverpool and the 12.30 night (i.e. in the early hours of 25 December) sailing from Liverpool to Douglas. By 1933, her main work was on the 9.00pm Douglas to Liverpool cargo sailing, a chore she shared with the purpose built freighter the **Peveril**. She was also used on some of the direct Ramsey sailings, as with this scene. She was sold for scrap in December 1938.*

(from page 77)

To some, this smelled of profiteering. Such a charge was in fact, untrue, for the paid up capital of £200,000 was an historic figure, dating back many years, and for decades profits had been ploughed back into building up the fleet. The four new turbine steamers built in the decade prior to the outbreak of war had collectively cost £351,275, the **Ben-my-Chree** alone weighing in at £112,100. The cost of those four vessels was approaching twice the paid up capital of the company, and there were another eleven ships, offices, a workshop and warehouses in Douglas, offices in Castletown and Ramsey, stock and stores etc. Even allowing for depreciation, the company's assets were valued at £889,502, or more than four times the paid up capital. Based on the value of the assets actually employed, the 20% dividend was a little below 5%, but historical accident had converted a modest dividend into apparent profiteering. In 1919, it did not matter, but a similar

situation sixty years later was a key element in the chain of events leading up to the humiliating take over of the company in 1985.

The Company was also in a strange position. As eleven of its fifteen vessels had been requisitioned for war service, it was asset-weak. However, the government charters and subsequent purchases had left the Steam Packet with cash holdings that vastly exceeded the paid up capital. There were shareholders and board members who felt that this nest egg should be distributed to the shareholders, as it would be possible to return £5 to investors for every £1 share, an undeniably attractive option, which avoided the risks inherent in carrying on in business. Dalrymple Maitland, who had been chairman since 1900, was strongly opposed to such ideas, as he felt they would harm the Island, but with a strong lobby backing them, had no option but to call an Extraordinary General Meeting immediately after the conclusion of the Annual General Meeting scheduled for Tuesday 25 February 1919. A resolution proposed

by Mr E T Heys of Stockport was one of the most important in the 150-year independent history of the company. It read,

> *That, in the opinion of this meeting, in view of the unique financial position of the Company, the time has now arrived when the Directors should take the earliest opportunity of: -*
>
> *1 Offering the undertaking to the Manx Government on reasonable terms of purchase under a scheme of nationalisation: or*
>
> *2 Reconstructing the Company; or*
>
> *3 Disposing of the undertaking as a going concern to the best possible advantage, and in such a way that the business of the company may be in no way interrupted. That in the meantime the Directors should carefully conserve the funds of the Company which they now have at their disposal.*

The inclusion of nationalisation may seem surprising, but one effect of the Great War was a socialisation of attitudes. The Lenin "October Revolution" of 1917 in Russia, with the overthrow of a democratic government that had replaced the Czarist autocracy in the previous February was the most extreme example of this, but calls were being heard to nationalise the mainland railways in the UK, and in support of other measures that would have been viewed with abhorrence less than five years earlier. By 1919, nationalisation was "respectable", but there was no realistic chance of the IOM government adopting such a policy. The reason for including it, and option 2, reconstruction, was to make disposal for the best price seem less ruthless. If achieved, sale to some other shipping line would offer a massive financial windfall to shareholders. Faced with such a resolution, Maitland had no option but to put it to the vote.

It was expected that there would be a large attendance, so the Masonic Hall in Douglas was hired for the event, which was as well as there were some 300 shareholders present. Even before the start of the meeting, Maitland obviously felt the stress, as those who knew him well remarked that he appeared haggard. He welcomed shareholders and expressed his relief that hostilities were over, but that the price had been high. Many Manxmen had served gallantly throughout the war, and he touched

A handful of ships have become legends in their own lifetime, and their fame has endured long after they have gone. Their ranks include the **Queen Mary**, the **Mauretania**, the **Lady of Man** and a magnificent paddle steamer called **La Marguerite**. The Steam Packet never owned her, so why does she enter this book? In 1919, she was chartered by the Packet to help move the crowds that flocked to the Island in that first post-war summer. She was not a new boat, for she had been built in 1894 for the Palace Steamship Co and the London (Tilbury Pier) to Boulogne route. Tilbury was chosen as her London terminal because it was the highest point up river that a paddle steamer could make for at high speed and had good railway connections to London. She was 330 feet long, 40 feet over the hull and no less than 73 feet over her paddle boxes, and her compound diagonal engines gave her a speed in excess of 21 knots. She had been built by Fairfield's yard on the Clyde, the home of so many fabled ships and her maiden voyage was on 23 June 1894. Although the premier paddle steamer on the Thames, the market was too fragmented, and in 1904 she was sold to the Liverpool & North Wales Steamship Co Ltd, which, as its title implied operated coastal cruises from Liverpool along the North Wales coast as far as Anglesey. She was requisitioned for trooping duties in 1914-18, being released in April 1919. She was immediately chartered by the IOMSPCo to cover the desperate shortage of vessels in 1919, but in 1920 she returned to the North Wales services of her owners. Sadly hard war service had taken its toll, and as with the big paddle steamers of the Packet, most of which had preceded her to the breakers, her last sailing was in September 1925, after which she was broken up at Briton Ferry. On one occasion my father spoke of her, and to my surprise he remembered her not only on the Isle of Man service in 1919, when he was seven years old, but on the North Wales services as well, as his parents were then living in Liverpool. His family had travelled on her from Liverpool to Llandudno. Her "French" name actually related to the daughter of Arnold Williams, a steamship proponent on the Thames.

---

on the price the island had paid, "many of our promising youths have made the supreme sacrifice, and will never return to their friends and their island home". They were no empty words, for the lost generation included his only son, Lieut J D Maitland, killed in action on 21 February 1916, as many of his listeners would have known. He revealed that a provisional contract had been entered into with Laird line to acquire the **TSS Hazel** of 1907 as soon as she was released from government service. He had said it was provisional but one of his opponents on the board pointedly said it was "conditional". It was a harbinger of the acrimony that was shortly to erupt. Maitland would have liked to give his customary outline of what the Board thought should be their line of procedure for the coming season, but,

"Unfortunately, through a division of opinion on the Board, I am unable to adopt that course on this occasion. Let me say at once, most emphatically that, speaking for myself, I retract nothing of what I said at our last meeting. My policy then was to re-establish the fleet and "Carry On". . ."

He then moved the adoption of the annual report.

Often the deputy chairman seconded this, but in 1919, W A Waid, the deputy chairman, was the leading exponent of the sell-out policy, so another director C T Hughes-Games did so. Keen to "sit on the fence", he was critical of two shareholders, A H Teare and J D Clucas, who had issued a circular to shareholders in favour of Maitland's policy, but was careful to add "I was born on the island. I was

brought up here, and I have always resided here. All my interests and affections are centred here. I am prepared to make a sacrifice for the community in which I live". After Hughes-Games had spoken, keeping in with both camps, Alexander Robertson, the Town Clerk of Douglas, rose in his capacity as a shareholder. He delivered a bombshell, and there was no doubt on which side he stood. He proposed that instead of the annual report being adopted, it should only be done in part, and that a committee of five shareholders be appointed to consider "the policy of the directors and the advisability of increasing the capital of the Company from £200,000 to £600,000, by utilising part of the reserve fund, to issue to shareholders two additional shares for every share held by them". Robertson's plan was not to distribute money, but to issue bonus shares on a 2:1 basis. One result of that would be that the 20% dividend which was based on a capital figure that went back generations, but looked as if it was rank profiteering, would drop to a respectable 6.67%. It would also indicate that the company intended to stay in business. Used to marshalling complex arguments, Robertson was the most impressive speaker at the meeting, revealing that three of the directors had opposed the "Carry On" policy, and had backed E T Heys, one of the mainland shareholders, whose policy was "to end the company and divide its assets". Robertson waded into the opposition, proclaiming, "camouflage them as the promoters may, the avowed object was a raid upon the assets of the Company, involving the liquidation thereof." In a devastating speech, he pointed out that Hey's sympathisers on the board had sought to manipulate the proxy system in Heys interests, "thus, if Mr Heys had succeeded, contrary, we believe, to the wishes of the majority of the shareholders and to public policy, the Isle of Man Steam Packet Company, which for nearly a century has been the 'lifeline' of the people of the Island, would have come to an ignominious end, with disastrous results to the community". Robertson resolutely defended the Shareholders committee,

"At the eleventh hour, therefore, a committee of shareholders were compelled to take action and place the position before the shareholders who are unable, owing to distance and other unavoidable causes, to attend the meeting".

Revealing just how close he was to the Committee, he said,

"they are responsible, after careful consideration, for the proposals contained in the amendment I am proposing".

He rejected nationalisation as pie in the sky, and then paid a gallant tribute to Dalrymple Maitland, to whose aid he had come so powerfully.

"The magnificent response that has been made by shareholders on the mainland and in the Isle of Man to our appeal for proxies to support you in the "Carry On" policy, is a sincere and welcome tribute to the confidence and trust placed in you, which confidence, I am sure, will not be betrayed".

His use of the word "our appeal" made it clear how closely he was associated with the committee.

When two of Heys supporters suggested the resolution was out of order, Robertson received the support of no less a figure than the Attorney General, George Alfred Ring, who was present as a shareholder, but his opinion that it was merely a resolution to appoint a committee, so was in order, carried all the formidable weight of his office. Ring had been appointed to the Manx bar as far back as 1873 and served as Attorney General from November 1897 to October 1920. The amendment was put. It was a trial of proxy strength in which the "carry on" team triumphed, with A H Teare, J D Clucas, E C Thin and R C Cain representing them, and Heys being the only success for the opposition. The election of directors is seldom a controversial matter, but when the Vice chairman, W A Waid, stood for re-election, A H Teare let fly. Alfred Hugh Teare, although known to his friends as Hugo, was the son of Robert Hinds Teare of Ramsey and had been born in 1877. He worked for Robert Cowley, corn and timber merchant of Ramsey, before becoming pro-

prietor and editor of the *Ramsey Courier* newspaper in 1900. He became MHK for Ramsey in 1918, and was possessed of immense energy and zest. He was tough, outspoken and not renowned for suffering fools gladly, and had thrown his weight behind the campaign to save the Packet.

Hugo Teare hammered Waid mercilessly, accusing him of encouraging Heys in the break up plan, of failing to support his chairman, Dalrymple Maitland, who was the "captain" in the crisis they were passing through, and of mutiny. When one of the biggest mainland shareholders, E C Thin, heard what was happening, he had proposed to distribute his own shares amongst his immediate family to maximise voting strength in favour of Maitland. Hugo Teare blasted Waid for blocking that move, whilst encouraging Heys' drive for proxies. When one shareholder said bluntly "The wrecker-raiders are only out for blood and

plunder", the meeting descended into uproar. Maitland, always a figure of moderation, delivered a devastating blow against Waid when he revealed that after the previous AGM, he had objected to Mr Waid being appointed vice chairman on account of his known views. As the election had to be decided on proxy votes, the AGM was adjourned whilst the votes were being counted, and the Extraordinary Meeting was held to consider the Heys motion.

As the Extraordinary Meeting started, Heys opened fire on the shareholders committee and suggested that Maitland, with his association with the IOM Bank and the IOM Railway, was susceptible to pressure from the visiting industry. He was backed in this by W A Waid, who claimed that Maitland wanted to build two new "Ben-my-Chree's", a claim Maitland rejected, given "new build" prices at that time. Hey's argued that,

"If the Manx people wanted a steamship company, they should control it themselves and should pay for it, Nationalisation of the steamship service is being universally accepted".

John Donald Clucas led the response. Like Hugo Teare, he was a formidable character, and with his legal and political connections, was aware that nationalisation was a non-starter. Maitland and Hugo Teare backed him, but when Heys accused Maitland and his colleagues of acting improperly in giving the list of shareholders to the Committee to build up proxies against his own, the Attorney General joined in the fray once more, reading from the Companies Act to show they were right to do so. By now it was early evening, and the proxy votes had been counted. The meeting erupted in cheers as Maitland gave the figure. There were 2,327 votes in favour of the deputy chairman, and a devastating 7,042 against. The two meetings were adjourned to the following morning.

W A Waid, who had lost his vice-chairmanship, did not attend on the Wednesday, sensing, no doubt, how things were going. Maitland said they would now need to appoint a director in place of Waid. The two directors who had previously backed the Waid-Heys proposals had seen what had happened to Waid, and had promptly changed sides, whilst Hughes-Games saw no need to sit on the fence any longer. Instead of being divided, as

If ever there was a case of the poacher turned gamekeeper, the **Manxman I** epitomised that transition. She was built for the start of the "opposition" MR services from Heysham to Douglas in 1904, and was the first turbine steamer to serve the Island. She was purchased by the Admiralty for war service in January 1915, de-requisitioned in December 1919, and sold to the Steam Packet in March 1920. In 1921, she was converted to an oil burner, the first Packet boat to be so modified. The company had some anxieties about the change and explained 'The Company's steamer "Manxman" has been fitted to burn Oil fuel on the White patent low pressure system, and is the first channel steamer to burn Oil. The installation was fitted by Vickers at Barrow; special tanks forward of the boiler room carry the fuel, while the coal bunkers are left empty in case a return to coal was found to be necessary at any time. For the same reason the furnace bars and other fittings are carried on board, so that a quick change round could be effected and the service maintained either on Coal or Oil. The fuel used is heavy Mexican Oil of a calorific value of 18,500 B.T.U.'s per pound as opposed to 13,000 B.T.U.'s from coal.' Frequently used on the Liverpool services, she was also to be found at Ardrossan between the wars. She was again requisitioned at the start of World War Two, and did not return to the company after the war.   MIdwood

had been the case for months, the board now had a unanimous proposal to submit to the AGM. It was John Donald Clucas. Predictably some of Heys backers challenged this, but the Attorney General intervened once again, destroying their case. Clucas was carried by a large majority. There was a suggestion from Hugo Teare that Hughes-Games, who had done nothing to back Maitland, be invited to resign, but Maitland asked that the strife should end, and such was his aura as a disciple of moderation that Hugo Teare immediately complied. The last, but the most important business, was the poll vote on the Heys resolution. 4441 votes were cast in favour, but there were 7,273 against, so Maitland, with the support of Hugo Teare, John Donald Clucas, E C Thin,

One day, my father was talking about some of the Packet boats of his childhood and mentioned how puzzled he had been to discover that the **TrSS Snaefell** had a serpent at the bows. It was not until he bought a copy of the superb centenary history of the Packet, that he discovered that the **Snaefell** has started life in 1906 as the **Viper**. She had been a part of the celebrated G & J Burns fleet and worked between Ardrossan and Belfast. By the 1930s, **Snaefell** was frequently to be found on the Heysham services. Remaining with the Packet during the war, she showed her age, and became increasingly difficult and costly to keep in service. With vessels returning after the end of hostilities, she was sold in 1945, but laid up in Port Glasgow for three years before being broken up.

The **Mona's Isle** was built for the South Eastern & Chatham Railway as the **TrSS Onward** by William Denny of Dumbarton in 1905. She is the only Steam Packet ship to have nearly sunk a railway locomotive! On 24 September 1918, she had arrived on trooping duties at Folkestone, and shortly after she had unloaded, caught fire. Despite the efforts of fire fighting teams, the blaze spread, and the decision was taken to open the sea-cocks. As she sank, she developed a severe list to port. A small SE&CR 0-4-0ST, No 313, which had been built by Manning Wardle, had been hauling goods wagons away from the blazing ship, but one of the mooring lines broke and snared No 313 which was being dragged towards the quayside. Desperate work by the enginemen with a chisel, as their engine was being dragged towards a blazing sinking ship, parted the cable just in time, so the engine did not join the SECR boat at the bottom of Folkestone harbour. She was salvaged using compressed air and a battery of locomotives to haul her upright, repaired, and sold to the Packet in 1920. She is seen at the Queens Pier, Ramsey, on a Belfast sailing, which was one of her regular routes. Dublin was another common destination for the **Mona's Isle**. After requisition during World War Two, she returned to the Packet, but was broken up in 1948.

---

the Town Clerk of Douglas, and the Attorney General, had won. Clucas had been elected. Hugo Teare would soon join him on the board, as would E C Thin, whilst Alexander Robertson would do so in the fullness of time, Robertson eventually becoming an outstanding chairman of the Packet. E C Thin, though not playing a prominent public role, had placed his massive voting strength in the hands of the Carry-On campaign, and his comments that he was well satisfied with Maitland's policy may have helped sway other English shareholders. George A Ring had been in poor health for some time, and stood down as Attorney General in 1920, moving to the milder climate of the South Coast, where he died near Steyning early in 1927. His contributions, though succinct, were crucial, and were a fitting conclusion to half a century of outstanding service to the Island.

Maitland had presided over the meeting with his usual fairness and tact, but it had been a trying ordeal. The House of Keys had watched events with anxiety, and a few days after the Steam Packet meeting, the House passed a resolution conveying its thanks to him for the stand he had maintained. Despite the dissension that had tormented the Board, Maitland was conciliatory as always,

May 1920 was a busy month for the Packet. Apart from acquiring the **Mona's Isle**, the company also bought a small steam coaster, the **SS Ardnagrena**. She was soon renamed **Cushag**, after the Manx national flower. She was 125 feet long and of 223 grt. With a draft of just 9ft 2 ins, she was able to go into the small ports that were once served by the company, and regularly visited Port St Mary, Peel, Castletown and Laxey. She had been built at Greenock in 1908, and had two owners prior to joining the Packet. In 1943 she was sold and moved to Stornoway on the Isle of Lewis, and in 1947 to Kirkwall in the Orkneys. She was not finally broken up until 1957. Although it takes us outside the 1920s, I will outline her movements during a single week in 1933. On Monday 17 July, she sailed at 7.00pm from Peel to Liverpool, and the following day, Tuesday 18 July, left Liverpool at 8.00pm for Ramsey. On Wednesday she sailed from Ramsey at 9.00pm for Liverpool. On Thursday 20 July, she loaded cargo for Castletown, Port St Mary and Peel, sailing from Liverpool at 10.00pm for Castletown. At 10.00pm, on Friday 21 July, she made the short journey from Castletown to Port St Mary, and at 11am on Saturday morning, she left Port St Mary, rounded the Calf, and arrived at Peel, where she was ready to start the same pattern the next week. She was renowned in the south of the Island for her unofficial (and free) coastal cruises from Castletown to Port St Mary, and would often leave Castletown with a goodly complement of local folks on board. Whether the great ones in Douglas knew of this, and turned a blind eye to it, or were in blissful ignorance of what went on, is not something I know.

SEASON 1922 (FIRST EDITION).

Isle of Man

SAILINGS & HOLIDAY TOURS
also "The Lil Islan" by Agnes Herbert
THE ISLE of MAN STEAM PACKET Cº Lᵀᴰ
(Incorporated in the Isle of Man)

*For many years, the Steam Packet produced a smart 64-page brochure. From the early 1900s, the cover was a colourful scene showing one of the company's steamers and usually reflected current fashions as well. The 1922 issue showed a magnificent two funnel steamer entering Douglas harbour as a delightful flapper looks out at the reader. Hemlines had started to go up after the war, and after a brief reaction when they dropped to the levels we see here, climbed steadily for the next few years. The change was not always popular and Utah politicians actually introduced legislation making it a criminal offence to wear a skirt that ended more than three inches above the ankle! Although the legendary **Ben-my-Chree** of 1908 had been lost in 1917, the steamer that is entering Douglas bears a striking resemblance to her.*

and changes after the battle were minimal. Although a great load had been lifted from his mind, the strain had been immense, and at the start of March, he was stricken with bronchitis, which rapidly worsened, with congestion of the lungs, and he passed away early on the morning of 25 March 1919. Although born in Liverpool, making him a "Comeover", Maitland had served the adopted land he loved so well with dignity and courage. It is fitting that his name is commemorated on one of the steam locomotives of the Isle of Man Railway, of which he was also a director. Today, with the majority of shares in publicly quoted companies being held by pension funds and investment trusts, where a quick return is paramount, there is no doubt what the result of such a contest would be, but many families on the Island had held shares for generations, and had invested not for a quick buck, but to secure the financial future of the community. That spirit, in which individual members of the community felt that the best form of public ownership was by public spirited individuals, rather than an anonymous state authority,

was seized upon by Maitland. Robertson's idea of a 2-for-1 bonus share issue was adopted, raising the nominal capital to £600,000. On that basis, the 20% profiteering dividend would stand at 6.67%, a much more realistic figure. In this, the board showed their wisdom compared to their successors in the 1970s and 1980s, when the same issue was allowed to fester, poisoning public attitudes to the company, and making the appearance of a rival Manx Line welcome. Panic, when its rival fell into the hands of a formidable predator, completed the process.

With wartime losses and the run-down state of many of the requisitioned ships, the Steam Packet did not think it was worthwhile repurchasing older vessels such as the **Queen Victoria** or the **Prince of Wales**, both of which were over thirty years old, and went from the Admiralty to ship breakers in Holland. As a result, just four vessels returned to the fleet, the **Mona's Queen**, **Viking**, **Peel Castle** and **King Orry**. With a pent up demand for relaxation after the end of the war, the 1919 season was going to be a trying period, and with so much shipping lost to the U-boat offensive during the war, new tonnage had to be a long-term solution. Second-hand tonnage was sought, and the **TSS Hazel** was acquired on 21 May 1919 from G & J Burns of Glasgow, acting on behalf of Laird Line, with whom they were closely associated and were to merge within a few years. Laird Line had the amazing distinction of predating the Steam Packet, tracing its origin back to 1814. Its main business was between

Glasgow and Londonderry, but a regular service was instituted between Glasgow and Coleraine in Northern Ireland. A shallow bar at the mouth of the River Bann made Coleraine a difficult port to enter, and even after the 1884 improvements to the harbour that had made the service possible, vessels had to be of shallow draft. Laird Line had maintained the route until the outbreak of war in 1914, but with the increased costs of coastal shipping after 1918, decided not to reopen the route, meaning that the last vessel to be specially built for the service, the **TSS Hazel** of 1907 was surplus, and was sold to the Packet for £65,000. She was renamed **Mona**, entering service as soon as possible.

1919 turned out to be an eventful year. Seasonal arrivals, which had slumped to 34,108 in 1915, and had not exceeded 100,000 for the rest of the war years, soared to 343,332 in 1919. By immediate pre-war standards, it was not good and one would have to go back to the 1890s to find a lower figure, but the fleet was much smaller in 1920 than in 1913, and the Packet was hard put to cope. A relatively good season was a boost for the island and the businesses that had suffered during the lean war years, whilst the gross profit earned by the Packet, of £151,568, was more than twice the surplus in 1918, and despite £10,000 put to reserves and £75,000 towards reconditioning steamers, there was sufficient left to pay a 10% dividend on the revise capital of £600,000. As total assets were now close on £1m, the catching up exercise over share capital had been overtaken by events within a few months. Dalrymple Maitland, the company chairman, died in March 1919, his place being taken by Cyril Tomlinson Wynn Hughes-Games as chairman. Other than for the decisive rejection of W A Waid and his replacement by J D Clucas, it was the

(turn to page 86)

The Isle of Man Steam Packet Co., Ltd
[INCORPORATED IN THE ISLE OF MAN.]

ISLE OF MAN

Easter Holidays, 1923

The Express Steamers "MONA'S ISLE" (Turbine), "Mona," and "Tynwald" will sail during Easter.

Steamers are appointed to sail as under—
(Unless prevented by any unforeseen occurrence, and weather permitting)—

LIVERPOOL TO DOUGLAS :	DOUGLAS TO LIVERPOOL :
WEDNESDAY, 28th March :	**WEDNESDAY, 28th March :**
10-30 am.c; 12 night.D	9 am.B
THURSDAY, 29th March :	**THURSDAY, 29th March :**
10-30 am.A; 3 pm.B;	9 am,c; 4 pm.A
12-50 night.A	
GOOD FRIDAY :	**GOOD FRIDAY :**
10-30 am.c	9 am.B; 4 pm.A
SATURDAY, 31st March :	**SATURDAY, 31st March :**
10-30 am.A; 3 pm.c;	9 am.c; 4 pm.A
12-50 night.B	
EASTER MONDAY :	**EASTER MONDAY :**
10-30 am.A; 3 pm.c;	1 am.B; 9 am.c; 4 pm.A;
12 night.B	12-30 night.c
TUESDAY, 3rd April :	**TUESDAY, 3rd April :**
10-30 am.A; 3 pm.c	9 a.m.B; 4 p.m.A
WEDNESDAY, 4th April, to 30th April:	**WEDNESDAY, 4th April, to 30th April:**
Weekdays, 10-30 am.	Weekdays, 9 a.m.

A "Mona's Isle." B "Mona." c "Tynwald." D "Douglas." E "Fenella."

Liverpool to Ramsey : (DIRECT)	Ramsey to Liverpool : (VIA DOUGLAS)
Saturday, 31st March 2 pm.D	Easter Monday ... 1 pm.

☞ FOR FARES SEE BACK.

The Company reserve the right of altering these Services if found necessary.
Passengers, their Luggage, Live Stock, and Goods conveyed subject only to the conditions of carriage of the Company as exhibited in their offices and on board their Steamers.

TRAINS AND ELECTRIC CARS FROM DOUGLAS.

On Thursday & Saturday, 29th & 31st March, & Easter Monday, Trains will leave Douglas for Peel, Ramsey, and Port Erin at 9-0 p.m., subject to a delay of 30 minutes, if necessary, to await arrival of steamer leaving Liverpool on Thursday, 29th March, 3 p.m.; on Saturday, 31st March, 3 p.m., and on Easter Monday, at 3 p.m.
Other trains are conveniently timed to leave Douglas to accommodate passengers by the Ordinary Week-day Boat Service.
Electric Cars for Laxey and Ramsey from Derby Castle Station will connect with the arrival of all the above trains.

THE ISLE OF MAN STEAM PACKET COMPANY, LTD., IMPERIAL BUILDINGS, DOUGLAS; AND
T. ORFORD & SON, AGENTS, DRURY BUILDINGS, 21, WATER St., LIVERPOOL.

Printed at "Herald" Office, Douglas. (P.T.O.)

The Isle of Man Steam Packet Co., Ltd
[INCORPORATED IN THE ISLE OF MAN.]

FARES : SINGLE—First-class (Saloon) **12/6** ; Third-class (Steerage), **7/6** ; **Return Tickets** (six months) : First-class (Saloon), **20/-** ; Third-class (Steerage), **12/6** ; TRANSFER TICKETS—Steerage to Saloon, Single, **5/-** ; Return, **7/6**.
Easter Excursion Tickets will be issued on Thursday, Friday, and Saturday, 29th to 31st March, available for 15 days. First-class (Saloon), **18/6** ; Third class (Steerage), **11/-**. Transfer Tickets—Steerage to Saloon, Single, **4/-** ; Return, **7/6**.
Week-End Tickets will be issued on Saturday, 31st March, available to return on the following Monday or Tuesday. **Fares :** First-class (Saloon), **17/6** ; Third-class (Steerage), **10/-**. TRANSFER TICKETS—Steerage to Saloon, Single, **4/-** ; Return, **7/6**.
Children under 3 years of age, free ; 3 years and under 12, half-fares.

Day Trips
CAN BE MADE—

From LIVERPOOL--	RETURNING From DOUGLAS--
Wednesday, 28th March, 12 night.	
Thursday, 29th March, 10-30 am.	**Thursday,** ... 4 pm.
do. 12-50 night.	
Good Friday, 10-30 am.	**Good Friday** ... 4 pm.
Saturday, 31st March, 10-30 am.	**Saturday,** ... 4 pm.
do. 12-50 night.	**Easter Monday,** ... 1 am.
Easter Monday, 10-30 am.	**Easter Monday,** 4 pm. or 12-30 night.
do. 12 night.	
Tuesday, 3rd April, 10-30 am.	**Tuesday,** ... 4 pm.

Day Fares : 1st Class (Saloon), **12/6** ; 3rd Class (Steerage), **9/-**
Easter Monday Excursion—LONG DAY IN LIVERPOOL. From Douglas, 1 am. ; Returning from Liverpool, 12 night.

CONTRACT TICKET (SALOON) RATES :
Contract Tickets available between Liverpool or Fleetwood (when occupied) and Douglas or Ramsey (Steamer only)—

Fortnight	£2 0s 0d;	One Month	£2 10s 0d;
Two Months	£4 0s 0d;	Three Months	£4 10s 0d;
Four Months	£5 0s 0d;	Six Months	£6 0s 0d;
	Twelve Months, £10 0s 0d.		

Contract Tickets available by all the Company's Services, including any of their advertised Excursions (Steamer only)—

Fortnight	£3 0s 0d;	One Month	£4 0s 0d;
Two Months	£5 0s 0d;	Three Months	£5 15s 0d;
Four Months	£6 10s 0d;	Six Months	£9 0s 0d;
	Twelve Months, £12 10s 0d.		

For Contract Tickets apply at the Douglas or Liverpool Office.

GOOD FRIDAY ALSO EASTER MONDAY

HALF-DAY EXCURSIONS
From LIVERPOOL, 2-30 p.m.
For Four Hours' Coasting Cruise. FARE 4/-
(P.T.O.)

---

*It was not until Whitsuntide, a traditional holiday that was based on the religious calendar, that the summer season began in earnest, but Easter, which could fall over several weeks in March or April, heralded the break with the long winter months. I have selected this handbill for the Easter 1923 sailings, as it gives information on no fewer than five vessels, the **Mona's Isle** and **Mona**, which were part of the second-hand acquisitions after the Great War and the **Tynwald**, **Douglas** and **Fenella**, which had seen many years of service with the company. The **Douglas** was a bit bigger than **Fenella**, but to the same general design, and had been built for the London & South Western Railway in 1889 as the **Dora**, and acquired in 1901. The Easter 1923 handbill was one of the last times her name would appear on IOMSPCO publicity material as she was involved in a collision in the Mersey on 16 August 1923, and sank, thankfully without loss of life. Whilst the 22 knots of the **Mona's Isle** well merited the title "Express" steamer, the 14 knot **Fenella** and 15 knot **Douglas** hardly merits the compliment.*

To our eyes, the fares seem incredibly cheap, 12/6d (or 62.5p in decimal terms) for a Third Class (Steerage) return and 20/- (£1) for a First Class (Saloon) return, but they need to be seen in relation to wages and expenses of the time. At the Belvedere Hotel, on the Loch Prom in Douglas, dinner, bed and breakfast was available from 12/6d (62.5p) a night. On the Island, a general labourer could expect to earn a few pence either side of £2 a week, though an agricultural labourer would be lucky if his wage was three quarters of that. However he could expect to grow a good proportion of his own vegetables, a benefit that town dwellers lacked. A joiner or painter could expect £3 a week and a skilled fitter £3 10s (£3.50), for which they would put in a 48 hour week. Today, the minimum hourly wage for an unskilled worker is comfortably above what a skilled man would earn in a week in the 1920s. Women worked in lower paid jobs, and a domestic servant or shop girl might take home 10/- (50p) a week. Such jobs were not seen as a living occupation, but as a way of supplementing the income of the parents, so that a child was contributing to the family income, rather than being a drain. When she married, a girl would invariably stop work and look after the home, her husband being the breadwinner. Looked at in this context, a steerage return ticket was a day's wages for a joiner or painter, but for a shop girl, it was a week's work.

The four vessels acquired in 1919-1920 to augment the fleet after the severe losses during the Great War dealt with the worst problems experienced by the Packet, but the loss of the **Douglas** in 1923 called for urgent action. The London & South Western Railway took delivery of a triple-screw turbine steamer the **Caesarea** in 1910. She was 1504 grt, with a length of 284ft 6ins. In 1923, she went ashore near St Helier in Jersey and was sent to Birkenhead for repairs and a refit. The LSWR had become part of the larger Southern Railway at the start of 1923, and was reorganising its shipping services, and the decision was taken to dispose of her. The Steam Packet snapped her up for £9,000, but repairs and refurbishment took the total to £38,500 but at a quarter of the price of the second-hand **Snaefell (IV)**, she was a bargain. As has appeared in print elsewhere, some of the work was carried out at Cammell Laird in Birkenhead, but she was then sent up to the Vickers yard at Barrow, and emerged as the **Manx Maid**.   Midwood

The work required to refurbish the **Caesarea** as the **Manx Maid**, the first time the name had been used by the IOMSPCo, was considerable, as refurbishment was two and a half times the purchase cost. A maiden voyage, even of a second-hand vessel, was a momentous event, and in May 1924, leading figures in the Manx business and political community received invitations to travel by the 9.00am boat from Douglas to Liverpool as guests of the Steam Packet, and thence to Barrow, staying overnight at the elegant Furness Abbey Hotel for the inaugural voyage under Steam Packet auspices from Vickers Wharf at Barrow to Douglas on 22 May 1924. A versatile boat, she was widely used, with Fleetwood, Liverpool, and Ardrossan being common destinations.

(from page 84)

first change in the board since before the start of the Great War. E C Thin of Liverpool, who had rallied to the cause, was recommended to represent mainland interests. Towards the end of 1919, the **Vindex**, formerly the IOMSPCo **Viking**, the **Manxman**, which had been one of the Midland Railway boats on the rival Heysham route, and the **Onward** were acquired from the Ministry of Shipping. All three were fast twin funnel steamers, much better suited to the company's routes than the **Mona**, which was a stopgap, albeit an invaluable one.

1920 saw arrivals rocket to 561,124, a phenomenal result, the only time the figure had been exceeded previously being the bumper 1913 arrivals of 634,512. In the all time arrival results, 1920 still holds a place in the top ten seasons, a measure of just how keen the world was to get back to life as usual. With the three vessels acquired at the end of 1919 available for the season, the company was much better placed to handle the traffic, but the board was still keen to find additional tonnage, and on 22

March 1920 acquired the **TrSS Viper** from G & J Burns. She had been built in 1906 for the daylight service between Belfast and Ardrossan and had been requisitioned in 1914 by the Admiralty and returned to her owners in 1919. Although an important route, the troubles in Ireland with demands for Home Rule in the south and a strong backlash in the north, meant that traffic was well down, persuading Burns to dispose of her. She became the **Snaefell**. Wartime and early post war inflation was causing havoc with finances, and an idea of how difficult times were is given by the £160,000 cost of this second-hand 1906 steamer. When new in 1908, the much larger **Ben-my-Chree** had cost £112,100. The only dedicated freight boat was the **Tyrconnel**, an 1892 coaster that was scarcely any bigger or faster than the original **Mona's Isle** of 1830. The **Fenella** of 1881, by now the oldest boat in the fleet, split her time between freight duties and lightly used passenger sailings, but with rising freight traffic, prompt movement of goods was becoming difficult. The annual report for 1920 commented that the directors *"have also, in order to meet a pressing requirement, purchased a small cargo boat, now called the "Cushag"*. She was acquired in May 1920, her original name being **Ardnagrena**, her name being changed in August 1920. Despite the dramatic increase in traffic compared to 1919, the gross profits for 1920, of £98,770, were a third down on the previous year. It was a period of rapid and unpredictable price movements, making comparison of one year with another fraught. As in 1919, the board decided on a 10% dividend. At the end of 1919, the capital consisted of £600,000 in ordinary shares and £104,000 in debentures. A debenture is the corporate version of a mortgage, so bears interest, and if that is not paid, then the debenture holder can seize the assets as with a mortgage repossession of a house. Prudent financing in the old days demanded that debentures did not exceed fifty percent of the paid up share capital, but with the revised capital following the 1919 meeting, the Steam Packet increased its debenture stock to £300,000 during 1920. To the board's pleasure, the issue was substantially over-subscribed. In other words there were more would be buyers than stock, which was a measure of the company's standing.

1921 was not nearly as good. Seasonal arrivals fell from the bumper 561,124 of 1920 to 427,923. The "Arrivals" figure related to passengers landed between 1 May and 30 September and included all methods of travel, but air was not existent at this time and the Midland route via Heysham and the Silloth route carried a small percentage of the traffic. Although some arrivals would not be visitors, the majority would be, so a drop of 133,201 arrivals would suggest a fall in passenger journeys of twice that, and the Packet recorded a drop of 245,394 passengers indicating the correlation between Packet arrivals and overall arrivals. The main reason for the decline was general industrial unrest, and a major coal strike that lasted from 1 April to 1 July, required service cuts to conserve coal stocks. It meant that many potential holidaymakers from the mining districts could not afford to travel. As Lancashire and Yorkshire were both major coalfields and sources of visitors, the Packet and the island were badly affected. Receipts fell by no less than £86,142 and gross profits declined from £98,770 to £50,671. With a fifty percent drop in profits the board halved the dividend from 10% to 5%. Until the eve of the Great War, virtually all merchant ships were coal fired, but the reduction in manning levels with oil firing became attractive after the war due to wage inflation, and the annual disruption in the coal-fields was a powerful factor in encouraging ship owners to abandon coal firing, the intransigence of the mine owners and unions hastening their own decline. Although she was just over thirty years old, the **Tynwald** was reboilered in 1922, whilst the former Midland steamer, the **Manxman** had been sent to Vickers at Barrow for conversion to oil firing. F M LaMothe, a long serving director had been appointed Deemster, so had stood down from the board, his replacement being A H Teare of Ramsey. A member of the House of Keys, Hugo Teare had played a key role in the shareholders committee in 1919, and was a resolute and capable director who played a key role in saving the Isle of Man Railway in the 1920s.

1922 saw a further decline of £26,000 in receipts, although 87,484 more passengers were carried and cargo rose by 2,772 tons. The increase in passengers mirrored the improvement in seasonal arrivals, which reached 481,736. The decline in receipts, despite higher levels of traffic, was due to cuts in passenger fares and freight rates to try to bring in more business despite the depressed state of the economy. Bad weather for much of the summer was no help. With the fleet adequate for current traffic levels, and the weak economic climate, no attempt was made to add new or second-hand vessels in 1921 or 1922. Gross profits of £53,462 were marginally up on the previous year, but the board did not feel inclined to go beyond a 5% dividend, and unlike the profitable years at the immediate end of the war, nothing was set aside to reserves.

1923 was another mixed year, with receipts falling by £28,885, and 50,967 fewer passengers as well. Thankfully freight rose by 3,665 tons. On 16 August 1923, the **SS Douglas**, which had been built for the London & South Western Railway as the **Dora** in 1889, and acquired in 1901, was involved in a collision in the Mersey and sank. Thankfully there was no loss of life, but my father recalled a packet arriving one morning. Inside was a letter expressing the Postmaster General's regrets that the enclosed letter had been immersed in seawater, having gone down with the **SS Douglas**. The **Douglas** had been acquired in 1901 to plug a gap caused by the loss of the **Peveril** in 1899, and her demise prompted a fresh search. The London & South Western Railway competed with the Great Western Railway on the Channel Isles services, but in 1923, the LSWR became a part of the much larger Southern Railway. The **Caesarea**, of 1910 had gone aground near St Helier in Jersey during 1923, and was purchased by the Packet in December 1923, whilst undergoing repairs, for the bargain price of £9,000. Repairs and refurbishment added another £22,500, whilst conversion to oil firing added £7,000, but at a total price of £38,500, the **Manx Maid (I)** as she became, was a quarter of the price of the **Snaefell**. In part, this was due to her poor condition when bought, but the inflation and boom of the early post-war period had been followed by a long depression driving down prices. R T Curphey, a director from pre-war days, and a loyal backer of Maitland in 1919, passed away, and his successor was William H Dodd of Liverpool, the company long having a

(turn to page 89)

87

Private and not for Circulation

Electric Light to be switched on at Sunset for all Sailings between Sunset and Sunrise when Steamer is alongside Pier, Quay, or in Dock.

Sailing Arrangements—Saturday, July 31st, 1926, to Friday, August 6th, 1926.

SUMMER TIME	Saturday, JULY 31st, Wigan, Ince, Leeds, and Wakefield Wakes.	Sunday, AUG. 1st.	MONDAY 2nd. BANK HOLIDAY.	TUESDAY 3rd.	WEDNESDAY 4th.	THURSDAY 5th.	FRIDAY 6th.
High Water at L'pool	4·31—16·11 5·5—15·6	5·30—15·4 6·5—14·5	6·38—14·1 7·13—13·9	7·49—13·5 8·23—13·9	8·38—13·6 9·27—14·5	10·2—14·1 10·24—15·3	10·56—14·10 11·13—16·3
MANXMAN	L to D 9 a.m. 1st D to L 2.30 p.m. 1st L to D 12.50 night* Not to sail before 1.20 a.m. Sunday		D to L 12.30 a.m.* Oil L to D 10.30 a.m. D to Dublin 5 p.m.	Dublin to D a.m.* D to L 4 p.m.	L to D 10.30 a.m. D to L 4 p.m.	L to D 10.30 a.m. D to L 4 p.m.	L to D 3 p.m.
VIKING.	F to D 1.30 a.m. D to F 6.45 a.m. 1st F to D 10.30 a.m. 1st D to F 4 p.m. 1st		F to D 10.30 a.m. D to F 4 p.m.	F to D 10.30 a.m. D to F 4 p.m.	F to D 10.30 a.m. D to F 4 p.m.	F to D 10.30 a.m. D to F 4 p.m.	F to D 10.30 a.m. D to F 4 p.m.
KING ORRY.	D to L 1 p.m.* Friday and Coal L to D 10 a.m. 2nd D to L 4 p.m. 2nd		L to D 1 a.m.* 1st D to L 4 p.m. 2nd	L to D 10.30 a.m. D to F 6 p.m. And Coal	F to Llandudno 10.30 a.m. Llandudno to F 5.45 p.m. And Coal	F to D 9.35 a.m.	D to Ard. 8.30 a.m. Calls R Coal at Ard. Ard. to D 11.30 p.m. Not to Call R
SNAEFELL	D to F 8 a.m. 2nd F to D 10.30 a.m. 2nd Stand by D to F 4 p.m. 2nd		D to L 9 a.m. Fill up Coal L to D p.m.*	D to Dublin 8.30 a.m. And Coal Dublin to D 5 p.m.		D to F 6 p.m. And Coal F to L p.m.*	L to D 10.30 a.m. D to L 4 p.m.
MANX MAID	D to L a.m.* L to D 11 a.m. 3rd	D to Dublin 4 p.m.*	Dublin to D 8.30 a.m. 1st D to L 4 p.m. 1st And Oil	L to D a.m.* D to L 9 a.m.	L to D 3 p.m.	D to Dublin 8.30 a.m. Dublin to D 6 p.m.	D to L 9 a.m.
PEEL CASTLE.	D to L 7.30 a.m. 1st L to D 12.30 noon 5th	Coal at D D to Dublin 1 p.m.*	Dublin to D 8.30 a.m. 2nd	D to Belfast 8.30 a.m. Coal at B Belfast to D 4.30 p.m. Calls R to and from	D to L 9 a.m.	L to D 3 p.m.	D to Belfast 8.30 a.m. Coal at B Belfast to D 4.30 p.m. Calls R to and from
Mona's Queen	D to L 8.20 a.m. 2nd L to D 2 p.m. 1st		D to Ard. 11 p.m. Sun. Coal at Ard. Ard. to D 12 noon Calls R from Ard. D to L 12.30 night* 1st	L to D 3 p.m.	Round Island Calls Ramsey 11.30 a.m. Passengers return D to R by Rail	D to Llandudno 9.30 a.m. Llandudno to D 4.30 p.m.	D to L a.m.* Fill up Coal L to D 12.50 night 1st*
MONA	D to L 9 a.m. 3rd L to D 3 p.m. 2nd	D to L a.m. And Coal	L to D 3 p.m. D to L 12.30 night* 2nd	L to D 12.30 night* From Stage	Discharging Cargo	D to L 9 a.m.	L to D 12.50 night 2nd*
TYNWALD.	D to F 8.30 a.m. 3rd Coal at ... F to D 3.30 p.m.	No passengers* D to Workington* To enter p.m. tide	Workington Excur. Charter Workington to D 7.15 a.m. Calling R Coal at D	D to Workington 1 a.m.* Not to call Ramsey Workington to R a.m.*		R to L 9 a.m. Fill up Coal	L to R 12 noon R to F p.m.*
FENELLA	D to L a.m.* L to D 11 a.m. 4th And enter Harbour	D to L 4 a.m. Theatrical Company and Scenery	L to D 12.30 night* From Stage	D to L 8 p.m.* And Dock	L to D 12.30 night* From Stage	D to L 10 p.m.* And Dock	L to D 11 p.m.* From Dock
TYRCONNEL Cargo Steamer,	D to L 7 p.m.		Load for C, PSM, and P L to C 6 p.m.	C to PSM 7 p.m.	PSM to Peel 8 p.m.	Peel to L 9 p.m.	Load for C, PSM, and P L to C 9 p.m.
CUSHAG Cargo Steamer,	Load for D L to D 5.15 p.m.		D to L 8 p.m.	Load for Ramsey L to R 7 p.m.	R to L 9 p.m.	Load for D L to D 10.30 p.m.	D to L 10 p.m.
Wind and Weather							

(from page 87)

policy of including two mainland directors on the board. Gross profits, of £50,511, were slightly down, but the usual 5% dividend was possible.

1924 was the fourth consecutive year that receipts declined, but the fall, of £8,233 was less than in previous years. Passengers rose by just over ten thousand, but in contrast to 1922 and 1923, freight dropped by 1,370 tons. The UK economy remained weak, and the weather had not helped either. The **Manx Maid (I)** had entered service prior to the start of the summer, and in the words of the board, *"was highly popular with the travelling public"*. Although I cannot truthfully say that I recall her, as she was sold for scrap in November 1950, when I was just two and a half years old, my parents told me that I had travelled on her on at least one occasion. Profits at £53,564 hovered round the same figure as before and once again there was a 5% dividend. 1925 saw better tidings. For once, fine weather prevailed for much of the season. The economy seemed to be recovering and passenger journeys rose by 163,830. A protracted battle with the tax authorities in Great Britain came to an end, with no very happy results, and resulted in a heavier tax burden extending as far back as 1921. Profits were, as usual around the £50,000 mark, (£54,756 to be precise), with the customary 5% dividend.

1926 was a disaster. A fresh economic downturn put pressure on coal prices, and the coal owners decided on drastic wage cuts. Predictably the National Union of Miners was outraged and responded with a strike, and demanded support from the TUC. A General strike was called and lasted for ten days before collapsing, but the coal dispute dragged on for seven weary months, inflicting irreparable harm on the miners and the coal owners. Coal shortages became critical, and with the island tourist trade heavily dependent on the coal mining districts, passenger journeys slumped by 289,556. The reduced level of visitors resulted in cargo dropping by 5,172 tons. Receipts fell by £97,913, but working expenses had been drastically curtailed, because several of the larger steamers operated for a much shorter season, and there was no need to charter relief tonnage at peak periods. The profits, of £50,894 showed their usual immunity to change, and

once again, a 5% dividend was paid. The most exciting news, at the end of 1926, was that despite the grim economic situation, the Packet had decided to order its first new vessel since before the Great War. The contract was awarded to Cammell Laird of Birkenhead, and the guaranteed speed was to be 22 knots. This was a little slower than the legendary **Ben-my-Chree** of 1908, but still very impressive. It was expected that the new ship would carry 2,400 passengers. Needless to say, she would be oil burning, reducing the company's dependence still further on unreliable coal supplies. The seasonal arrivals of 384,705 in 1926 were the worst peacetime figures until the next prolonged miners' strike in 1984.

1927 saw the arrival of the new steamer, but with the results for 1926 so distorted by the miners strike, the Steam Packet took 1925 as a comparative year when preparing the annual accounts. In 1927, receipts dropped by £19,542 and expenses fell by £6.258 compared with 1925. Passenger numbers, although well up on 1926, showed a decline of 27,554 compared to 1925, but the net profits were of the usual magnitude, £54,908. E C Thin who had supported the "carry on" policy, and had been one of the Liverpool directors since the death of Dalrymple Maitland in 1919, died in 1927, and was succeeded by his son, Lt-Col E G Thin. The main news of 1927 was the delivery of the **Ben-my-Chree**, which entered service on 29 June. She was the fourth vessel to bear the name, and at 2,586 grt was the largest vessel in the fleet, although twenty feet shorter than her legendary predecessor of 1908. When her construction was announced, the board commented, *"After a careful consideration of the requirements of the trade and the more favourable conditions for building new tonnage, the Directors have placed an order with Messrs Cammell, Laird & Co Limited for a Geared Turbine Twin Screw Steamer"*. Shipyards were desperate for business, and were willing to construct at bare cost, but Lairds slipped up and incurred a loss of £17,000. Because the builders met a tight delivery deadline, and had done a superb job, the Steam Packet voluntarily increased their payments to the yard from £185,000 to £200,000, a remarkable gesture that reflected well on the company and its business standards. Although eclipsed in size and prestige for most of her career by the

Although 1926 was affected by the miners strike, so that sailings were trimmed, the Sailing Arrangements for the week commencing Saturday 31 July, show how the fleet was used. The **Manxman** was mostly on the Liverpool service, but with a trip to Dublin. **Viking** was the Fleetwood boat, a role taken by the **Lady of Mann** after 1930. **King Orry** ran to Liverpool, but on Tuesday went to Fleetwood, where she coaled before an unusual Fleetwood to Llandudno round trip on Wednesday. On Thursday it was Fleetwood to Douglas, with an Ardrossan run on Friday. **Snaefell** worked to Fleetwood, Liverpool and Dublin. Many boats were still coal burners, and coaling was common at Liverpool, Fleetwood, Ardrossan, Belfast or Dublin, as this avoided shipping coal to the Island. **Manx Maid** sailed to Liverpool and Dublin, oiling at Liverpool. **Peel Castle** ran to Liverpool, Dublin and Belfast. **Mona's Queen**, the last paddle steamer, worked out and back to Liverpool on Saturday, an Ardrossan out and back on Monday, and a night sailing to Liverpool. Tuesday was Liverpool to Douglas, with a Round the Island cruise on Wednesday. Llandudno on Thursday, and Liverpool on Friday completed a busy week. **Mona** started the week as "D to L 9 a.m. –3rd" which means she was the third boat on the busy 9.00am sailing from Douglas to Liverpool on Saturday morning. She was the 2nd Liverpool to Douglas at 3.00pm. On Sunday she sailed light ship to Liverpool. Monday

2nd August was Bank Holiday, and she did a Liverpool-Douglas return. On Tuesday she loaded cargo, but departed from the Landing stage carrying passengers as well. She spent Wednesday discharging cargo, and Thursday and Friday were taken up with Liverpool. **Tynwald**, ran a return trip to Fleetwood on Saturday, but was light ship to Workington on Sunday for an early charter sailing to Douglas on Bank Holiday Monday. It was a full day excursion, leaving Douglas at 1.00am on Tuesday. She sailed light ship to Ramsey to take the 9.00am Ramsey-Liverpool direct sailing on Thursday. Friday was the direct Liverpool-Ramsey working at noon, and then light ship to Fleetwood. **Fenella**, was the 4th boat on the busy 11.00am Liverpool-Douglas sailing on Bank Holiday Saturday. On Sunday she sailed from Douglas at 4.00am with a theatrical company and scenery for Liverpool, travelling theatrical groups changing venues on Sundays. On Monday, it was Liverpool to Douglas. Tuesday was an 8.00 pm sailing to Liverpool, entering dock after unloading passengers to pick up cargo. She returned to the Landing Stage for a late sailing on Wednesday, repeating the pattern on Thursday and Friday. **Tyrconnel**, one of the two freight only boats, worked Douglas-Liverpool, and also the Liverpool-Castletown-Port St Mary-Peel-Liverpool round, which occupied four days. **Cushag**, the other cargo boat worked Liverpool to Douglas and to Ramsey.

*Had it not been for the delivery of the **Lady of Mann** in 1930, the **Ben-my-Chree (IV)** of 1927 would have gone down as the finest vessel ever built for the Packet. Although she was slower than her legendary namesake of 1908, her internal fittings were even finer. She was launched at the Cammell Laird yard in Birkenhead on 5 April 1927, was 366 feet in length and of 2,586grt, and had a notional maximum speed of 22.5 knots, though she was able to exceed this in service. She was often seen on the 10.30am Liverpool to Douglas sailing, returning on the 4.00pm departure from Douglas. She was sold to ship breakers in Belgium at the end of the 1965 season. Except for the first three years of her life, she was overshadowed by her bigger and more celebrated sister, but she was a magnificent boat. If I am to be honest, I have to put "the Lady" as my own favourite and the finest vessel ever to serve the Island, but it was a close run thing and I was sorry to see her go.*

Centenary Steamer, the **Lady of Mann**, she was a magnificent ship, and served the company until 1965. In many ways the "Ben" and the "Lady" were reminiscent of the Cunarder liners, the **Queen Mary** and the **Queen Elizabeth**, both built within a few years and the younger sister eclipsing her older sibling. The uniform colour scheme heightened this impression. The "Ben" was to be the culminating achievement of William M Corkill, who had served the company for fifty-five years, and had been general manager & secretary for twenty years. He was no longer in good health, and retired on 31 December 1927. Although relinquishing active control of affairs, he was asked to remain in a consultative capacity. His successor, from 1 January 1928 was Thomas Craine, moustached, as was still common amongst senior managers, but for the first time in the company's history, clean-shaven. As with William Corkill, he had served the company for over fifty years. An amusing study might be made of the beards of the Company's first four general managers from 1830 to 1927, for each, in his own way, typified the fashion in beards of his own era. Ill health also persuaded John Donald Clucas to stand down after a decade on the board.

By 1928, the Steam Packet was looking forward to its centenary. In that long period, it had seen many rivals appear and usually disappear after a short while. The most persistent mainstream challenge came from the Midland Railway and its allies. In

*When the LMS reorganised the former MR, LNWR and LYR routes from Heysham and Fleetwood, the Irish routes were concentrated at Heysham, but the LMS asked the Steam Packet to take over the seasonal route to Douglas. This would require at least three additional steamers, two of which were available from the LMS. For the third steamer, the Packet approached the Southern Railway, buying the **TrSS Victoria** on 2 March 1928. Although specifically bought for the Heysham route, she was to be found at Liverpool, Llandudno, and Fleetwood as well. She was 1641 grt, and at 22 knots was one of the fastest channel packets available. She had been built for the South Eastern & Chatham Railway in 1907 for the Dover-Calais service and with reconditioning, cost the Steam Packet £37,550. A year younger than the second-hand **Snaefell**, she cost less than a quarter as much, an indication of how sharply costs had fallen since 1920. She retained her original name, serving the Packet until the end of the 1956 season, and was sold for scrap in January 1957. She was the last coal burner and the last two funnel steamer in the fleet, and I can recall sitting on the beach and seeing this majestic two funnel "liner" departing from Douglas shortly before the end of her long and successful career.*

The **Rushen Castle** was one of the two LMS ships for the Heysham route. She had been built as the **Duke of Cornwall** in 1898 by Vickers, Sons & Maxim for the joint London & North Western Railway and Lancashire & Yorkshire Railway service from Fleetwood to Belfast. She was purchased on 11 May 1928, together with the **Antrim**. Including refurbishment, she cost £29,254, but at 17.5 knots, was considerably slower than the **Victoria**. She was an economical ship and a good sea boat, and although bought for Heysham, was put on the winter sailings to and from Liverpool at the end of her first season with the Packet. She was a regular winter boat for several years, but by the mid-thirties was a weekend boat, being tied up in Douglas harbour for much of the week. As one of the older boats, she was not requisitioned at the outbreak of the Second World War, so became a familiar sight to travellers going to and from the Island. My parents after several years in the Western Desert, Sicily and Italy returned to the UK, and made their first trip to the Island for some years in 1944, travelling one way on the **Rushen Castle**. For much of the war, the Douglas service had been diverted to Fleetwood, and it was the **Rushen Castle** that re-opened the Liverpool sailings in April 1946. She was sold for scrap in January 1947.

1851, the MR reached Morecambe and commenced a Belfast service, which ran twice weekly with a call at Ramsey. The Ramsey call only lasted for a few years, but the route was not financially successful. In 1867, the MR, working in conjunction with the Furness Railway, transferred its maritime base to Barrow, and services ran to Belfast and to the Isle of Man under the auspices of the Barrow Steam Navigation Co. In 1904, the Midland deserted its partner, opening a new harbour at Heysham. As in the 1850s, the venture was not a success financially, but company prestige was at stake, so it survived. When the MR was absorbed into the London Midland & Scottish Railway in 1923, the London & North Western and Lancashire & Yorkshire Railways also fell into the LMS orbit. The new company decided to discontinue the Fleetwood operations, concentrating its Irish services at Heysham. However, the LMS invited the Steam Packet to take over the Heysham – Douglas route in 1928. Three further steamers, all second-hand, were acquired to cover the new route. The **Victoria** came from the Southern Railway and had been part of the South Eastern & Chatham Railway fleet operating between Dover and Calais. She retained her name in

Packet service. The **Antrim**, built in 1904 for the inauguration of the MR Heysham-Belfast service, became the **Ramsey Town**, whilst the LNWR & LYR joint steamer, the **Duke of Cornwall**, which had been on the Fleetwood-Belfast service, became the **Rushen Castle**. With an additional busy route, receipts, expenses, passengers and service miles all rose sharply. The increase in passengers, of 114,500 was largely due to this new route for the company, which under Packet management showed a 12% increase on the last year of LMS operation in 1927. An additional 22,000 sea miles was largely due to the Heysham operation.

Hughes-Games explained the impact of the Heysham service,

> '*The three steamers mentioned in the report as having been purchased for the Heysham service from the London Midland and Scottish and Southern Railway Companies, the cost of which, together with necessary alterations, was paid for last year and charged against the accounts, have proved satisfactory and have been most serviceable. The pressure of the Heysham Saturday traffic required four steamers for some weeks during the very busy*

> *time, so that in addition to the three steamers purchased, we had to charter a fourth from the London Midland & Scottish Railway Company for a few Saturdays. The **Rushen Castle** has been in commission for a considerable part of this winter, and the comfort of her accommodation has been much appreciated by the travelling public who have made use of her. The **Victoria** is equally suitable for winter work, and could at any time when occasion arises be utilised for such purpose.'*

Seasonal arrivals had always shown a Saturday peak, and many boarding houses would only quote Saturday to Saturday for that reason in high season, but the weekend peak became more pronounced in the 1920s. In 1913, the last full peacetime year before the Great War, 47.65% of the week's total arrivals were on Saturday. By 1928, it had reached 58.3% of arrivals. Translated into human terms it was an average of 2,500 more passengers every Saturday, or slightly more than the capacity of the new **Ben-my-Chree**. On the simplest analysis that meant that to carry the same number of passengers in the season to and from the

The **Ramsey Town** was the remaining ship acquired for the Heysham service in 1928. She had been built in 1904 as the **Antrim** for the Midland Railway Heysham-Belfast service. Her cost, including refurbishing was £14,612, and she was much the cheapest of the three vessels, and the shortest lived, being taken out of service in 1936, and broken up in Preston the following year. As the chairman had spoken of the other two vessels acquired in 1928 in laudatory terms, but had not mentioned the **Ramsey Town**, it is possible that she was not seen as a particularly good acquisition even then. As with the **Rushen Castle**, she was a weekend boat by the early thirties, so was an obvious candidate for the axe, when new vessels arrived in the late thirties.

Island, the company would require one additional large steamer compared to 1913, which during the week, would be under-employed. C T W Hughes-Games, the chairman, ascribed this to a higher proportion of holiday makers "who are for the most part engaged in work where it is customary for the holidays of employees to commence and terminate at the weekends. But whatever the cause may be, the result to this Company is that it is becoming increasingly costly and difficult to cope with the passenger traffic presenting itself." He was correct, but another factor he did not mention was that the proportion of saloon or first class traffic was declining, as the number of managerial and professional people who would holiday abroad increased. We tend to think of competition from overseas resorts as being a modern phenomenon, but professional and managerial families were discovering the continent. In the halcyon days before World War One, many businessmen in Lancashire would send their families to the Island at the start of the summer, and would travel over themselves every weekend, and numerous examples exist of senior officials on the UK railways applying for concession travel facilities on the Island's railways and shipping lines. By the 1920s, this traffic was in decline. To give one example, my father's parents

were living in England in the 1920s, where Dr Robert Applegarth Hendry was a gynaecologist with a rising reputation. His father had owned the Rothesay Hotel on the Loch Prom from the 1880s to the start of the 1920s, and his wife, Emily Hendry, nee Preston, was a Douglas girl, but despite those close Manx connections, the family regularly visited the south of France in summer.

Despite the dramatic changes brought about by the additional route, gross profits remained around the £50,000 mark, though at £57,984, they were the highest for several years, and prompted a 6% dividend, a welcome improvement after a long spell at 5%. Seasonal arrivals in 1928, of 550,572, were not as good as 1925 or the bumper year of 1920, when there was frantic pressure to get away from the drab war years. Although the proportion of professional families was declining, those who continued to come were increasingly profitable to the Packet, as motor vehicles, which were once the exclusive preserve of the very rich, were now affordable by professional people. At the AGM on 2 March 1929, the chairman revealed that the company was not only aware of this trend, but had considered far reaching technological issues as well. The diesel engine had become practicable before the Great War, and the

first motor ships dated from that era, but the engines were very bulky for their power output and cost several times the price of a comparable steam plant. In his speech, Hughes-Games announced that a new vessel was on order.

'You will see from the report that an order has been placed with Messrs Cammell, Laird & Co Ltd, for a new single-screw cargo steamer. Such a steamer is very much needed. The carriage of motor vehicles alone has called for the provision of additional tonnage. This new ship will be specially adapted for such traffic. She is to be ready for service in June next, and is to be called the **Peveril**. In relation to the building of the vessel, the Board very carefully considered the question of propulsion by internal combustion engines. This question has been occupying the attention of the Board for some time past, but became more particularly a subject for consideration in the case of a steamer such as that now on order, as she will be practically continuously in commission, and the saving of fuel cost might justify increased capital expenditure, though at the present time it could not be said to do so in the case of a passenger steamer made use of for only a short time in each year, and for no more than a proportion – frequently a small one – of each day. It must be remembered that these motor vessels, as compared with steamers, cost considerably more, and take considerably longer to build. These are necessarily very serious disadvantages. The Directors are also keeping in view the future possibilities of pulverised fuel and superheated steam, and are watching all experiments directed towards these developments".*

1929 dawned well. In America, and throughout the civilised world, the stock markets were rising, and the mild recessions of some years previously seemed to be a chimera. The economy was on the march, and pundits proclaimed that recession had been banished forever. Passenger traffic was buoyant in 1929, and at 555,211 seasonal arrivals were only a few thousand short of the bumper figure of 1920. The Roaring twenties had come in with a roar and were set to go out that way. A statistician could tell you that in all the years since 1887, there had only been two more successful years for Manx tourism than 1929, the legendary years of 1913 and 1920. The new freighter, the **SS Peveril** had entered service in June 1929, and had been a great success. Although passenger traffic was up, cheaper fares and greater use of contract tickets led to a slight fall in revenue, but the profits, as ever were around £50,000, or to be precise £56,785.

Whit week, which was the traditional start of the season, came early in 1929, so it was going to be a long season in any case, but suggestions had been advanced that a better service to the end of September would extend the season, and the board took this up. They noted 'This experiment was not a success, and will not be repeated'. A spasmodic service had been provided from the Cumberland ports to the Island from the earliest days, and the chairman spoke of what had been essayed in 1929, 'We also, in response to much urgent request, instituted for tentative purposes a periodic service between Workington and Ramsey during the months from June to September. This service proved unsatisfactory, and we cannot undertake it again. The direct passenger services between Liverpool and Ramsey, which we have conducted for many years, and have given the fullest trial, exhibit

no inclination to develop, but rather the reverse, and can be said only very barely to justify their continuance'. The **Fenella**, now approaching her fiftieth birthday operated the new Workington route, but it was to be her swansong. She was auctioned in September 1929 by Messrs Kellock & Co of Liverpool, and with the **PS Mona's Queen**, was sold for scrap for £7,972. The **Mona's Queen** was another distinguished veteran. She dated back to 1885, and during the Great War when on war service had been stalked by a U boat, whose captain was not perhaps aware of the uncanny manoeuvrability of a paddle steamer. The **Mona's Queen** turned on her assailant, and quite literally beat it to death with her paddle wheel. She left Douglas for the last time on 7 October 1929, en route to the Clyde and the ship breakers, bringing an end to the paddle steam era in the Steam Packet after 99 years. The "Three Legs" emblem from her paddle sponson was attached to the end wall of the Royal Buildings in Douglas for many decades. The chairman explained the reason for the two disposals,

'In September last, we sold the steamers **Mona's Queen** *and* **Fenella**. *Each of them had for a very long period served us well. They were, however, too old to justify the expenditure which Board of Trade requirements would have involved if we had asked for a renewal of their certificates, and the sale of them was the only course open to us to take. The prices obtained were only for breaking-up purposes and were regarded as very satisfactory. As stated in the report, they exceeded the book values of the vessels.'*

If you had asked if there was a cloud on the horizon in September 1929, a sentimentalist might mention the imminent departure of two much loved vessels. Within the Company's head offices, Imperial Buildings, which had been the former Imperial Hotel and fronted on to the Red Pier, there was concern that Thomas Craine, who had succeeded William Corkill as manager & secretary on 1 January 1928, and who had served the company for 52 years, 22 of them as Assistant Manager, had been taken ill. C T W Hughes-Games, the chairman, commented in 1930, 'He was taken ill early in September last, after months of strenuous work in preparation for and during the summer season, and, owing

*As we discovered in the text, serious thought was given to fitting the **Peveril** with diesel engines before she was built, but the lower cost of steam triumphed. She was launched at the Cammell Laird yard in Birkenhead on 25 April 1929 and cost £42,600. At 798 grt, she was the largest freight boat until the **Fenella** of 1951. A sturdy workhorse, she was broken up at Glasson Dock in May 1964. For some years, her chief engineer was a great character who shall remain nameless. He had false teeth, and the habit of leaving them out, but this had a dire effect on his ability to communicate intelligibly, which was a trial to the deck officers and especially to the engineering staff. A capable engineer, he was fond of a drop of drink off duty, so mischievous members of the crew would wind him up by inventing some fantastic calamity that required his immediate presence in the engine room when he was off duty and had "drink partaken". He would arrive hurriedly, garbed in vest, trousers and braces, but minus teeth. The more he attempted to communicate, the less his orders would be understood until it finally dawned on him that he had been "had", and he would stalk back to his cabin in high dudgeon.*

The Isle of Man Steam Packet Company, Limited.
(Incorporated in the Isle of Man).

NEW PASSENGER SERVICE.
DOUGLAS,
RAMSEY and WORKINGTON.

By s.s. FENELLA. 3½ hours sea passage.

	Douglas Depart.	Ramsey Depart.	Workington Arrive.	Workington Depart.	Ramsey Arrive.	Douglas Arrive.
SATURDAY, 29th June	10- 0 a.m.	11-30 a.m.	3- 0 p.m.	4- 0 p.m.	7-30 p.m.	9- 0 p.m.
SATURDAY, 6th July	6-45 a.m.	8-15 a.m.	11-45 a.m.	12-45 noon	4-15 p.m.	5-45 p.m.
SATURDAY, 13th July	10-30 a.m.	12- 0 noon	3-30 p.m.	4-30 p.m.	8- 0 p.m.	9-30 p.m.
SATURDAY, 20th July	7- 0 a.m.	8-30 a.m.	12-0 noon	1- 0 p.m.	4-30 p.m.	6- 0 p.m.
SATURDAY, 27th July	9- 0 a.m.	10-30 a.m.	2- 0 p.m.	3- 0 p.m.	6-30 p.m.	8- 0 p.m.
FRIDAY, 2nd August	4-30 a.m.	6- 0 a.m.	9-30 a.m.	10-30 a.m.	2- 0 p.m.	3-30 p.m.
FRIDAY, 9th August	9- 0 a.m.	10-30 a.m.	2- 0 p.m.	3- 0 p.m.	6-30 p.m.	8- 0 p.m.
FRIDAY, 16th August	4-45 a.m.	6-15 a.m.	9-45 a.m.	10-45 a.m.	2-15 p.m.	3-45 p.m.
SATURDAY, 24th Aug.	9- 0 a.m.	10-30 a.m.	2- 0 p.m.	3- 0 p.m.	6-30 p.m.	8- 0 p.m.
SATURDAY, 31st Aug.	4-30 a.m.	6- 0 a.m.	9-30 a.m.	10-30 a.m.	2- 0 p.m.	3-30 p.m.
SATURDAY, 7th Sept.	8- 0 a.m.	9-30 a.m.	1- 0 p.m.	2- 0 p.m.	5-30 p.m.	7. 0 p.m.

For train Services between Workington, Maryport, Carlisle, Whitehaven,
and Barrow, see special handbills.

FARES:

SINGLE—Saloon, 8s. 6d.   Steerage 5s. 6d.
RETURN TICKETS, available for the Season :— Saloon, 13s. 0d ;
Steerage, 9s. 6d.
DAY EXCURSION TICKETS FROM RAMSEY :—Saloon, 8s. 6d ;
Steerage, 5s. 6d.   From Douglas: Saloon, 9s. 0d ; Steerage, 6s. 6d.

There are frequent services between Ramsey and Douglas by the L.o.M.
Railway Co., Manx Electric Railway Co.; also by The Isle of Man Road
Omnibuses.   The journey occupies about 1¼ hours.   Time Tables and
Fares will be forwarded on receipt of stamped address, sent to these
Companies' Head Offices, Douglas.

Return portions of Workington to Ramsey tickets will be available
from Douglas to Liverpool or to Fleetwood, or to Heysham (boat only),
on payment of 4s. Saloon, 1s. 6d. Steerage.   The Rail journey from these
ports to Workington is extra.
Contract Saloon Tickets available by the above services, £3 3s. 0d.
For conditions, form of application and contract tickets, apply at the
Douglas or Ramsey Office.
Passengers and their accompanied luggage will only be carried on the
conditions exhibited in the Company's Offices and on board their steamers.
Acceptance of a ticket issued by the Company binds the passenger to
these conditions.
The Company reserve the right of altering or withdrawing any of the
services if found necessary.
For List of Apartments and Illustrated Guide to Ramsey and District,
apply to Tourists Bureau, Town Hall, Ramsey.

Breakfasts, Luncheons, Teas, and Refreshments can be had on Board.

For Isle of Man Guides and Sailings, apply to W. Sandwith & Co., 26,
Station Road, Workington, Enquiry Office L.M. & S. Railway, Carlisle :
Isle of Man Steam Packet Co., Offices, Ramsey or Douglas.

THOS. CRAINE, General Manager and Secretary.
Douglas, 18th June, 1929.

S. K. Broadbent & Co. Ltd., Printers, Douglas, I.o.M.

*This handbill, although the worse-for-wear, is the only copy I have ever seen advertising the experimental service that ran between Douglas, Ramsey and Workington at weekends in 1929, and gave the venerable **Fenella** of 1881 her final opportunity to open a new route. As the only vessels to exceed her 48 years of service were the **Viking** and the **Ellan Vannin**, each with 49 years, neither of which opened a new route in their last years of service to the best of my knowledge, I believe that the **Fenella** can claim the distinction of being the oldest vessel in Packet history to inaugurate a new route. The handbill is also of interest as it is one of the very few items to be issued during Thomas Craine's tragically brief reign as General Manager & Secretary.*

modestly on the stock exchange found that they too, were ruined. American investment and confidence dried up, and the malaise spread across the globe. In far away Australia, 25% of employees found they were without a job, and millions joined the dole queues from Norway to the antipodes. Hitler's rise to power was fuelled by despair in Germany. By 1931, visitor totals had dropped by over 100,000 in the Isle of Man, and the steady £50,000 surplus earned by the Packet each year had fallen by a third, despite the most stringent economies. C T W Hughes-Games, who was appointed chairman upon Maitland's death in 1919, passed way at Hango, on the outskirts of Castletown on 8 August 1933, having resigned as chairman due to ill health some months previously.

When I started work on this book, the modern world was living in the same sort of fairytale world that existed at the start of 1929. Our politicians preached of their own wisdom and bankers basked in multi million pound bonuses. In the autumn of 2008, that bubble burst, and the contagion spread across the world, just as it had done in 1929. In the UK, companies that were household names on every High St collapsed into ruin. Living through times that have an uncanny similarity with the events of the Great Depression, brings the end of the Roaring Twenties into a sharper focus for us. The politicians and bankers whose recklessness created this situation tell us that they are so much wiser than their predecessors eight decades ago. I suspect that few people have any great faith in their so-called palliatives. History will record whether our politicians and bankers are right to have such a high opinion of themselves, or whether they are no better than their predecessors, or a lot worse.

to a determination, I fear, to get back into harness whilst only partially convalescent and before complete recovery, suffered a relapse which unhappily resulted fatally.' W G Barwell, who had completed 41 years of service, and was to guide the company until 1937, succeeded him.

To replace the old ships that were going, and to herald the centenary of the company, a contract had been signed with Vickers Armstrong & Co of Barrow before the end of the year for a new steamer that would gross 3,104 tons. To mark the long association of the Dukes of Atholl with the Lordship of Mann, the Board decided to invite the Duchess of Atholl to perform the naming ceremony, which was to be in March 1930, and would have liked to call the vessel, **Duchess of Atholl**, but there was already a ship of that name in the British register, and it could not be duplicated. As the Duke had been Lord of Mann, an alternative name was selected, **Lady of Mann**. She was to become a legend.

In October 1929, the bubble burst. The era of endless boom, where there could be no recession, evaporated in a flash as stock prices collapsed on Wall St. The folklore story of ruined millionaires jumping out of skyscraper windows as the extent of their ruin dawned on them really did occur, and millions of ordinary people who had gambled

CHAPTER NINE
In the Air, on Land and Sea

In writing this section, I toyed with many titles. "Steam Packet Freight" was one option, but would rule out some of the properties that have been owned by the IOMSPCo, and whilst a separate chapter was possible, the two themes were so closely interlinked that it was wrong to split them. As I gathered material, other items complicated the issue, including the "Flying Packet", and a splendid ship that never put to sea. It was our daughter, Anastasia Elaine, who provided the solution, though she is not yet two years old. Anastasia likes music, but it has to have a rousing beat. One of her favourites is the US Marine Corps march. The words of the Marine Corp hymn extols the versatility of the Corps, "in the air, on land and sea", so I had a title. Given the title, I will start with aviation, as most people will see planes and the Packet as mortal enemies. For a brief period in the 1930s, this was not so, as we shall discover. When the company had taken out limited liability status in 1885, it had powers to build and operate ships, deal in all sorts of goods such as coal, timber or meat, and to act as warehousemen, but when the idea of the Flying Packet emerged, the board found they had to rely on a useful catchall phrase "To carry on any other business which may seem to the Company capable of being conveniently carried on in connection with the above". When air operations seemed to be firmly established, the Steam Packet amended its powers in 1937 "To establish operate and maintain Air Services". The clause was so widely worded that it would allow the IOMSPCo to compete with Boeing, as they could manufacture,

(turn to page 98)

The first demonstration flights had taken place in the Isle of Man before the Great War, but commercial air services were many years in the future, and awaited aircraft that were safe enough to attract passengers and large enough to carry an economic payload. In August 1934, Railway Air Services, in which the mainland railways had a stake, introduced flights to the Island, ceasing in September. During the winter, the Steam Packet and the London Midland & Scottish Railway negotiated over a joint service to be called MANX AIRWAYS. The Annual Report for 1935 explained, "The year 1935 marked another epoch in the history of this Company, as on the 15th April last, we, in collaboration with the London Midland & Scottish Railway Company, added to our transport facilities TRAVEL BY AIR between Manchester, Liverpool, Blackpool and Ronaldsway Airport in the Isle of Man. Negotiations are at present in progress for expansions of these Joint Air Services, and, if arranged, they will in all probability operate from Whitsuntide to Mid-September." The cover of the 1936 brochure shows Manx Airways working closely with RAS to provide a network of trunk routes.

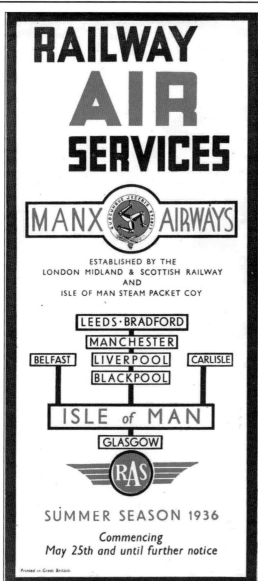

RAILWAY AIR SERVICES

MANX AIRWAYS

ESTABLISHED BY THE
LONDON MIDLAND & SCOTTISH RAILWAY
AND
ISLE OF MAN STEAM PACKET COY

LEEDS·BRADFORD
MANCHESTER
BELFAST — LIVERPOOL — CARLISLE
BLACKPOOL

ISLE of MAN

GLASGOW

RAS

SUMMER SEASON 1936

*Commencing
May 25th and until further notice*

GENERAL INFORMATION AND NOTICES

The aircraft employed are, for the most part, **8-SEATER TWIN-ENGINED MACHINES**, with a top speed of 157 miles per hour—cruising at 132 miles per hour. They are luxuriously appointed and furnished with wireless and all the most modern navigational aids. They include:—

" The Star of Mona."   " The Star of Ulster."
" The Star of Lancashire."   " The Star of Renfrew."
" The Star of Yorkshire."   " The Star of Scotia."

FOUR-ENGINED AIR LINERS will also be operated by R.A.S. on these routes.

SHORT SEA CROSSINGS.

The approximate times occupied on the actual over-sea crossings are only:—

15 minutes on the	GLASGOW—ISLE OF MAN Service.	
20	BELFAST—	
20	CARLISLE	
35	BLACKPOOL—	
40	LIVERPOOL—	

AVAILABILITY OF TICKETS.

Single and outward portions of return tickets—valid only for the date and services specified thereon. Return tickets—valid for three calendar months from date of outward journey.

Passengers desiring break of journey can be supplied with appropriate sectional tickets at the sectional fares and reservations effected accordingly.

INTERAVAILABILITY OF TICKETS.

Air passengers may return by rail or steamer by exchanging the return half at a railway booking office for a first class single ticket available by any recognised railway route and/or the services of the Isle of Man Steam Packet Company to the terminal point of the air ticket.

Rail or steamer passengers may return by air on payment of an appropriate supplement on their Ordinary, Tourist, Monthly Return, or Week-end tickets issued for a journey between the places served by the air service.

BAGGAGE.

Each passenger is allowed 35 lbs. of personal baggage free of charge. No free baggage is allowed to children travelling at half fares or travelling free. Baggage in excess of the free allowance—Air Freight Rates. Passengers travelling together may bulk their baggage for the purpose of calculating excess weight.

PASSENGERS' LUGGAGE IN ADVANCE.

The difficulties and cost often attending air travel with heavy luggage are non-existent for passengers by Railway Air Services, for whom are available the ordinary railway and steamer luggage-in-advance arrangements at the following nominal rates per packet up to 150 lbs. weight per passenger:—

	Per Package. s. d.
To and from Douglas (I.O.M.).	
Collection and Conveyance (" C.L.")	1 6
Conveyance and Delivery (" D.L.")	1 6
Collection, Conveyance and Delivery (" P.L.A.")	2 6
In Great Britain.	
Collection and Conveyance (" C.L.")	1 0
Conveyance and Delivery (" D.L.")	1 0
Collection, Conveyance and Delivery (" P.L.A.")	2 0
To and from Interior Stations (I.O.M.).	
Collection in Great Britain and Conveyance (" C.L.")	1 6
Conveyance and Delivery in Great Britain (" D.L.")	1 6

CONCESSIONS TO RAILWAY SEASON TICKET HOLDERS.

Railway season ticket holders, including the holders of contract tickets on the Isle of Man Steam Packet Company's boats, are allowed a special discount on the air fare for journeys by air between points within the area of availability of their season tickets, merely by presenting the season ticket at the time of effecting an air reservation at any R.A.S. office or railway station and signing a voucher entitling the season ticket holder to the concession.

RAILWAY BULK TRAVEL VOUCHERS.

Railway Bulk Travel vouchers are changeable for Air Tickets at all R.A.S. offices and railway stations.

"THE MANX AIRWAYS" {L.M.S. & I.O.M. S.P. Co.} Joint

ENGLAND and ISLE OF MAN — Daily—Sundays included, except where otherwise stated.

		a.m.	a.m.	a.m.	p.m.	a.m.	Mons., Tues., Fris. and Sats. only.	p.m.	p.m.	p.m.	p.m.	p.m.
London (Croydon. ... dep.		...	...	9*30	...	...		...	...	...	...	...
Birmingham (Castle Bromwich) ... ,,		...	...	10*25	...	11n50		...	...	...	...	...
Stoke-on-Trent (Meir) (on request) ... ,,		...	...	10*45	...	12 10		...	...	...	...	...
Liverpool (Speke) ... arr.		...	...	11* 5	...	...		...	...	...	...	...
Manchester (Barton) ... ,,		...	...	...	...	12 50		...	...	...	...	...
CARLISLE {Carlisle Station (dep. by Road)		...	...	...	1k15	...		...	Mons., Tues. and Sats. only.	...	...	...
{KINGSTOWN AIRPORT ... dep.		...	...	...	1k30	...		...		...	...	...
LEEDS-BRADFORD {New Station (dep. by Road) ...		...	7 50	...	...	12 40		...		...	...	6 0
{Forster Square Station (dep. by Road)		...	7 50	...	...	12 40		...		...	...	6 0
{YEADON AIRPORT ... ,,		...	8 30	...	...	1 25		...		...	...	6 40
{BARTON AIRPORT ... arr.		...	8b50	...	...	1b45		...		...	...	7b 0
MANCHESTER London Road Station (dep. by Road)		7 45	8 15	10 15	...	1 15		...	3†15	4 0	5 25	
Parker Street Bus Stn. (dep. by Road)		7 50	8 20	10 18	...	1 20		...	3†20	4 5	5 30	
Midland Hotel (dep. by Road) ...		7 55	8 25	10 21	...	1 25		...	3†25	4 10	5 35	...
Victoria Station (dep. by Road) ...		8 0	8 30	10 25	...	1 30		...	3†30	4 15	5 40	...
BARTON AIRPORT ... dep.		8 30	9e 0	10 50	...	2 0		...	4†10	4 45	6 30	...
LIVERPOOL {Adelphi Hotel (dep. by Road) ...		...	9g 5	10 45	...	...		2 15	4 5	...	6 30	...
{SPEKE AIRPORT ... ,,		...	9 35	11 20	...	...		2 50	4 45	...	6 55	...
§BLACKPOOL— SQUIRES GATE AIRPORT ... ,,		8 55	...	11 45	...	2 25		...	...	5 10	7 20	...
§ISLE OF MAN— RONALDSWAY AIRPORT ... arr.		9 30	10L20	12 20	2 15	3 0		3 35	5L30	5Lp45	7 55	...

		a.m.	a.m.	a.m.	a.m.	a.m.	p.m.	p.m.	p.m.	p.m.	p.m.
§ISLE OF MAN— RONALDSWAY AIRPORT ... dep.		...	8 15	10 0	11k15	11mq30	1 45	3 0	3 30	5 0	7dm0
{BLACKPOOL— SQUIRES GATE AIRPORT ... arr.		...	8 50	10 35	...	12 5	...	3 35	...	5 35	7 35
LIVERPOOL {SPEKE AIRPORT ... ,,		...	9h15	11 0	...	...	2 30	...	4c15	...	8 0
{Adelphi Hotel (arr. by Road) ...		...	9 35	11 25	...	...	2 55	...	4 40	...	8 20
MANCHESTER BARTON AIRPORT ... ,,		...	9 40	11 35	...	12 30	...	4 0	...	6 0	8 25
Victoria Station (arr. by Road) ...		...	10 5	12 5	...	1 0	...	4 30	...	6 30	8 55
Midland Hotel (arr. by Road) ...		...	10 8	12 8	...	1 5	...	4 35	...	6 35	9 0
Parker Street Bus Stn. (arr. by Road)		...	10 11	12 11	...	1 10	...	4 40	...	6 40	9 5
London Road Station (arr. by Road)		...	10 15	12 15	...	1 15	...	4 45	...	6 45	9 10
BARTON AIRPORT ... dep.		8a 0	...	...	...	12an50	...	...	...	6a10	
LEEDS-BRADFORD {YEADON AIRPORT ... arr.		8 20	...	...	...	1 10	...	...	...	6 30	...
{New Station (arr. by Road) ...		9 0	...	...	...	1 55	...	...	...	7 10	...
{Forster Square Station (arr. by Road)		9 0	...	...	...	1 55	...	...	...	7 10	...
CARLISLE {KINGSTOWN AIRPORT ... ,,		...	...	...	12 0	...	...	...	...	...	...
{Carlisle Station (arr. by Road)		...	...	...	12 15	...	...	...	...	...	...
Manchester (Barton) ... dep.		...	...	...	...	...	...	4†10	...	...	...
Liverpool (Speke) ... ,,		...	9*25	10*30	...	...	...	4†30	...	...	...
Stoke-on-Trent (Meir) (on request) ... arr.		...	9*45	10*45	...	...	...	4†45	...	...	...
Birmingham (Castle Bromwich) ... ,,		...	10*e0	11* 5	...	...	...	5†f5	...	...	...
London (Croydon) ... ,,		...	...	12* 0	...	...	...	...	...	...	...

NOTES. RONALDSWAY is the nearest Airport for DOUGLAS, CASTLETOWN and SOUTH of the ISLAND.

The above services will be augmented according to traffic requirements. Such aircraft as are fully loaded from and to Manchester or Leeds will fly without intermediate stop, accomplishing the journey in about 50 minutes to and from Manchester, and 60 minutes to and from Leeds. Such through flights will not, however, reduce the facilities to and from Blackpool.

Arrivals at intermediate points are 10 minutes before the departure times stated. * Not on Sundays. † Mondays, Tuesdays, Fridays and Saturdays only. § At Blackpool and Isle of Man, public road services to and from the aerodromes are available. a—Cars will leave Parker Street 'Bus Station, Manchester, at 7.15 a.m., 11.55 a.m. and 5.30 p.m. to connect with aircraft departures for Leeds. b—Cars will meet aircraft arrivals and convey passengers to the town terminals. c—Connection

to 5.25 p.m. train (Weekdays), 5.50 p.m. train (Sundays) from Lime Street Station, Liverpool, to Stoke-on-Trent, Birmingham and London. d—Commencing September 6th, will leave Isle of Man 6.30 p.m. and operate 30 minutes earlier throughout. e—Connects to West and South of England, Sundays excepted. f—Connects to West and South of England, Mons., Tues., Fris. and Sats. g—Leaves at 8.55 a.m. on Sundays. h—Connects with 10.10 a.m. train (Weekdays), 10.0 a.m. train (Sundays), Liverpool (Lime Street) to London. k—Operates daily (Sundays included on and from July 5th). L—Connects daily to Glasgow, Sundays included. m—Connects daily from Glasgow, Sundays included. n—Connects from West and South of England, Mons., Tues., Fris. and Sats. p—Connects daily to Belfast (Sundays included on and from July 5th). q—Connects from Belfast daily (Sundays included on and from July 5th).

TRANSPORT TO AND FROM AERODROMES.

Except where adequate regular transport services exist, cars or other special vehicles to and from the aerodromes are provided free of charge in connection with the aircraft arrivals and departures.

BELFAST.—Free transport by special R.A.S. cars, as shown.
BLACKPOOL.—Frequent services of omnibuses and trams to and from Blackpool, Lytham-St. Annes, and all parts, pass the entrance to the Airport. Squires Gate L.M.S. Station is adjacent to the Airport.
BRADFORD.—Free transport by special R.A.S. cars, as shown.
CARLISLE.—Free transport by special R.A.S. cars, as shown.
GLASGOW.—Free transport by special R.A.S. cars, as shown.

ISLE OF MAN.—The omnibuses of the Isle of Man Road Services, Ltd., connect, with the aircraft arrivals and departures to and from Douglas, Castletown, Port St. Mary, Port Erin, Peel, and all parts.
LEEDS.—Free transport by special R.A.S. cars, as shown.
LIVERPOOL.—Special road conveyances provided to and from the Airport by the Liverpool Corporation, Liverpool terminus is Adelphi Hotel. No charge to R.A.S. ticket holders. In addition, Crosville omnibus service "B" operates between Liverpool Pier Head and to within two minutes of the Airport entrance, and affords connections to all parts of Liverpool.
MANCHESTER.—Special road vehicles provided by the Manchester Corporation at the times stated above. No charge to R.A.S. ticket holders.

The 1936 RAS and Manx Airlines timetable revealed the rapid progress, with routes from the Island to London, Birmingham, Liverpool, Manchester, Blackpool, Carlisle, Glasgow and Belfast. With the massive time required for check-in nowadays to combat the curse of hijackers and terrorists, it recalls a more civilised era when we discover that 'Passengers should present themselves at the Departure Booking Offices or Airports about 10 minutes previous to the advertised departure of the connecting road service or of the aircraft, to admit of the embarkation formalities'.

The Steam Packet Annual Report for 1935 had referred to air travel as 'another epoch in the history of this Company', and it meant that services in which the Packet had a direct stake now operated to Croydon Aerodrome, the furthest that a vehicle operating a service in which the Packet was interested has voyaged with paying passengers on board. This portrait of Croydon Aerodrome was taken from the control tower in September 1938, by which time Manx Airways had been reorganised as Isle of Man Air Services Ltd, in which the LMSR, the IOMSPCo and Olley Air Services all had a one third stake. Services were drastically curtailed in 1939, and the advent of a Labour Government in the UK in 1945, which was committed to wholesale nationalisation of transport and basic industries meant that air services were transferred to the state owned BEA in 1947. G-AEPW X8510 was a De Havilland DH 89A Rapide, new to Olley Air Services of Croydon on 1 December 1936, which was one of the partners in Isle of Man Air Services. G-AEPW was impressed into RAF service on 4 March 1940 and struck off charge on 11 December 1941.

The 1935 air service was largely experimental, but for 1936 the Lady of Mann shared the cover of the IOMSPCo official guide with a single engined white painted biplane. It was an odd choice, as the Manx Airways brochures emphasised that the planes were twin-engined, as this was rightly seen as an important safety feature. One assumes that the artist used a photo he happened to have of "a plane" to create the cover, oblivious to what was relevant. The guide ran to 96 pages plus a colour cover. It included a detailed write up of the most recent vessel, then the **Mona's Queen** of 1934, a fleet list, addresses of Agents in different towns, many pages of service schedules, railway connections in the UK and Ireland, the Steam and electric railway timetables on the Island, hotel adverts and other useful information for the traveller. A modern marketing man would criticise it for being heavy reading, but it contained far more useful information than its glossy modern counterpart, where slick presentation comes before usefulness. Today professional marketing men write stylish guides that are of little value. In those days, senior managers wrote them with the aim of providing useful information.

*The **Tyrconnel** had been built by Fullerton of Paisley in 1892, and was a single screw freighter with engines amidships. She had been registered in Glasgow and then in Londonderry, but was bought by the Manx Steam Trading Co of Castletown in 1902. The Company had been formed in 1888, with a capital of £5,000. A local advocate, C W Coole, who had been admitted to the Manx bar in 1877, became its first secretary. The **Tyrconnel** was acquired by the Packet as their first freight only vessel on 6 May 1911, and is seen at the West Quay in Ramsey. If her funnel looks too light for the customary red of the Packet, it is because the **Tyrconnel** never received conventional Packet house colours, retaining her old funnel colours which were a very pale cream. My mother described it as being like full cream milk. She was sold to W Coe & Co in 1932, and broken up at Danzig two years later. It is to be hoped that some of her steel did not come back to the British Isles after 1939, through the good offices of Herr Hitler, who had assumed power in Germany in 1933.*

(from page 95)

hire, charter, buy or sell aircraft of any description! Improbable though it may seem, Imperial Buildings were entitled to manufacture jet fighters for the Soviet Union or the United States Navy, had they so wished!

Until air travel became the norm for many people, most Manx residents and visitors were familiar with the passenger ships that sailed in and out of Douglas, but at various times of day, often in the early evening, the company's freighters would slip out to sea, unheralded and unnoticed. As the freight berths opposite the old Imperial Buildings and at Liverpool were tidal, the precise time depended on tidal conditions. A night passage meant that the cargo loaded in the day would reach its destination in the early hours of the morning to be unloaded. The container revolution, with the familiar rectangular ISO container that appeared in the 1960s, and the subsequent triumph of the roll-on roll-off concept with the juggernauts that now clog our roads, has meant that the old style freight service is but a memory. For every hundred views that were taken of the passenger boats, I would be surprised if one was taken of freight operations, and most of them were of the cargo boats themselves, rather than the overall freight operation, with its warehouses, flatbed trailers and lorries, mechanical horses, containers, and supporting apparatus. It was a vital service, but one that passed largely unnoticed by the public, unless their consignment happened to be delayed, damaged or lost. Through the courtesy of many seagoing and shore based officers, I was able to record the last years of traditional freight services. The term "forgotten" is often used, but implies some familiarity to begin with, and the ramifications of the freight operation were so unfamiliar at the time that "unknown" might be a better term. The offices at Ramsey were a natural extension to this theme, as was the Orford connection that endured for 120 years in Liverpool. To conclude this section we looked at a Steam Packet boat that never set sail.

The chairman revealed that the company had considered a motor vessel as far back as 1929, when the **Peveril** was being built, but steam had won the day, due to the much higher costs of motor ships at that time. By the time the next freighter was ordered after the war, there had been another twenty years of progress in diesel engineering, and the costs were now firmly in favour of motor vessels for freight, but with passenger vessels, winter lay-ups and the vibration that was still associated with diesel engines meant that most cross channel operators still preferred steam turbines. I have been on board the **Fenella** in harbour when her diesels were running, and there was a perceptible tremor. I have also travelled on a motor ship that was built for North Sea service a few months after the **Fenella**, and compared to the smoothness of a steam turbine, there was vibration. The **Fenella** is at the seaward end of the freight berth on 20 August 1972. At this time, the Packet freighters were still using the Coburg docks in Liverpool, which were up river, but the Mersey Docks & Harbour Board closed them in September 1972, the Steam Packet boats transferring to the Hornby Dock, which was down river.

The **Fenella** of 1018 grt, was launched at the Ailsa Shipbuilding Co yard at Troon on 6 August 1951. She was powered by a 7-cylinder British Polar diesel engine developing 1184 ihp, and was capable of 12.5 knots. Despite the change in power plant, she followed the same general design as the **Peveril**, with the superstructure amidships and cargo spaces fore and aft. Although some Irish passenger boats regularly carried cattle, the Packet preferred to segregate this important but malodorous traffic, so the **Fenella** was equipped to handle cars, livestock and general freight. Derrick posts and winches were provided for the fore and aft holds, and movable wooden partitions permitted different types of cargo to be separated, or could serve for livestock. We are looking at the aft cargo space on the **Fenella** on 4 Sept 1971. By the start of the seventies, the container revolution was well advanced, and **Fenella**, with her separate holds with limited access, was not suitable for container traffic without a massive rebuild that was uneconomic on a twenty-year old vessel. She was sold to E Mastichiades of Pyraeus, Greece in January 1973.

Until the 1960s, the **Fenella** of 1951 remained the only motor vessel in the fleet, but between 1963 and 1965, the old steam driven **Peveril** of 1929 was replaced by a new motor vessel bearing the same name, whilst the steam coaster **Conister** was replaced by a new diesel coaster, the **Ramsey**. Both came from the Ailsa Shipbuilding Co at Troon, and bore a striking family resemblance to one another. The "little sister", the **Ramsey**, is seen at her name port of Ramsey on 7 July 1970. She was 149 feet x 28 feet, with a draft of 12 ft 1 ins, and had been specially designed to get in and out of Ramsey harbour, as the Packet continued to run freight boats to the town long after the services to the other minor ports on the Island had been discontinued. The Steam Packet office is immediately behind the foremast. Although they are not as "pretty" as views where the tide is in, I have selected views with the tide out wherever possible, as this provides a chance to study the underwater lines of the vessels.

Many of the readers of this book will have travelled on a passenger steamer, but few will have set foot on a freight vessel. I was in a privileged position with friends of my parents on the shore and seagoing staff of the Packet, so had the opportunity to visit some of the ships, though with hindsight, I wish I had made better use of those possibilities. This portrait of the telegraph, ships wheel and binnacle of the **Ramsey** was taken on 6 September 1971. Although purely a freighter, the brass work on the telegraph and on the wheel gleamed, as did the woodwork. The wooden spoked wheel and the brass telegraph were developed in the early days of steam ships, and even though the power plant had changed, were still being fitted to newly built vessels in the sixties. Within a few years, direct control of the engines from the bridge had rendered the telegraph obsolete, and the "wheel" started to resemble the steering wheel on a motorcar. It was practical, but sad.

I suspect that everyone will have heard of the "ship's galley", which is the maritime name for the kitchen. On the **Ramsey** there was accommodation for up to 18 crew members. Even in this day and age of equality, I suspect that lady readers will be more at home in the kitchen than the men, and I wonder how many of them would relish preparing a meal for 18 guests in a kitchen this size. If that is not daunting enough, this kitchen could roll from side to side and pitch longitudinally, or even worse do both simultaneously in a gale. To counter these proclivities, the work surfaces and cooking range have a raised edge to prevent pots and pans sliding off when the ship was encountering heavy weather. A crew member told me it was excellent unless the weather was "raal baad". He added that the language of a ship's cook in bad weather after a few pots had ended up on the floor, and he had burnt himself on hot surfaces, was a revelation even to a hardened seaman. I am prepared to believe this.

The **Ramsey** was launched on 5 November 1964, joining the fleet the following year. She was sold in December 1973, one of the shortest careers in the Packet history up to that time. Why was this? She had been built for traditional cargo handling, with individual consignments of goods stowed in her hold. Containers had been around for generations, and were used for furniture removals, but in the 1960s, the great container revolution got under way, and things changed rapidly. Traditional cargo handling was costly, led to high levels of damage, and sad to say, of pilferage. My mother, when she was doing her nursing training in Liverpool, became friends with the family of a Liverpool docker. He was a decent and honest man, but regaled her with tales of cargo that had been badly slung on purpose, so that it would fall when lifted, smashing the crate, which would then be set aside in the warehouse, pending a claim. A good proportion of the contents would "walk" thereafter. He said that the dock authorities turned a blind eye, as a proportion of genuine accidents were unavoidable, and deliberate ones, within reason, were seen as a perk of the job. Understandably, this did not go down well with shipping companies or their customers, and when a more secure way of handling cargo came along, it was avidly seized upon. Part of the fierce opposition to containerisation by the dockers was a realisation that such pickings would cease, but in doing so, they merely hastened the demise of their own jobs. As we see here, the **Ramsey** could carry containers in her hold, but moving them into the corners was slow and difficult, and whilst it was acceptable in a part cargo, it was not ideal when a shift to 100% containerisation was imminent. Container traffic rose by over 30% in 1973 alone, and at the end of the year, the **Ramsey** was sold. The propeller, or screw, secured to the forecastle, is the emergency screw. Unlike the toughened bronze of the genuine screw, this was a cheap iron screw that would not last long, but would get the ship moving again in an emergency. The opening beneath the forecastle deck is the tonnage opening, and means that the space does not count towards the vessels net tonnage, which is what harbour dues are based on.

The alterations that have taken place at the foot of the King Edward VIII pier between 1970 and the present day have changed this area out of all recognition, but as it represented the hub of activity and power within the Packet, it merits coverage. The Imperial Hotel was located at the foot of the Red Pier, which was later rebuilt as the King Edward VIII pier. It had once been a successful hotel, as it was close to the harbour, but the noise and bustle of the harbour and the newer hotels that were appearing along the Loch Prom meant it was losing popularity. In 1887, the hotel, which was a tall but narrow building in the French Chateau style, was purchased by the Packet, and became the company's head offices. I took this view on 10 August 1969, as a replacement office block was being built near the Sea Terminal, a phased transfer taking place in November 1969. The Royal Buildings, which faced the inner harbour, and the now demolished Lord St bus station, housed the freight offices, and had been another former hotel. It was decided to leave the freight offices in their existing location, and demolish Imperial Buildings to make more space for container storage. With over 30 containers visible in this view, with just a narrow passage left for the public to visit the Head offices, the need for space is clear, but it was a shame to see the old building go. I recall one old Packet employee complaining bitterly to me, "They never should have done it, they'll have no luck. Mark my words" Ironically he was right, for within fifteen years, the company had been given away to James Sherwood's Sea Containers Group.

The Steam Packet site stretched along the quayside from Imperial Buildings at the foot of the Red Pier almost as far as the swing bridge that spanned the harbour, roughly on the same site as the present vehicular lift bridge. Most of the space from Imperial Buildings to the swing bridge was occupied by a warehouse, which we see on 4 September 1971. The Royal Hotel, which was at the Eastern end of the site was at right angles to the quay and faced Lord St bus station. More warehouse accommodation was provided at the northern end of the Royal Hotel, and this continued towards the site of the modern Imperial Buildings, which are a few yards from the Sea Terminal. Beyond the Royal Hotel the road ran at approximately a 45-degree angle. Until the replacement of horses with internal combustion engines, a stables block and yard was located in the midst of the site. This area is now largely cleared, and the amount of warehouse and office accommodation may seem excessive to modern readers, but in the days before the container revolution, when freight was moved in individual consignments, one of the biggest expenses facing any carrier was to provide warehouses to protect goods that were waiting shipment by sea, or collection by the consignee in the case of inbound traffic. Another major expense was the production of the mountains of paperwork that was required for every single consignment.

Instead of an 8ft x 8ft x 40 ft container or a juggernaut lorry that the sender loads, there would be hundreds of individual packages, crates, barrels and oddments, all of which had to be entered up when they were delivered to the Packet, and moved to the right section of the warehouse, as the sender would not be too impressed if the goods he wished to send to Liverpool were unloaded in Dublin. Then they had to be loaded on the right steamer, and checked off and a cargo manifest completed. Then there was the job of unloading them, and when you thought you had got everything dealt with there was the next day's work to begin, and complaints about breakages and shortages.

In the days when the inner harbour was a genuine working port and North Quay was a proper road, as it had been for generations back, the IOMSPCo Royal Buildings, which were on Parade Street, dominated the seaward end of the quay, as in this view from 21 July 1968. The building dated from about 1790 and had been built as a town house for the Bacon family of Arragon, who had first moved to the Island c1724. It became a hotel in 1848, under the charge of Mr William Hill, a highly regarded hotelier of his day. (See "100 Years of Mann"). It passed to his son-in-law about 1875, and was acquired by the Steam Packet in 1913, becoming the goods offices, but was demolished in recent years along with the warehouses. In contrast to Castletown or Peel, with a splendid array of early properties, most of Douglas dates from mid-Victorian times, so the loss of Imperial Buildings and Royal Buildings has removed two of the finest older buildings left in this part of Douglas. I am glad I knew the area when the Peveril Hotel, Villiers building and the old terminal arcade survived, as together they made an impressive group of structures, all torn down since the start of the 1960s. A visitor arriving in Douglas for the first time in 1960 saw imposing buildings the moment he stepped off the boat. Today we see modernist mediocrity. We are the poorer for their passing.

When freight arrived off the boat, it was taken to the inward section of the Warehouse, and the consignee was advised by postcard that the goods were awaiting his collection, and that Warehouse rent would be charged if they

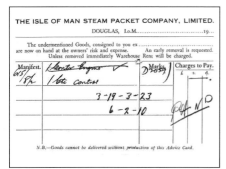

were not removed promptly. This particular card was sent to the GPO Repeater Station at Port Erin, and is just one of the myriad of forms that were needed to handle freight traffic. A shipping company is sometimes seen as ships and seafarers, but an army of land-based staff was required to process the mountain of paperwork.

To the end of its days, the raised entrance to Royal Buildings boasted an elegant mosaic floor with the company title in a garter, and the Manx motto in smaller letters inside a second garter. A paddle steamer attested the maritime connection. Sadly the passage of thousands of feet every year, decade after decade, had wrought havoc on this delightful mosaic. I would make a plea to our legislators. We can look back with gratitude on the legacy of fine building left by our ancestors from Castle Rushen hundreds of years ago, to the superb sweep of Douglas Prom in Victorian times. Your legacy has been the destruction of vast numbers of fine buildings and their replacement by structures such as Summerland, which has already had to be torn down. There is something to be said for ignoring the siren voices of the property developer, who stresses the benefit of his latest plan to destroy a little more of our heritage. In my lifetime, the architectural merit of Douglas has been sorely diminished. We have lost many fine buildings, and what has replaced them justly merits the words of the Gilbert & Sullivan ditty, "There'd none of them be missed". Our politicians and planners were the guardians of that heritage, and they let it go. Will a future generation say "they did a good job'? It would be nice to think so, but I have some doubts.

The Isle of Man Steam Packet Company Limited
(Incorporated in the Isle of Man)

Steamer _K Orry_   From _Lpool_   To Douglas   17/12 19

WAYBILL OF THROUGH BOOKED PARCELS, LUGGAGE, Etc.

Carter _1 MR_   Delivered _17/12/54_

"EXAMINER" PRINTING WORKS

STATION	CONSIGNEE	ADDRESS	NUMBER & DESCRIPTION OF PACKAGES		PAID		TO PAY			SIGNATUR
41 Bangor	Read (Read)	Ballaugh	1 case		3 7	CL			✓	
2 Caine	Owen	Peel	1 ctn	36	9 10		1 6	✓	
3 Trowbridge	Quayes	PE	1 "	16	5 10		1 2	✓	
4 Greasides	Moore	St Johns	1 bale	64	18 0		1 7	✓	
5 Bradford	Harding	Ctown	1 pce	27	5 10		1 2	✓	
6	O'Brien	"	1 "	7	2 7		10	✓	
7 Trowbridge	Quayes	PE	1 ctn	19	5 10		1 2	✓	
8 Crewe	Kiggin	"	1 trunk		3 7	CL			✓	
9 Stockbridge	Moore	Ctown	1 bale	14	5 5		1 0	✓	
50 St Monance	Wood	Peel	1 case		3 7	CL			✓	
1 Kewston	DeHaine	Braddan	1 wd box	27	8 9		1 2	✓	
2 "	Quayes	RM	1 cc		7 4		-	× Vock	
3 Halifax	Stout	Legayne	1 trunk		3 7	CL			✓	
14	"		1 "	16	5		1 2	✓	

In the last few days before Christmas 1954, the **King Orry** and the **Mona's Queen** were on the passenger service, and although their main role was passenger, rather than freight, the "Waybill of Through Booked Parcels and Luggage, Etc" for a single sailing of the **King Orry** on 17 December 1954 ran to three large sheets of paper, each measuring 13 x 16 ins. In order to reproduce it to a reasonable size, we have included only the heading and the first few lines of a sheet that is more than twice the size of a modern A4 sheet of paper and which covers 40 individual consignments. These waybills merely related to consignments booked to continue by the Isle of Man Railway, and separate sheets were prepared for other Island carriers such as the Manx Electric Railway or road hauliers, and goods being delivered by the Steam Packet's own lorries in the town. Traffic was modest in December, and there might only be a few dozen passengers on board, but in high season, some of the boats could carry over 2000 passengers. Many would carry their own luggage, but the load rose dramatically, and the boats would not make a single passage but on a peak day might make 3 or 4 sailings. The volume of paperwork that was generated in a single day was formidable, which explains why there were two large office buildings within a few yards of one another.

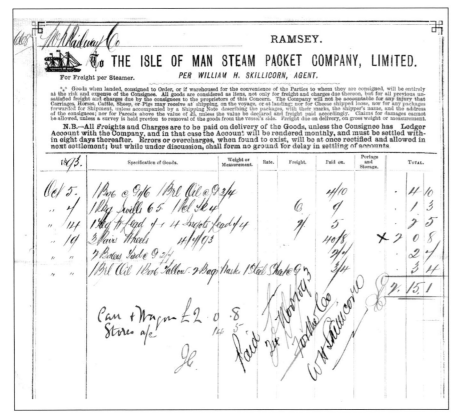

After Douglas itself, the longest-lived agency on the Island was at Ramsey. One remarkable feature of the Packet was the length of service of many of its staff, senior officers frequently completing 40 or 50 years. The agents were equally long-serving, and at Ramsey, William H Skillicorn, James Bell, and Geoff Bell served the company for many decades between them. This freight account from 1893 refers to goods shipped on the direct Liverpool – Ramsey service, almost certainly on board the **SS Ellan Vannin**. The vignette, of a fully rigged paddle steamer with ornamental gun ports painted on the side, will be a stock item from the printer's type drawer. With its very tall funnel, dummy gun ports and paddle mounted well forward, it is a very early vessel. It could represent the three masted paddle steamers built for the Packet between 1845 and 1853, but if so, it is a very poor likeness. It is much closer to James Little & Co's **City of Glasgow** of 1822. (See Page 24) If so, the block would have been prepared for locally printed handills and adverts some seventy years previously. Indeed it may date from the era of Thomas Sayle or Josiah Heelis, both of whom we encountered in Chapter 2.

The Ramsey premises comprised a two-story office block and freight warehouse on the corner where the quay gives way to the south pier. They had been built for an 1850's Ramsey Steam Packet Co, which operated a vessel called the **Manx Fairy** for some years to and from Liverpool. For many years the agent was J G Bell. My mother used to book via Ramsey, as the more business that went through the office the better the chance of it surviving. She had known Geoff Bell since they were children, and on one occasion with a Force 11 forecast, she phoned Geoff to see if we could rearrange our crossing. Geoff, who was not travelling, said it would be a comfortable passage, as the wind was directly behind us, and when she expressed some doubts, said he could rearrange the booking, adding that he would buy a chicken to present to her when we arrived. That solved the problem, and we travelled on the **Manxman**, and to give Geoff his due, it was an excellent passage, one of the few times I have enjoyed a force 11 crossing. We called in to see Geoff the following day, but as we had crossed, he said that we were not entitled to the chicken! The dialogue reflected the mutual regard that existed between Geoff and the people who used the office.

With a heavy volume of freight after the close of World War Two, the Steam Packet chartered three freighters from J S Monk & Co, the **Seaville**, **Sprayville** and **Monkville**. The **Seaville** at 717 grt, was much larger than the other two, and comparable to the **Peveril** of 1929 at 798grt. On 20 November 1951, the **Seaville** was in collision with the Mersey Docks & Harbour Board **Mersey No 30**, and sank with the loss of one life, Mr William Davies. The following day, A E Teare, the Packet's manager sent out a letter to shippers and consignees to advise them of the loss. In early December, a further letter went out, and caused outrage, as two consecutive sentences read, 'in the meantime, by reason of our Conditions of Carriage, we have to decline liability for the loss or damage to the goods . . . We enclose debit note for the freight in accordance with Clause 7 of our Conditions.' The juxtaposition of these sentences, to the effect that your goods are at the bottom of the Mersey, and we decline any responsibility, but here are our charges for your ruined goods, was tactless to say the least. Waiving the charges, as the voyage had not been completed, would have been wiser. In August 1952, the MD&HB, as owners of **Mersey No 30** were held solely responsible for the collision, and instituted proceedings, which were permissible under Maritime law, to obtain a Decree of Limitation under which they paid a maximum of £15 per ton on the appropriate tonnage of **Mersey No 30** plus interest and costs in settlement of all claims. Part of this fund was reserved to the owners of the **Seaville** and the dependents of the man who lost his life, and the balance was largely available to cargo owners. Any cargo owner would need to employ solicitors to make a claim, and the proportion of the value would depend on all other claims. The Packet was also a victim, but did not come out of the episode looking good. It was an early manifestation of the arrogance that was to make the appearance of the rival Manx Line in 1978 welcome to so many people, and to bring the company to its knees.

ALL TRAFFIC CARRIED SUBJECT TO THE CONDITIONS OF CARRIAGE OF THE COMPANY AS EXHIBITED IN THEIR OFFICES AND ON BOARD THEIR STEAMERS.

THE ISLE OF MAN STEAM PACKET CO. LIMITED.
(INCORPORATED IN THE ISLE OF MAN)

TELEGRAMS:
STEAMERS, DOUGLAS.

TELEPHONE No.
DOUGLAS 1101 (5 LINES)

A. E. TEARE,
GENERAL MANAGER.

12.

General Manager's Office,
Douglas.

6th. December 1951.

Dear Sir/s,

1 Carton & 3 Cases Cones ex Hampson, P.S.Mary to Mono.London.

With regard to the above goods which were laden in the "Seaville" when she was sunk by reason of a collision with the "Mersey No. 30" we understand that the salvage operations are in the hands of the Liverpool and Glasgow Salvage Association, we do not yet know with what results.

In the meantime, by reason of our Conditions of Carriage, we have to decline liability for the loss or damage to the goods.

We enclose debit note for the freight in accordance with Clause 7 of our Conditions. 3x'11

The question of liability for the collision between the "Seaville" and the "Mersey No.30" is a matter which is doubtless being investigated by or on behalf of the Owners of such vessels and it is to be inferred that the right to recover damages against either or both will depend on the outcome of litigation failing a settlement by negotiation. If therefore you wish to protect your rights in the matter it is desirable you should seek independent legal advice with the minimum of delay.

Yours faithfully,

A. E. TEARE

General Manager

A. M. Sheard Esq.,
The I.O.M.Railway Co.,
DOUGLAS.

At each end of the main journey, transport companies, whether they are railways or shipping lines have to get the goods to or from the customer. Some commodities were collected or delivered by the customer, but from the early days of commercial transport, companies found that road cartage was essential. At first this was in the hands of the horse, and the Packet retained some horses until after the war, but Scammell had developed a three-wheel tractor unit before the war as an alternative to the horse. With the benefit of hindsight, we regard the defeat of the horse as inevitable, but the low capital costs of the horse and its flexibility gave it powerful advantages. The post-war Scammell Scarab was tiny compared to the modern juggernaut, and ideally suited to the Island's narrow roads and the tight confines of many industrial premises in Douglas. No 3, 1844MN, which was registered in 1960, is seen on the King Edward VIII Pier on 17 July 1971. A loader is adding more goods to the typical assortment of crates and cartons on the detachable trailer.

Although registered for highway use in the spring of 1962, so it could operate along the quayside, IOMSPCo No 16, 5354MN, a 4-wheel tractor unit by David Brown, was primarily intended for the tight confines of the Steam Packet warehouse and yard. The front end has taken even more damage than lorry No 3, the reason being that freight that was craned off the boats could swing back and forth, and the tractor units were in the line of fire. No 16 is outside the Packet warehouse at the foot of the King Edward VIII pier on 10 September 1970. Steam Packet road vehicles were painted blue, the exact shade seeming to vary, but was close to Cobalt Blue.

Although the Scammell mechanical horse had dominated the Steam Packet road fleet in the early post war years, the economics of using larger trailers and four-wheel power units were attractive. IOMSPCo lorry No 11, 735PMN, is near the tollhouse for the old 1895 harbour swing bridge in Douglas on 27 August 1969. This Austin tractor unit had only been registered for a few weeks, and in contrast to the battered Scammell, or the Brown tractor in the previous two views, is in pristine condition. The move to containerised loads in the early seventies and then ro-ro brought this whole freight system to an end.

"Agents" were established in various ports and major towns in the UK to represent the Packet. In the early days, even Edward Moore, who acted as the General Manager & Secretary, was defined as Agent. The term probably arose because the lack of rapid communications before the telegraph and telephone meant that companies appointed "agents" to look after their interests in different towns. Unlike the branch manager in many High Street chain stores today, who has little real autonomy, these old time agents were expected to take important decisions, and enjoyed great prestige in their individual fiefdoms. The term "agent" carried

[Memorandum]

IN YOUR REPLY
EA

TELEGRAPHIC ADDRESS: "ORFORDS, LIVERPOOL."
CITY OFFICE--TELEPHONE No. 6228 (CENTRAL.)
DOCK OFFICE ,, 371 (BOOTLE.)

REFERENCE TO

YOUR LETTER.

GIVE THIS REFERENCE

Joseph Orford

Memorandum. 30th Decr 1910

From
THOS. ORFORD & SON, AGENTS,
Isle of Man Steam Packet Company, Ltd.,
(INCORPORATED IN THE ISLE OF MAN).
17, DRURY BUILDINGS,
21, WATER STREET,
LIVERPOOL.

PASSENGERS, THEIR LUGGAGE, LIVE STOCK AND GOODS ONLY CONVEYED SUBJECT TO THE CONDITIONS OF CARRIAGE OF THE COMPANY EXHIBITED IN THEIR OFFICES AND ON BOARD THEIR STEAMERS.

17015

To Thomas Stowell Esq
Secy & manager
Isle of Man Rly Co Ltd
Douglas.

Dear Sir,

I enclose the expired pass for the current year, and thank you for the 1911 permit just received. With all good wishes for the coming year.

I am, Dear Sir,
Very truly yours
Joseph Orford

such standing that the agents guarded their title jealously, even after improved communications meant that major decision making became centralised. The Liverpool agency was special, as it was not even a part of the IOMSPCo until 1970, but a separate company. The first agent, until his death in 1833 was Mark Quayle, followed briefly by James Duff, before Thomas Durie Moore (1812-1851) became agent, at first with J Christian, and then alone until he died. His father was James Moore, one of the founders of the Steam Packet, whilst the Douglas agent and manager, Edward Moore, was his cousin. Following T D Moore's death in 1851, Thomas Orford was appointed to the post. A bluff 40 year old, Orford had trained with John Bibby & Co before becoming a ship-broker. He was joined in the business by his three sons, Joseph, Thomas and William, and survived until 1903, taking an active role until not long before his death. At the end of December 1910, Joseph Orford wrote to Thomas Stowell, manager of the Isle of Man Railway returning his expired free pass, the officers of the Island transport companies exchanging this courtesy with one another of an annual basis, so that Stowell enjoyed free travel on the Steam Packet, etc. The memo testifies to the independent nature of the Agency, with the Orford name in a prominent bold typeface, and Isle of Man Steam Packet in a less prominent style. I do not think this is accidental.

Joseph Orford's sons, William and Thomas joined the firm, and further generations of the Orford family continued to run the Liverpool agency under the name of Thomas Orford until Harold F Orford, who had become agent in 1947, retired in 1970, after completing 45 years of service with the agency. It was only in 1970, when Harold retired, that the Steam Packet finally purchased the business, which employed a staff of 20. The Company then appointed one of its Liverpool based directors, Mr Andrew Alexander, to act as the notional head of the Liverpool agency. 346DLV, came from BMC, and is seen in Orford colours of bright red and black at the Liverpool Landing Stage on 21 May 1970.

Although furniture removers had used their own containers in the nineteenth century, the big railway companies in the UK developed the general purpose container between the wars. It owed much to its Victorian forebears, which had to be small enough to be moved on a horse-drawn flat. It was 15 to 16' long, to fit on a standard railway flat wagon, 7' wide, and 7' 6" to 8' tall. It normally had doors at one end, and lifting points so it could be craned on and off wagons, lorries and boats. With household removals and furniture handled by container, the Packet was used to dealing with them, and a growing proportion of freight was moved in this way, but when a ship arrived, it was important to discharge the cargo quickly so the vessel could load and sail within a few hours. The inbound containers could not all be dispatched to the customers instantly, and containers being shipped to England would not arrive the moment they were required for loading. Lorries or trailers were too valuable to use as static storage units, but a grounded container was immobile. The answer was a crude wooden trolley with solid-tyres and a swivel axle at one end connected to a simple handle. The UK railways had used luggage trolleys at passenger stations for decades, and the container trolley was just an enlargement of this. These Steam Packet trolleys were at the old freight berth next to the original Imperial Buildings at the foot of the King Edward VIII pier on 4 September 1971. They were painted bauxite, a shade similar to the container in the background. This is BR type BK furniture container, No BK8984B. It was one of 450 diagram 3/127 containers built by the BR Earlestown wagon works in 1956. To the right of the container are some IOMSPCo open containers. These varied from the same length and width as a closed container through half length versions to small type H containers which were 7 ft x 4 ft, and were about 2ft 4ins deep. Steam Packet containers, which were often second-hand ex BR, were painted blue, sometimes with a vertical orange band.

With wooden construction and a rounded roof, traditional containers were not suitable for stacking on top of one another. In the early Sixties, British Railways led an international drive to modernise containers with the ISO 20' x 8' x 8' steel bodied container. The Packet set up a committee of Directors, Management, and the Liverpool Agent, Andrew Alexander, to look at cargo services. At the AGM in 1972, the chairman reported '… the Directors decided to adopt their report on the reorganisation of cargo services to enable all suitable traffic to be unitised. This will involve a reconstruction of the cargo space on the **Peveril**, which will be carried out later in the year. A 28 ton crane has been purchased for erection at Douglas.' The crane is depicted on 20 August 1972, along with some of the new 20' steel containers. There are also a couple of the old round-roofed wooden containers still to be seen, but it was a dramatic change from a couple of years previously.

The history books tell you that there have been two vessels called **Lady of Mann** in the history of the Packet, the centenary steamer of 1930, and her motor ship successor in 1976. Here is the third **Lady of Mann** in the Packet yard at the back of the 1969 Imperial Buildings in August 1984. Her history was complex. She was launched from the well-known Leyland "shipyard", in Lancashire in 1963, and began life as Leyland Titan PD3A/1 double decker bus, with a Willowbrook 73 seat front entrance body. She joined the fleet of Stratford-upon-Avon Blue Motors Ltd, where she became No 1. It is hard to get much further from the sea in the UK than Shakespeare's birthplace. Stratford Blue was a subsidiary of Midland Red, a leading UK bus company, and was merged into the Midland Red fleet a few years later, the erstwhile No 1 becoming No 2001. After a few months in Midland Red ownership, it was sold to the Isle of Man Road Services, where it became IMRS No 44, and later IOM National Transport 44 and then 61. Its Steam Packet career began a few years later.

CHAPTER TEN
Secret "Not to be Exhibited"

In 1914-1918 and again in 1939-1945, the majority of the Steam Packet fleet went to War, and put in distinguished service. Retaining many of their own crews, a number of Manxmen lost their lives in far waters in the defence of freedom in both wars. Although the wartime record of the Steam Packet boats has seldom been given its just recognition, it has at least received some mention in print. The work of the boats that stayed at home, maintaining the vital lifeline for passengers and general freight, has been all but forgotten, and I would like to redress that here. At the outbreak of war, the chairman of the Packet was Edwyn Kneen, who had taken over after the death of Sir George Clucas in November 1937. W G Barwell, who had been Manager & Secretary since Thomas Craine's premature death after only a few months in office in 1929 was suffering from ill health

and retired on 31 December 1937, his role as general manager being taken by R W Cannell, and as secretary by T O Fisher.

Unlike 1914, when war broke out at the start of August, traditionally the peak month of the season, it was 3 September 1939, that hostilities were declared. Hopes for a good September were dashed, and within a day or two, traffic was falling off, and soon after that, the newer and larger vessels were requisitioned for war service. Within weeks, all that was left was the **Rushen Castle** and the **Victoria**, later replaced by the **Snaefell** for the passenger traffic, and the **Peveril**, **Conister** and **Cushag** for freight. With traffic light in the winter of 1939-1940, considerably higher running expense due to the onset of wartime inflation and a massive increase in insurance rates, due to the risk of enemy action, the winter loss climbed steeply, without the prospect of making good during the 1940 sea-

son. Fares were increased on 1 January 1940, but freight receipts were also boosted by the demise of Manx Cargo Services Ltd. Edwyn Kneen, speaking in February 1940, referred to a significant cost cutting decision,

"For many years we have maintained a weekly cargo service between Liverpool and Castletown, Port St Mary and Peel. Of late it has not been a paying proposition, the main cause being lack of support by importers and lack of outward cargo from the Isle of Man due in part to the decrease in the quantity of oats and turnips exported of late years. After the fullest consideration, we reluctantly decided to close the service."

The Castletown sailings had once been handled by the **Tyrconnel**, and after her departure, by the **Cushag**.

*With all five of the modern passenger vessels requisitioned for war service in 1939, the Steam Packet was left with a pair of boats, initially the **Rushen Castle** and the **Victoria**, but after the latter was mined, she was replaced by the **Snaefell**, an unwelcome change, as she was already ailing and costly to maintain. It was on the **Rushen Castle**, illustrated here, that the brunt of the work fell, although she was several years older than the other two vessels. She re-opened the Douglas-Liverpool route on 6 April 1946, but with the Cammell Laird twins, **King Orry** and **Mona's Queen** being delivered that summer, she was laid aside later in the year.*

Manx Cargo Services competed with the Steam Packet for a number of years, but with the adverse trading conditions arising as a result of the outbreak of war, MCS ceased trading before the end of 1939.

With wartime uncertainties, she was retained for the time being, despite the loss of her main duty, which normally occupied Thursday to Saturday and Monday, Tuesday and Wednesday being taken up with a Ramsey sailing.

On 27 January 1940, the Island was lashed by an easterly gale and snow, and the **Rushen Castle**, arriving from Liverpool, was unable to enter Douglas, so was diverted to Peel, but by the time she arrived, conditions were so bad, and the bay was so congested with vessels sheltering from the storm, that she could not safely approach the breakwater until Tuesday 30 January, after a 71 hour passage. To add to the company's embarrassment, His Excellency the Lieut-Governor, Vice Admiral Leveson Gower, 4th Earl of Granville, was a passenger. Wartime secrecy with radio messages about weather conditions being directed to the captain, rather than the vessel, and cryptic go to the east or west instructions added to the confusion. Kneen added:

"Such an experience was without precedent in the Company's experience, and no regulations appear to have been laid down by our predecessors for the guidance of our caterers. You will, I am sure, be glad that your Board immediately made regulations, and in the future, when one of the Company's vessels is at sea in an emergency under similar conditions, all passengers will be provided for at the Company's expense".

Compared to the tactless action that was to be taken over the **Seaville** eleven years later, it was a wise and sensible policy.

In February 1940, the annual report still showed the fleet at its pre-war strength of 16 vessels, and Kneen said how pleased they had been with the conversion of the **King Orry** to burn oil, making her much more useful though she was by then engaged on war work. Within three months, three of the ships were to be lost at Dunkirk, during which the IOMSPCo vessels rescued 1 in 14 of the total evacuees from France. Two of the three newest ships, the **Fenella** and the **Mona's Queen** were casualties, as was the recently refurbished **King Orry**. 40 officers and men were reported missing. During 1940, services operated on a wintertime basis throughout the year, and after the 556,519 arrivals of 1939, slumped to 25,841, which was much less than the lowest figure recorded in the Great War. With traffic low, and with costs having risen between 25 and 140% of pre-war levels, profits were just £38,909. An idea of the magnitude of the slump is that Passenger Tax in 1939 had been £16,815. In 1940, it was just £1,652. During the summer of 1940, aerial mining of the approaches to Liverpool became a problem, with the port often closed for several hours, but in late September, Goering switched his bombers to nightly raids, known as "the blitz", and Coburg dock was hit badly. Aerial mining continued, as did air raids in the run up to Christmas, and the company's freight accommodation at Liverpool was blitzed. On 27 December 1940, the **Victoria** was mined shortly after leaving Liverpool. As the Battle of the Atlantic was heating up, Liverpool was increasingly in the front line, and with disruptions due to mining and air raids, and the need to free the Mersey for vital war work, the passenger service was switched to Fleetwood a few days after the damage to the **Victoria**.

On 24 January 1941, Edwyn Kneen passed away after several months of ill health. Although he was in his seventies, Alexander Robertson, the former Town Clerk of Douglas, who had played such a decisive role in saving the Packet in 1919, took over as chairman. During 1940, several of the ships that had been requisitioned were laid up by the Ministry of War Transport, so that not only were they not earning from summer traffic, but they were not even being used or earning a hire fee. Passenger traffic rose in 1941 through the increased use made of the Island by H M Forces, and cargo tonnages rose due to the forces requirements. At the AGM on 25 February 1942, Robertson was circumspect in discussing the move from Liverpool to Fleetwood, after the mining of the **Victoria** in December 1940,

"we are using a port in the United Kingdom other than our customary one. In this connection we are not altogether free agents, and whilst there is the advantage of a shorter sea passage and a saving in fuel, we hear many complaints of inconvenience and of lengthened and more costly railway journeys".

Although arrivals had more than doubled, to 61,942, profits for 1941 had dropped slightly compared to 1940, and stood at £37,352. The events of 1919, when a section of the Board and stockholders had wanted to sell off the remaining assets and enjoy a bumper cash distribution, though always referred to in muted terms, were not forgotten. Robertson was the last member of the team who had defeated the wreckers in 1919, and expressed his belief that when the war was over,

"whoever is in charge, will continue on the lines that the Directors, backed by a large number of stockholders did, about 25 year ago".

As it happened, it was to be Robertson himself, who guided the company through the war and into the start of peace. He was a worthy successor to Dalrymple Maitland.

After a period when part of the fleet was laid up, not required for war

The discovery, from old papers, that the Steam Packet had maintained an office in Castletown intrigued me, but the information given on old Sailings handbills, "The Quay, Castletown" was not particularly detailed, so I decided to have a look and see if any traces still survived. It was 19 August 1972, and I knew that the office had closed more than thirty years previously, but that was the total of my information, so my hopes were not high. As I walked along the quay, I discovered a double property with a painted sign that was faded, but was still clearly readable above the ground floor windows. It read, ISLE OF MAN STEAM PACKET COMPANY LTD. To my surprise and pleasure, I had found the building I was seeking. (Inset) A single story extension existed at the seaward end of the building. This bore a commemorative plaque with raised lettering, and included the date, 1912. The office remained in use until the early months of World War Two, and thirty years on, had altered very little. It was subsequently converted to residential accommodation, with a projecting Oriel bay window on the upper floor, whilst the single story extension was rebuilt to two stories, the ornate gable being reused. The building is now very smart, although it has changed considerably from its days as the Packet office in Castletown, which is why I have selected these rare views which show the office little altered

service, the accelerating pace of war meant that the newer ships all returned to active war duties, and during 1942, this created problems when the time came for the annual survey of the two passenger ships.

"Throughout the greater part of the year, the whole of our tonnage has been employed on Government or Home Service. We thus have not had an available relief vessel, and in consequence on two occasions, each of a few weeks' duration, were compelled

to restrict our Passenger Service to alternate day sailings while one or other of the steamers engaged thereon was overhauled".

From 15 November 1942, all passenger and cargo services operating to the UK came under official requisition. The Packet continued to operate them, but as an agent of the UK government, receiving a fixed hire fee. For the next three years, profits were between £40,000 and £42,000, but with the hire arrangements and the need for

Very little paperwork has survived for the Castletown office of the Steam Packet, which is not surprising, as the office closed more than sixty years ago. The last Agent at Castletown, W F Anderson, who had taken over from the long serving William Henry Kneale prior to the start of the 1934 season, sent this letter in December 1939, shortly before the office closed down. With the need to conserve paper during the war, left over stationery from the office had the Castletown address overprinted with a black X, and was reused at Douglas in 1941-42. Recycled letters are rare, but this is the only letter I have seen actually issued by Anderson.

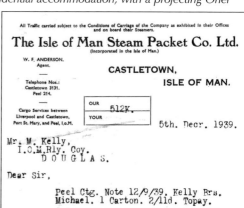

ALL TRAFFIC CARRIED SUBJECT TO THE CONDITIONS OF CARRIAGE OF THE COMPANY AS EXHIBITED IN THEIR OFFICES AND ON BOARD THEIR STEAMERS

TELEGRAMS—"STEAMERS, DOUGLAS."

THE ISLE OF MAN STEAM PACKET CO., LTD.

(INCORPORATED IN THE ISLE OF MAN)

R. W. CANNELL.
GENERAL MANAGER

GENERAL MANAGER'S OFFICE.

DOUGLAS.

7th. October 1940.

INCREASED PASSENGER FARES, AND ALTERED TIMES OF SAILINGS,
TO OPERATE ON AND FROM MONDAY OCTOBER 14TH 1940.
- -

Notice is hereby given that in consequence of further
increased expenses incurred in maintaining the present
Passenger Steamer Services between Liverpool and Douglas, it
has been found necessary to INCREASE THE PASSENGER FARES.
The New Fares on and from MONDAY, OCTOBER 14TH 1940 will be:-

SINGLES - 1ST. CLASS 20/-   3RD. CLASS   12/-

RETURNS - 1ST. CLASS 30/-   3RD. CLASS   20/-
(3 Months)

Children over 3 years and under 14 years - half fares.

- -

ALTERED TIMES OF SAILING

ON AND FROM MONDAY OCTOBER 14TH, 1940, it is intended
to maintain one sailing every week-day in each direction between
LIVERPOOL AND DOUGLAS, passengers to be ready for embarkation at
the Liverpool Landing Stage not later than 1-45 p.m., and at
Douglas not later than 8-20 a.m.

R. W. CANNELL

General Manager

With rapid inflation, two fare increases were needed in 1940, and with rail schedules being eased, the Liverpool departure was put back to later in the day to allow more time for passengers from the South of England to make their connections. Within a few months, Liverpool would become a memory for travellers until the end of hostilities.

secrecy, the annual reports were uninformative. The number of arrivals reached 93,203 in 1943 largely due to the heavy forces presence on the Island, a figure that dropped by around ten thousand the following year as troops were committed to the D-Day landings. 1945, the first partial year of peace saw a late season boom, and arrivals reached 167,089.

Because of official secrecy surrounding forces movements to and from the Island, information was shared on a need-to-know basis, and sixty years have drastically purged the surviving records, but some idea is possible. Jurby RAF Station was an important training base as far away as possible from the attentions of the Luftwaffe. Regular movements of forces personnel on leave took place. On 9 January 1941, forty-eight RAF men were booked to sail from Douglas to Fleetwood. One leave was cancelled, but the remainder travelled. Once they had disembarked at Fleetwood, they continued on to no fewer than 36 different destinations, which ranged from Lossiemouth and Montrose in Scotland to Bodmin in the West Country, and from Newport (Mon) to Peterborough. Three of them would require another sea journey. Two of them travelling to Belfast and Larne in Northern Ireland and one to Dublin in the neutral Republic of Ireland. Their leave numbers had been 1053 to 1100. Four weeks later, on 30 January, a group of 46 aircraftsmen going on leave were issued with no's 1637 to 1682. Their destinations were as varied, and the geographical spread included Thurso, Whitby, Cardiff and Bournemouth. By 25 June 1941, the Jurby leave numbers had reached 2558, or fifteen hundred

forces personnel from that one base in six months. Before the end of 1941, and as Jurby expanded, weekly leave drafts for 120-150 airmen were being issued. Although the most important RAF station on the Island, there were numerous other RAF stations including RAF Dalby, RAF Scarlett and RAF Cregneish, plus RAF Andreas, which was a major air station in the north, each with its own leave requirement. Coordinating the transport requirements of these RAF stations was the work of the Officer Commanding the RAF Embarkation Unit at Douglas. Apart from the RAF presence, the Royal Navy had taken control of Ronaldsway aerodrome, which became a naval air training station. Radar units were established on Douglas head, and whilst this profusion of radar and radio units testifies to the important work that was taking place on the Island, older forms of communication were not forgotten, such as the Army Pigeon Service, with its own unit in Douglas, which had occasion to forward crates of carrier pigeons by sea. Although the majority of Forces traffic was of personnel being posted on duty to or from the island, and leave movements, there was a steady stream of Manx men and women who were serving away and who wanted an opportunity to see their loved ones. My father, as a peacetime doctor in the Royal Army Medical Corps, had his first overseas tour of duty to Egypt for two years in 1939. In 1944, after fighting his way up and down the Western Desert and into Sicily and Italy, he and my mother were posted back to UK, and managed to see their families again as autumn was giving place to winter.

Apart from such joyous homecomings, there were others, thankfully much rarer, of a sadder nature, as on 27 August 1940 when the remains of Flying Officer Eastoe and Flying Officer Ives were taken by sea en route to their families in Chingford and Tonbridge. A party of five Polish officers who had fled from Hitler to the UK to continue the fight against tyranny provided light-hearted relief. With negligible English between them, and a lack of Polish speakers on the boat, their trip to the Island was a source of confusion all round. Apart from moving people, the Steam Packet found it was moving all sorts of equipment, and consignment notes for strange sounding radio valves and components to 77 Wing, Woolton, Liverpool and other RAF stations in

"NOT TO BE EXHIBITED"

The purpose of a handbill is to advertise something, so the wider publicity the better, but during World War Two there were fears that German spies would see such information, and relay it to U boat commanders who could lie in wait to torpedo the passenger steamers with heavy loss of life. As it happened, no torpedo attacks were launched on IOMSPCo vessels in home waters during the war, but it was a wise precaution. Due to the extraordinary success of British counter intelligence, which neutralised the entire German espionage network in the British Isles throughout the war, it would not have mattered, but this was not known with certainty at the time. As Alexander Robertson mentioned during the AGM in 1943, sailings had to be reduced to thrice weekly twice during part of 1942 to allow for survey and overhaul of the **Rushen Castle** and the **Snaefell**. The sailing time, of 12.15 from Fleetwood was much later than the normal Liverpool departure because of the longer rail journey from much of the United Kingdom and slower train services due to war conditions. Fleetwood had replaced Liverpool due to the blitz on the Liverpool docks and regular mining of the Mersey estuary, but with the importance of Liverpool to the Battle of the Atlantic, transferring the Steam Packet ships out of the way helped reduce congestion in the Mersey.

England became routine. Less esoteric items included a sack of worn out sweeping brushes. With rationing of petrol, a push bike was a useful form of transport, and the army transported my parents cycles from Egypt to the Isle of Man. Sadly I have never seen the paperwork, but written records do survive for less dramatic moves of push bikes, such as from Bride to Formby in Lancashire.

In the early months of the war, the boarding houses along Douglas Promenade had become an Alien internment centre, and the area around Port Erin and Cregneish was made into a restricted zone wherein internees were confined. Few had any nefarious intentions against the British Isles, but the existence of Quisling collaborationist movements in various occupied countries and a hard core of Hitler devotees meant the authorities were disinclined to take chances. After hostilities began, a new name began to figure in Steam Packet correspondence, "Headquarters, Alien Internment Camps, Douglas" Movement of aliens between different camps on the Island and for work details at farms throughout the Island was the responsibility of the local rail and bus operators, but moves to and from the Island fell to the Packet. A popular assumption is that aliens were rounded up quickly, shipped to the Island, and other than for the necessary food supplies, that was an end of the matter. The reality was very different. Aliens were also moved from one camp to another, and as the war widened and additional countries became belligerents, the pool of aliens expanded, but other were vetted and no longer seen as a threat. Except in the latter case, all such moves required an escort, so Imperial Buildings could expect to receive regular directives from Headquarters, AIC, requisitioning accommodation on the boat for aliens plus escort.

Apart from moving service personnel and aliens, much of the food required by these all year guests on the island placed a strain on the freight boats. The cargo manifests soon came to reflect this. The **Peveril** arrived in Douglas on an overnight sailing on 7 February 1941. Eight consignments of alien's luggage were included. Two suitcases were for Ranische at Rushen, and there were 3 packages of goods to the commandant of Rushen camp. Internees Schuster and Steinharst at Port St Mary had three items between them, whilst Dunbech, Gruenberg, and an internee whose name defeated the Steam Packet staff, their best guess being Modelah, had four items. A solitary Peel internee, Shapeiro, also appeared. The NAAFI, which provides sustenance for servicemen, seems to have been particularly unlucky with damage to its shipments, not least because everyone realised that NAAFI consignments were likely to include rationed foodstuffs and even cigarettes, so they were frequently pilfered. A regular correspondence grew up between the NAFFI, the road and rail carriers on the Island, the Packet and the UK railways.

Whilst military traffic was controlled by the voluminous directives that emanated from the War Office,

the Admiralty and the Air Ministry, it was also subject to the eccentricities of Dora. To the modern reader, Dora may sound like a benevolent aunt, but benevolent is a word few who encountered her would apply. The full title was the Defence of the Realm Act, and the regulations made under it. The UK Dora had a little sister on the Island, the Manx Dora, who although small, was equally forceful. In 1945, a hapless LAC (leading aircraftsman) at RAF Andreas had produced a small bedside cabinet as a test piece during training at the woodworking class at Andreas, and not unreasonably hoped he could send it to his family. This infringed no fewer than three sets of regulations made under DORA, and required an authorisation by His Excellency the Lieutenant Governor, before LAC Ryan's cabinet could be accepted on board. Without that vital piece of paper, not only LAC Ryan, but also the officers of the IOMSPCo, who might be tempted to spirit the cabinet off the Island, would incur the wrath of Dora. The case of Mr Sperni, an alien with 24 cans of food, went all the way to the government secretary, and involved his former

NOT TO BE EXHIBITED

All Traffic carried subject to the Conditions of Carriage of the Company as exhibited in their Offices and on board their Steamers.

THE ISLE OF MAN STEAM PACKET CO. LIMITED.
(INCORPORATED IN THE ISLE OF MAN).

TELEGRAMS :
"STEAMERS, DOUGLAS"

TELEPHONE NO.
DOUGLAS 1101 (5 LINES)

R. W. CANNELL.
GENERAL MANAGER.

General Manager's Office, Douglas.

REDUCED PASSENGER SERVICES, with Embarkation Times, between Fleetwood and Douglas.

Notice is hereby given that **ON AND AFTER MONDAY, 28th SEPTEMBER, 1942,** the Passenger Services, with Embarkation Times, will be as follows :—

From DOUGLAS to FLEETWOOD,

Each **MONDAY, WEDNESDAY** and **FRIDAY** - - **9 a.m.**

From FLEETWOOD to DOUGLAS,

Each **TUESDAY, THURSDAY** and **SATURDAY** - **12-15 noon.**

The Passenger Fares are—

	First Class.	Third Class.
SINGLE - - -	20/-	12/-
RETURN (valid 3 months) -	30/-	20/-

IDENTITY CARDS must be produced before embarkation.

10th September, 1942.

R. W. CANNELL,
General Manager.

IT IS EXPECTED THAT THESE REDUCED SERVICES WILL REMAIN IN OPERATION FOR ABOUT SIX WEEKS, BUT THEREAFTER IT IS ANTICIPATED THAT A SERVICE EACH WEEK-DAY IN EACH DIRECTION WILL BE MAINTAINED.

Printed at "Herald" Office, Douglas.

camp, AIC HQ in Douglas, government office, the Customs & Excise, the Isle of Man Railway and the Steam Packet. I have illustrated the key document in this bizarre episode, as it casts remarkable light on the official mindset.

A few months after Mr & Mrs Sperni were trying to ship 24 cans of food on the Douglas to Fleetwood boat, the *Tynwald (IV)* of 1937 was operating as an anti-aircraft cruiser off Bougie in French North Africa. She was a part of the Torch landings, and her crew had rather more to worry about than cans of pineapples. She was sunk in action, bringing the number of vessels lost in the war to four, including the three most modern ships. R W Cannell, the general manager, and the superintendent engineer, R B Moore, started planning a new fleet to cope with post war demands, for unlike 1918 when there were members of the board who wanted to take the money, that attitude had no place under Alexander Robertson. Al-though the *Tynwald* and *Fenella* had only entered service in 1937, they had proved to be outstanding boats, big enough for summer needs, yet economical in winter, and R B Moore fine tuned the design, and after official permission was received, ordered two new ships from Cammell Laird early in 1945. With hostilities drawing to a close in Europe, *Viking*, *Mona's Isle* and *Manx Maid* were de-requisitioned, and *Viking* and *Mona's Isle* were hurried back into service in July 1945. *Mona's Isle* had been reconditioned, but *Viking* was still in a dreadful state. *Snaefell*, which was now hopelessly uneconomic to maintain, and a ceaseless worry to R B Moore during the war, was laid up as soon as the other two vessels re-entered service and was sold for scrap in the autumn, an indication of how dire her condition was, given the shortage of shipping. *Rushen Castle*, the other wartime boat, was in reasonable order, giving the company three vessels by the end of the

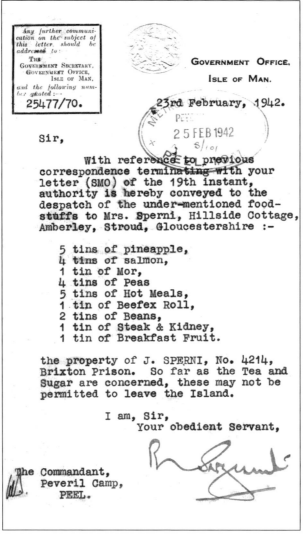

Any further communi-
cation on the subject of
this letter should be
addressed to:-
THE
GOVERNMENT SECRETARY,
GOVERNMENT OFFICE,
ISLE OF MAN,
and the following num-
ber quoted :-
25477/70.

GOVERNMENT OFFICE,
ISLE OF MAN.

23rd February, 1942.

25 FEB 1942

Sir,

With reference to previous correspondence terminating with your letter (SMO) of the 19th instant, authority is hereby conveyed to the despatch of the under-mentioned food-stuffs to Mrs. Sperni, Hillside Cottage, Amberley, Stroud, Gloucestershire :-

5 tins of pineapple,
4 tins of salmon,
1 tin of Mor,
4 tins of Peas,
5 tins of Hot Meals,
1 tin of Beefex Roll,
2 tins of Beans,
1 tin of Steak & Kidney,
1 tin of Breakfast Fruit.

the property of J. SPERNI, No. 4214, Brixton Prison. So far as the Tea and Sugar are concerned, these may not be permitted to leave the Island.

I am, Sir,
Your obedient Servant,

The Commandant,
Peveril Camp,
PEEL.

The masters of the Steam Packet boats had to weave their way through aerial mines and bombing raids, and to combat the perils of the sea, but this fascinating letter, shows the bureaucratic perils they also encountered. Mr J Sperni, an alien who had previously been at the Metropole Internment Camp, otherwise the Metropole Hotel, in Douglas, had been transferred to the Alien unit at Brixton prison. During his stay on the island, he had managed to save 24 tins of food, including 2 cans of beans and 5 cans of pineapple, plus a little tea and sugar. When he was transferred to Brixton, he wanted to send this vast cache of food to his wife, who resided in the small village of Amberley in Gloucestershire. This momentous act required a personally signed letter from the Government Secretary, Bertram E Sargeaunt, who, amazingly, had filled the same post during the Great War. Alas for Mr & Mrs Sperni, although the Steam Packet could convey the 24 cans, "So far as the Tea and Sugar are concerned, these may not be permitted to leave the Island". If the hapless Mr Sperni thought all was now in order, he was mistaken. The tea and sugar would remain, but a customs permit was still required and some of the cans contained a substance called sugar. Once the quantity of sugar had been ascertained, the internment camp at Peel obtained a one shilling (5p) postal order on behalf of Mr Sperni. This was sent to the Isle of Man Railway Co, who paid the collector of customs, and only then, with a letter from the government secretary, and an export certificate from the customs, could the goods be handed to the Steam Packet. I sincerely hope that the couple had a celebration meal of Salmon and peas, with pineapple to follow. Without such clearance from on high, not only Mr Sperni, but also the officers and master would have been guilty of a breach of the Defence of the Realm Act.

summer, with *Manx Maid* due out of refit early in 1946. To R B Moore's pleasure, the first of his new steamers, the *King Orry* was launched in November 1945. With 53 years of service, he was now well beyond retirement age, but had shouldered the burden of keeping the fleet in running order during the war, when maintenance was almost impossible. He stood down as superintendent engineer on 31 December 1945, but sadly passed away on 27 January 1946. The *King Orry*, the vessel of which he was so proud, was expected to arrive in April, and to be followed a few months later by a sister ship, *Mona's Queen*. For the first time in the company's history, there were to be three identical ships, triplets, as Alexander Robertson described them, the third vessel being laid down in July 1946 with a 1947 delivery date. She would be named *Tynwald*. For the last two and a half years, T W Craine had been assistant marine superintendent and had the unusual distinction of having been promoted direct from chief engineer on the smallest of the freighters to the same post on the *Ben-my-Chree*, and subsequently to R B Moore's assistant.

Like the superintendent engineer, the general manager, R W Cannell, was beyond retirement age, but had hoped to stay on to see the new steamers launched and if possible, in service, but in 1945, he suffered increasingly severe eye troubles, and in June was told that he must give up his duties as soon as possible. He stood down at the end of June 1945. He was destined for a brief retirement, dying in August 1947. His successor, Alfred E Teare, had been assistant manager for eight years, and was another long serving officer. Captain J J Keig, a senior master, and who had commanded the *Victoria* during the D-Day landings when she had operated as an assault ship, landing some of the first commandoes to set foot on occupied soil, also died in 1945. The retirement of the chief cashier, T C Hogg, the accountant W H Shimmin, and of other senior engineering and seagoing staff attested to the strain all had been under for six long years.

Alexander Robertson OBE, JP, was the last of the Steam Packet's wartime leaders to leave the stage. He had played a key role in saving the Company in 1919, and had subsequently joined the board, becoming chairman in 1941 when he was already in his late seventies. He was taken ill early in 1947 and was unable to preside at the AGM that year. Although he made a recovery, he decided to stand down as chairman, but remained on the board until his death at the age of 86 on 8th January 1951. His successor, J F Crellin MC, spoke of his qualities,

"Possessed of wide knowledge and a great personality, he was at all times kindly and generously disposed, yet he could, when necessary, vigorously emphasise and uphold any point upon which he held strong views. This applied particularly when pressing for ships and still more ships, for he was noticeably progressive in his outlook regarding new tonnage."

Having played a key role in resolving the crisis of 1919, he laid the

foundations for the renaissance of the Steam Packet and of Manx Tourism from the late forties to the sixties. It would be hard to determine whether Maitland or Robertson was the greatest chairman in the history of the company. Both were outstanding. Although the Packet had carried the main load throughout the war, the sterling efforts of the officers and staff of the Ramsey Steamship Co should

Alexander Robertson was christened at St Barnabas Church, Douglas on 13 November 1864, his parents being Helen and Robert Alexander Robertson. He was educated at King William's College, and then joined Richard Sherwood, (later Deemster Sherwood) for a year. Next, he spent eight years in the Manx Bank, being appointed Deputy Clerk to the Douglas Commissioners in 1890, and Town Clerk in 1898, a post he held until his retirement in 1930, when he was made a freeman of the borough. This portrait dates from his appointment as Town Clerk.

In 1919, Alexander Robertson had played a decisive role in saving the Steam Packet from the "Wreckers" and joined the Steam Packet board after his retirement as Town Clerk in 1930. Appointed Chairman when he was already in his late seventies during the dark days of World War Two, he laid the foundations for the magnificent fleet that served the Island so well from the 1940s to the 1970s. Probably the most outstanding chairman in the history of the IOMSPCo, he has received scarcely any mention in the many books written about the company. I am pleased to rectify that omission, for the Island owes him an incalculable debt.

not be overlooked, for their coasters carried most of the bulk freight that was required during the war years, the original **Ben Veg** of 1914 having been run down and sunk in 1941.

---

*The **Tynwald** of 1937 was the last of the three modern ships to be lost during the War. In common with her sister, the **Fenella**, she was 314' 6" long x 46', and of 2376 grt. Their loss prompted R W Cannell and his superintendent engineer, R B Moore, to plan a post war fleet. The new ships, of which there were eventually to be six, the first being the **King Orry**, which was laid down early in 1945, were to serve the company until 1982, and are the subject of our next chapter. Compared to the 1937 twins, they were 10' 6" longer and had one foot greater beam. The design of the funnel, which looked slightly awkward on the 1937 pair, as the top was horizontal, was modified so that it was an exact right angle to the rake of the funnel itself, a small alteration that transformed their appearance.*

CHAPTER ELEVEN
The Six Sisters

The *Tynwald* and *Fenella* of 1937 were excellent boats, and after both were lost through enemy action, R B Moore, the Superintendent Engineer adopted the design as the basis of a new class, which had to be small enough to be economical in winter, yet large enough to handle the summer Saturday peaks, for a feature of the 1920s and 1930s was the way in which traffic was increasingly channelled into the Saturday peak periods. The biggest visual difference was that the top of the funnels on the 1937 boats was horizontal, but with the stylish rake given to the funnel, this looked ungainly. In the post war boats, the top of the funnel was also raked. Six identical boats might seem

daunting and even boring compared to the diversity of the past, but my father realised that there were constructional differences that made identification simple, even if it was not possible to read the name. On one occasion some school friends and I were making the ascent of Snaefell as a boat was approaching Douglas harbour. It was an exceptionally clear day, and we could eliminate the freight boats, the car ferries and the 1930 *Lady of Mann*, which removed half the fleet. As the Snaefell car rattled up the mountainside, we discussed each option and ended up with only one possible candidate, to the surprise of other passengers who had not expected some school kids to identify a boat entering Douglas from

a moving Snaefell car! After we got to the summit, I had a look in my pocket, as I had a copy of the sailing arrangements. We had not cheated, and I merely wanted to confirm that we were correct. We were! Although that knowledge is now only of use in identifying old photos, I have shared the recognition points here, as I have often heard people bewail the difficulties of identifying a group of ships in Douglas harbour. In "A Century of Manx Transport in Colour", published by Manx Experience in 1998, I used a view taken by my father showing seven different IOMSPCo vessels in Douglas. Within a few minutes, I was able to identify every one of them with absolute certainty using the tips that follow in this section.

*The **King Orry** was launched on 22 November 1945, and took her maiden voyage on 19 April 1946. She was of 2485 grt, and was sold in October 1975. She is depicted entering Douglas harbour in August 1970. The first three sisters, **King Orry**, **Mona's Queen** and **Tynwald**, had pairs of triple windows to the first class passenger saloon immediately below the wheelhouse. The last three ships had this triple pattern and a fourth window closer to the side of the vessel. Aft of the first class saloon was the promenade deck, sometimes known as the boat deck, and in the earlier boats the side was largely unglazed. Initially only a short section was roofed, but it was later extended as in this view. A study of the third vessel, the **Tynwald** will reveal how rectangular glazed windows replaced the unglazed supports from then on. On the shelter deck, the glazed area also extends further back on the **Tynwald** compared to the earlier pair of ships. The side windows to the first class saloon are small, as are the first four windows on the shelter deck, but from the **Tynwald** onwards, the large side windows commence immediately. At the bows, there is no "Three Legs" roundel, whilst there is one circular fairlead opening for the mooring ropes followed by two rectangular slots. The cowling or cravat at the top of the funnel was removed at an early date, providing an instant recognition feature for the **King Orry** at almost any distance.*

The greatest similarities within the class were between the first two boats, the **King Orry** and the **Mona's Queen**. She was launched on 5 February 1946, just over a week after the death of her designer. Her maiden voyage was on 26 June 1946. With the growth in car traffic, she was sold in October 1962, being replaced by the first car ferry, the **Manx Maid (II)** in 1963. This portrait of **Mona's Queen**, taken in August 1961, shows how similar both vessels were. Until the covered but unglazed section of the promenade deck was extended backwards on the **King Orry**, it was very difficult to tell them apart, other than for the funnel. This view is useful in that "the Queen" is moored alongside the **King Orry** revealing the difference in appearance after the removal of the cowl.

Dr R Preston Hendry

The **Tynwald**, launched on 24 March 1947, made her maiden voyage on 31 July 1947, and was 2493 grt, an increase of 8 tons over the earlier two boats. She is approaching Douglas on 20 August 1969. The covered section of the promenade deck immediately aft of the first class saloon received large windows instead of openwork supports, whilst the forward portion of the shelter deck had large windows instead of small ones. These two changes immediately distinguished her from the first two ships. Between the second and third lifeboats, the promenade deck is recessed. This was to provide a craning-off access for cars, which were carried on the shelter deck, and except when tidal conditions were right at Douglas, craned on or off. The first pair of ships did NOT have this opening on the port (left) side so had to berth with the starboard right hand side adjacent to the quay. The **Tynwald**, with openings both sides, could use any berth.

The **Snaefell**, launched on 11 March 1948, served for thirty years, being broken up in 1978. Unlike the first three ships, she had an additional window fronting the first class saloon on the promenade deck. The 3+1 pattern is clearly visible for the port side windows, the starboard windows being masked by the foremast. This alteration plus a "Three Legs" roundel in red and yellow on the bows made her instantly recognisable compared to the earlier boats. On the forward portion of the promenade deck there were 10 small windows instead of 8 as hitherto, and there was a car access in the promenade deck on the port side as with the **Tynwald**. Instead of open struts supporting the promenade deck on the aft portion of the shelter deck, this too was glazed with large windows. This combination made her easy to recognise. She is approaching Douglas on 26 August 1970. The funnel colour looks very pale in this view, and after several weeks in service, exposed to the bleaching effects of the sun and sea spray, the Steam Packet orange red could fade to a bleached out pink, whereupon the bosun would issue paint pots to some of the seamen, and wooden platforms would be slung from anchor points high on the funnel and you would see four or five men industriously restoring the funnel to its proper colours. The ability to do this depended on time in port and good drying weather, and in summer the former depended on how demanding the schedules were, and the latter on what the clerk of the weather had ordained. When I took this photo, **Snaefell** was suffering a severe case of pink funnel.

The **Mona's Isle**, the fifth member of the class was launched at Cammell Laird's yard on 12 October 1950 and was sold in 1980. She closely followed the **Snaefell** in design, but with two important visual differences. Unlike her predecessor, she did not have a "Three Legs" roundel on the bow, and the small fairlead opening just behind the bow was no longer round but rectangular, although not as large as the other two openings. She is at the Liverpool Landing Stage on 23 May 1974. Ever since my father was a child, the Liver Building, which dominates the skyline, was a sombre grey black, and we had assumed it was built from some very dark stone. In 1974 we were astonished to discover that it was a very light coloured stone, in so far as it was visible, as cleaning was still taking place on the sides. The building is topped at both ends by statues of the mythical Liver bird, which is pronounced "Liva", not as in the bodily organ. Many of the company's seafarers have haled from Liverpool, and an "old Salt" of Merseyside ancestry, told me that the Liver bird had truly remarkable properties, for whenever a virgin passes the structure, the Liver bird is said to flap its wings approvingly. I have not been able to verify the truth of this story, but would not wish to cast doubts on the veracity of my nautical informant!

After a five year gap, the last of the six sisters, the **Manxman** was launched on 8 February 1955. Technically there were numerous improvements including a higher boiler pressure and steam superheated to 650 degrees F, but I have concentrated on the physical recognition features in this section. She retained the four windows to the front of the first class saloon on each side of the foremast along with the 10 small windows at the forward end of the promenade deck. The roundel, which had appeared on the bows of the fourth vessel, the **Snaefell**, but not on **Mona's Isle**, reappeared, whilst the rectangular fairlead introduced in **Mona's Isle** was adopted, providing a unique blend of features. The forward pair of lifeboats on the bridge deck were carried as usual at deck height, but the other four lifeboats, on the promenade deck, were carried on Walin gravity davits and mounted above head height so that the deck space could now be used for passengers, a very sensible improvement, and an instant recognition feature. She is seen at sea in July 1982, her final year of service.

The wheelhouse on the **Manxman** was provided with excellent forrard and side vision through numerous windows and with the all-important wood and brass ships wheel. On the **King Orry** class, the design was unusual, as the wheel was carried on two A brackets by means of a polished horizontal shaft. The quartermaster, who steered the boat, stood astride this, so it was not a job for anyone with short legs! Ahead of the wheel is the ships compass or binnacle. In the far corner is the radar. The radar screen was housed at an angle in the top of the sloping rectangular box. The officer who had the watch looked down the shroud as the image was very faint and would be invisible in strong sunlight. It took a great deal of skill to interpret the flickering blips on the screen, and the celebrated collision between the **Andrea Doria** and the **Stockholm** in the North Atlantic is thought to be the result of a wrong interpretation of a radar reading, as both ships had observed one another on radar long before the collision. Even this basic radar was a remarkable advance on the days when ships had to grope forward in fog relying on the instincts of their officers and crews. A few years after photographing this installation, I was on board the **MV Lady of Mann** of 1976, and her radar had a target acquisition system, which drew its nomenclature from its military origins, but enabled one to set an intercept (collision) or a "miss" course. After some instruction, I was given the opportunity to carry out a few plots whilst we were at sea, the captain suggesting I refrain from applying the intercept option.

On this occasion, the **Manxman** was moored at the landward end of the North Victoria pier. She is secured by no fewer than five separate ropes, all three fairleads being in use. It is worth studying how this is done. Seamen do not tie knots in the heavy hemp cables they use, but take the rope in a figure of eight pattern over the two mooring bollards. As the tide comes in or out, it will be necessary to adjust the cables, hauling in or paying out as necessary, so the crew cannot just knock off and go to sleep when the vessel is alongside. A plentiful supply of hemp rope is kept just abaft the steam driven anchor engine. The last portion of the chain is painted white, so that when the engineman is recovering the anchor, the appearance of white links would alert him that the anchor has nearly been recovered. Otherwise he might try to drag it through the side of the boat, with dire results. Ahead of the windlass and between the white painted chains is the bow capstan. This was steam powered, but in the event of a loss of power, heavy wooden beams could be inserted in the square slots at the top of the capstan, and a gang of seamen put on them to turn it by hand. The rhythmic sea shanties of old were created by seafarers in the days before steam to co-ordinate their efforts when doing heavy work such as hoisting sails or pulling in cables or anchors. Between the steam capstan and the rope enclosure is the ship's bell.

In the days when the Steam Packet boats were two class, with saloon and steerage accommodation, the forward lounge immediately below the wheelhouse was reserved for first class or saloon passengers. Elegant polished veneers, fluted columns, carpets, comfortable armchairs, loose cushions and tables, provided a splendid passenger environment. In summer, it was often difficult to get a seat in the main lounge, but in winter it was much easier, and I look back on many passages on the six sister ships of the King Orry class with affection. Sometimes my parents travelled first class, especially in winter, but in summer, when we might be on the open deck enjoying the sun, there was little point in paying the higher fares. I always wanted to explore the boat, but at the age of 3 or 4, I was not allowed off on my own for obvious reasons. My father accompanied me on what must have been many hundreds of tours of exploration. Sometimes if my parents knew the master, that might include a visit to the bridge, or very occasionally to the engine room. I got to know the six sisters, and although it is more than twenty-five years since I last set foot on the **Manxman**, I do not think I would find the slightest difficulty in finding my way from the wheelhouse to the shaft tunnel.

From Victorian days, the idea of frosted glass windows with company devices emblazoned on them was popular with railway and shipping lines. The **Manxman** of 1955 held true to this tradition. Sadly repeated painting has resulted in the complex "Greek" corners being partially obscured.

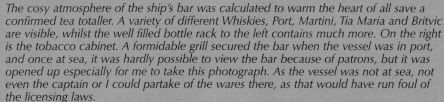

The cosy atmosphere of the ship's bar was calculated to warm the heart of all save a confirmed tea totaller. A variety of different Whiskies, Port, Martini, Tia Maria and Britvic are visible, whilst the well filled bottle rack to the left contains much more. On the right is the tobacco cabinet. A formidable grill secured the bar when the vessel was in port, and once at sea, it was hardly possible to view the bar because of patrons, but it was opened up especially for me to take this photograph. As the vessel was not at sea, not even the captain or I could partake of the wares there, as that would have run foul of the licensing laws.

The advent of competition from Manx Line in 1978 hit the Steam Packet hard, especially after Manx Line fell into the hands of BR Sealink, and had the bottomless pocket of the British taxpayer at its back. The Packet had to trim cost, and the last of the six sisters, the **Manxman**, was prematurely withdrawn on 4 September 1982. As the Steam Packet had warned, the "benefits" of carrying passengers on what was basically a ro-ro freighter cost the Island the excursion trade it had benefited from since Victorian days, and arrivals plummeted between 1979 and 1985. Sadly, the warning was ignored, as the Company was despised, on account of its "exorbitant" dividends, which were because the nominal capital had not been adjusted in line with the value of the assets employed for years, as in 1919, and the tactlessness that had first been demonstrated with the **Seaville** letter. It was a lethal cocktail, made worse by needlessly insulting the powerful IOM Harbour Board. A farewell excursion was arranged from Liverpool to Douglas on 4 September, and I photographed the purser checking tickets at the Landing Stage for the last time. The value of the high slung boats on the Promenade deck is apparent in this view, as deck space that had to be fenced off on the earlier boats is available for passengers on the **Manxman**.

On the main deck there was a steel door that was divided horizontally. At sea, the lower half was kept closed but the upper half was open, and if Dad lifted me up, I could peer down into the exciting and mysterious world of the engine room. He had seen the reciprocating engines that drove the last IOMSPCo paddle steamer, the **Mona's Queen**, but for me, it was the steam turbine age, which lacked the myriad of moving parts of the older designs. Even so, on the rare occasions when we were able to venture down the steep ladder, which is why I was debarred when I was small, it was wonderful. There were two main sections, a boiler room, where a row of oil-fired furnaces generated the steam to power the ship, and the engine room itself, where the turbines were located. Unlike the old coal fired boats with their firing doors, oil fuel was sprayed into the combustion chamber, but a door still existed for inspection purposes, and this was provided with small peep holes, and the white hot fire can be seen through the near pair of peepholes. The next furnace has not been lit, but the one after that is in use.

Captain David Hall, one of two masters assigned to the **Manxman** in her last season, commanded on the outward leg on 4 September 1982, and made sure that the ship was dressed overall for her final departure from Liverpool. She pulled away from the landing stage, and made an emotive close pass, blowing her triple whistle repeatedly in answer to the salutes from another distinguished Mersey veteran, the celebrated **Royal Iris**, which can be seen off the **Manxman's** bows. My father and I had been chatting to the Chief Engineer, and Dad had remembered the clouds of smoke that poured from the old coal burners with their reciprocating engines, and the chief had heard a few tales from the chiefs he had worked with when he was a young feller. As we sailed, a column of black smoke rose into the sky, providing a departure scene reminiscent of a lifetime ago.

As the **Manxman** headed down river, the sound of her own triple whistle and the siren from the **Royal Iris** echoed and re-echoed from the buildings on both banks of the Mersey. They were joined by the **Manx Maid**, which was to take the scheduled morning sailing to Douglas. She was the next boat to join the Packet fleet after the **Manxman** of 1955, and had been launched at Cammell Laird's yard on 23 January 1962. With her more modern "pepperpot" funnel she looked very different to the traditional **Manxman**, and was the first car ferry in the fleet. Because of the variety of ports the company used, which would have made linkspans hopelessly uneconomic, the IOMSPCo had developed a spiral ramp at the stern, and a side-loading concept. It was a brilliant and economic solution to the problem, and from the appearance of the "Maid" in 1962, and until the switch to ro-ro operation in the 1980s, motorists enjoyed an unrivalled standard of service. They were fine sea boats, and unlike the grim ascent from the bowels of the ship to passenger accommodation high above water level on today's ro-ro craft, which is a severe challenge for the elderly, the infirm or those with children, motorists had a short walk from their car to the passenger accommodation. For those with mobility problems, it was possible to use the inclined car ramp that connected the car decks with the passenger accommodation. As the **Manxman** headed down river, I filmed from the Landing stage, whilst my father filmed from the Wirral side of the river. We both knew that the era of classic ships that we had come to love had drawn to an irrevocable end.

CHAPTER TWELVE
Johnny Kee's Legacy

People and their interaction determine the course of events, and nowhere is this more apparent that with the Ramsey Steamship Co, which was the result of the interplay between Captain Johnny Kee and his wife, Eliza, although Eliza does not appear in any formal history of the company.

John Thomas Kee, the son of a Ramsey blacksmith, was born on 22 May 1854. He went to sea, becoming a blue water master for the Liverpool shipping line, William Lowden & Co. Seafaring in the nineteenth century was not for the fainthearted and you did not become a blue water master without great strength of character and ability. His wife, Eliza, was the daughter of a wealthy farmer from Andreas, John Mearns Brown, and his wife Isabella Christian of Ballakey, Andreas. In the introduction, we discovered the tragic fate that befell Isabella Christian's great grandfather and great great grandfather, both of whom were lost at sea in 1751. Eliza was born on 12 March 1855. The daughter of a powerful and proud

Captain John Thomas Kee died on 16 June 1926, his wife Eliza passing away on 28 December 1929. Eliza's family had strong links with Andreas and Bride, her parents being buried at Andreas parish church. John Kee and Eliza lie in the family plot at Andreas, together with their son, John Brown Kee, who served as manager of the company until his premature death on 12 May 1934.

family, Eliza was a good match for "Johnny Kee", as she called him. With her husband away at sea for long peri-

ods, Eliza had to run the home and bring up a family. When Captain Kee retired from the sea in the early 1900s, he and Eliza soon realised that however fond they were of one another, that two captains on the same bridge was a crowd.

Wisely, Johnny decided to take up an interest, so he established a coal business. The business prospered, and soon Johnny was regularly chartering steamers or sailing ships to bring in cargoes of coal. After a while, it occurred to him that with his knowledge of shipping, it would be possible to found a shipping line to bring in the coal they needed, and the Ramsey Steamship Co was formed in 1913. Two brothers, Robert and Frederick Brew were also involved putting up part of the finance, and Robert Brew became chairman, but the real impetus came from Johnny Kee. Captain Kee's son, John Brown Kee, who was born in 1883, was appointed secretary & manager, as Johnny Kee, like many men who followed an active career, had no great love for office work.

The first ship for their new company, the **Ben Veg**, was launched by the Larne Shipbuilding Co, and delivered to Ramsey in August 1914, a few days after the outbreak of World War One. Johnny Kee's choice of house colours and emblem was controversial, for the **Ben Veg** carried a Maltese Cross on its funnel. Although the RSS version was a white cross on a red ground, the Maltese cross was not popular at the time, as it was the emblem of the Kaiser's Germany, and war had broken out a fortnight before the **Ben Veg** sailed into Ramsey. Popular or not, it stayed in place, for Johnny Kee was not a blue water master for nothing. Further vessels came in 1916, 1917, 1918 and 1919, a remarkable rate of expansion. The **Ben Rein (II)** of 1919 replaced a ship of the same name acquired in 1916, but sunk by a U-boat two years later.

The second **Ben Rein**, seen here, had been launched in Paisley in 1905, and was purchased on 6 June 1919, but was sold to a Pembroke owner in October 1921. After these two short-lived ships, the name was dormant until 1956. The name means "Girl Queen".
Midwood

The RSSCo was extremely busy during the First World War, and under John Brown Kee's shrewd management, the fleet had increased to five ships by 1920. A sixth vessel was purchased in April 1924. She was the **SS Jolly Basil**, which had been built in Rotterdam in 1919. This letter, from 28 March 1924, probably relates to her first sailing under RSSCo auspices at the start of April. The acquisition was so recent that the letterhead had not been revised to include the additional vessel, nor had she received the traditional "Ben" name, becoming the **Ben Jee** a few weeks later. The Company soon became known as "the Ben Boats". She served the company from 1924 to 1933.

The original board of the Ramsey Steamship Co included Robert and Frederick Brew, who were the sons of John Brew (1816-1879), a butcher, and his wife Catherine Kennish. Robert Brew, who was born in 1856, and was a grocer and butcher in Ramsey, was the first chairman, but died on 26 April 1914 shortly before the **Ben Veg** entered service. Frederick Brew subsequently became chairman. He had been christened in Maughold on 24 March 1867, and was educated at King William's College, before joining the "The Manx Bank", which had been established in 1882 as an independent Island bank. One of the founding directors of the bank was the centenarian, William Waid, father of W A Waid, the Steam Packet director who lost his seat on the board in 1919. W A Waid was joint owner of the **SS Sarah Blanche**, which sailed for the Ramsey Steam Ship Co from 1923 to 1933 as the **SS Ben Blanche**. By 1895, Frederick Brew had become manager of the Ramsey branch, but with the Dumbell's collapse in 1900, the Manx Bank decided that investor confidence would be better preserved by amalgamating with a UK bank, so in 1900, it became part of the Mercantile Bank of Lancashire. That was absorbed by the much larger Lancashire & Yorkshire Bank in 1904, Brew remaining manager during these rapid changes. By the early twenties, Frederick Brew was chairman of the Ramsey Steamship Co, and with the Kee family, founded the Island Steamship Co in 1923. This was closely associated with the RSSCo, and its first ship, the **SS Pembrey**, is illustrated in this chapter. Although retired from the bank, Frederick Brew remained as chairman of the RSSCo until his death on 16 September 1933, his wife Lucy having predeceased him by two years. He left an estate of approximately £2,000.

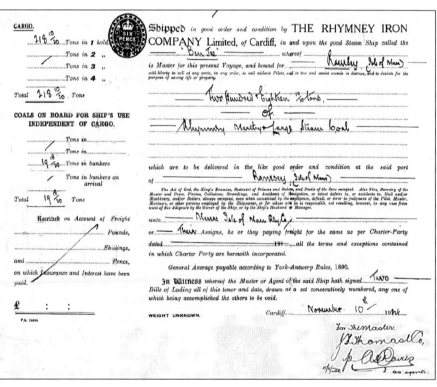

Students of maritime law soon get accustomed to the term, "Charter Party". This does not relate to a jolly time had by all, but is the term used for a contract for carriage of goods by sea. This charter party relates to the movement of a cargo of 218.5 tons of Rhymney Merthyr steam coal from Cardiff to Ramsey. Apart from moving coal for their own coal business, John Brown Kee soon persuaded the Isle of Man Railway Company to become a major customer, a tradition that endured for almost half a century, and is an interesting reflection of how the Island's transport companies were interlinked. One effect of this was that the Scottish steam coal that had been imported on the Paton & Hendry coasters was replaced by South Wales steam coal. It is noteworthy that between the letter of March 1924 and the charter party in November 1924, the **Jolly Basil** had become the **Ben Jee**. The Ben names, used by the RSSCo, mean "Girl" or "Woman" in Manx, **Ben Veg** being Little Girl or Little Woman, **Ben Vooar** – Big Girl; **Ben Varrey** – Sea Girl, or Mermaid, etc. **Ben Jee** means Goddess.

124

A curious episode in the history of the RSSCo began at the start of the twenties when Captain Kee, his son J B Kee, and Frederick Brew, then chairman of the RSSCo, bought a small freighter which they ran for a few months. She was unsuitable and disposed of, but in 1923, J B Kee, Frederick Brew and another RSS director, T B Cowley formed a second shipping line, the Island Steamship Co Ltd. They acquired a second-hand coaster, the **SS Pembrey** for £7,500, and she made her first voyage for the new company in July 1923. The late Fred Henry told me that her first inbound cargo was a load of fertilizer from Bremerhaven to Ramsey. The RSSCo board were happy for J B Kee to act as managing agent for the new venture, but freight rates were falling, and the **Pembrey** made few trips to and from the Island, and before the end of the year was offered for sale. Through connections with Liverpool shippers, some sailings to the continent were arranged, but the **Pembrey** was laid up in 1925 and sold to Belgium three years later. She had been launched in Holland in 1920, and was 549 grt. After sale in 1928, she stranded in fog off Prawle Point in 1930, becoming a total loss.

The Island Shipping Co ceased trading in 1930, its one remaining ship being taken over by a new company, J B Kee (1930) Ltd, John Brown Kee managing both companies until his death in 1934. Following the loss of **SS Bradda** in 1936, James Ramsay, who had taken over as manager of the group after J B Kee's death, purchased a second-hand coaster, renaming her **J B Kee** in honour of his predecessor. She served the company for 21 years, foundering in Liverpool Bay after a cargo had shifted, thankfully without loss of life. Although the RSSCo and its associated companies did not provide passenger services, the Island transport companies worked harmoniously over the years, so RSSCo employees were accorded privilege ticket rates on the steam and electric railways and the Road Services buses. This Privilege ticket order from December 1940 is headed RSSCo although the **J B Kee** was not, technically, a part of the RSSCo fleet.

RAMSEY STEAMSHIP Co., Ltd.

THE RAMSEY STEAMSHIP CO. LTD.

24, WEST **PRIVILEGE TICKET ORDER.**

RAMSEY, I.O.M.

To ISLE OF MAN RAILWAY COMPANY.

Please issue a Privilege Ticket from

.......*Peel*........ to ......*Port Erin*......

to Mr. *W. W. Cregeen*

a member of the crew of S.S. ....*J. B. Kee*....

Signature of Captain ....

Signature of Applicant ......*W Cregeen*......

Date..*9/12/1940*..

Privilege Tickets used by persons other than those in whose favour they are issued, render the user liable to prosecution.

Although the "Ben Boats" were regarded as coal boats by most Manx folk, which was their origin, J B Kee realised that diversification was vital if the company was to survive in the early 1920s, and the company was soon moving gravel, and because Anglo-Irish relations were fraught following Irish independence, the company even obtained a contract to service lighthouses on the West Coast of Ireland. This led to RSSCo boats wandering up and down the Atlantic coast of Ireland, an area where the Dublin government had little more influence than their Imperial predecessors. Crewmen who returned from the lighthouse trips spoke of the elastic opening hours of the shebeens or pubs, a process often facilitated by the presence of the local Garda as customers. The Ben Boats also turned a blind eye to rules and regulations, their skippers realising that the Red Ensign was more of a "red rag to a bull" in those wild parts not long after the bitter struggle for independence. A red ensign was carried for legal reasons, but preferably very tattered and grimy, but was totally eclipsed by a large "Three Legs of Mann". Improperly bedecked though they were under the terms of the Merchant Shipping Act, 1894, the Ben boats could then expect a friendly welcome. Quite soon, they could be seen anywhere in the Irish Sea, and occasionally further afield. William A Mackie was the IOM agent for Lancashire Associated Collieries for many years, and was in regular touch with James Ramsay, who took over as RSSCo manager after J B Kee's untimely death. When the **Ben Ain** was to make an unusual voyage in 1948, Ramsay invited Mackie to join the ship. They travelled north to Fort William, and then through the Caledonian Canal. This view shows the **SS Ben Ain** at Corpach, where the navigable section of the River Lochy debouches into waters of Loch Eil where they join Loch Linnhe.   W A Mackie

The flight of locks at Banavie at the south end of the canal, known as "Neptune's Staircase" was an unusual challenge for the crew of the **SS Ben Ain**. Although it was a wet day, calling for oilskins, William Mackie managed to photograph the gates at one of the locks being opened as the vessel negotiated this slow but important part of the route. The idea that Manx coal boats threaded their way through the Highlands of Scotland to Inverness may come as a surprise to readers, as, indeed, it did to me, when I first saw these fascinating scenes that were recorded by a skilled and dedicated photographer more than sixty years ago.   W A Mackie

Bill Mackie had a "photographer's eye" for an appealing or unusual shot. Realising that every lock had its own dog, and aware that the Chief Engineer of the **Ben Ain** had a soft heart, he secured this enchanting photo of a bedraggled Collie being rewarded with a titbit. This wonderful sequence of views on the Caledonian canal were part of a collection of glass slides that I rescued at the eleventh hour, as they were about to go in the bin, and it is a pleasure to share them with you, and to recall the work of a talented photographer.   W A Mackie

Life on the Ben boats, as on all steam coasters, was tough. On the **Ben Ain**, seen between Corpach and Loch Lochy in June 1948, steep sided iron companionways led to an open bridge, which was no place to be on a cold wet day, but that was what generations of seafarers were used to. A heavy jersey, seaboots and a stout oilskin provided protection from the elements, and with radar still only to be found on a few vessels, navigational aids were minimal, and losses through grounding and other hazards were considerable. The **Ben Ain** was built by Manchester Dry Docks Co Ltd at Ellesmere Port in 1924 as the **Doris Thomas**, later becoming the **Dennis Head**. She was acquired by the RSSCo in 1938 and quickly renamed **Ben Ain**, and served until 1963. This portrait with the ships bell in the foreground, and the makers' plate below the open bridge epitomises these sturdy craft.
W A Mackie

Photographs taken on board the RSSCo vessels in steam days are understandably rare. This view was taken in 1951, when the **Ben Jee** was outward bound light ship from Londonderry having taken a cargo of bagged cattle feed from Liverpool to Ireland. To catch the tide, she has sailed without the hatch covers being refitted, and as she is making her way down the Foyle with the coast of Southern Ireland visible on the north side of the estuary, the crew are refitting the strongbacks, after which the hatch covers will be replaced. The **Ben Jee (2)** was built in 1920 as the **SS Stertpoint**, acquired by the RSSCo in 1946, but sold for scrap in 1953, after grounding near the Point of Ayre in November 1952.
W A Mackie

James Ramsay had joined the RSSCo in 1928 and had become manager in 1934 following J B Kee's untimely death. In the fifties he decided that the company needed to switch to motor vessels if costs were to be kept down. Problems with delivery dates and firm prices for new tonnage prompted him to look at the second-hand market, and to the Dutch-built **Tamara**. She had been launched by Scheepswerf Delfzijl v/h Sander, of Delfzijl on 31 July 1947 as the **Lita** for a Norwegian owner, changing owners and name to **Tamara** but not her flag in 1954. She was acquired for £50,000 in July 1956, and became **Ben Rein (III)**. It was a wise choice, as the Dutch had achieved a commanding lead in motor coaster design after the war, and Norwegian ship owners had a deservedly high reputation for the upkeep of their vessels. The **Ben Rein** is seen at Peel on 17 July 1968. She was to serve the company until 1972 when she was sold to Greek owners, moving to

Panamanian ownership in 1980. Although funnel colours were unchanged, the motor coasters heralded the adoption of a pale grey hull. One day, my mother and I watched a cargo boat arrive in Douglas. A mother with a small child stood nearby, and she told the little boy to find out the name of the strange ship. He came galloping back and produced a somewhat mangled version of "**Ben Rein**". The mother, looking at the Maltese Cross on the funnel, announced sagely, "I said it was one of them Russian or German Boats". We met Bernie Swales, the manager of the RSSCo, a few days later, and Bernie was enchanted that one of his boats should have been identified thus. After a few moments to digest this news, he announced that he would give serious consideration to changing the house flag to a hammer and sickle! I reminded Bernie that another of his boats already carried a large red star on the bows!

James Ramsay purchased a second Dutch motor coaster second-hand in 1959, but passed away in March 1962. His successor, Bernard Swales, had joined the RSSCo from school, and acquired a new-built Dutch motor coaster, the **Ben Varrey** in 1963. All three had been a little over 400 grt, but the RSSCo still regularly traded to the smaller Island ports of Castletown, Port St Mary and Laxey. Of the three ports, Laxey was the most confined, but with regular cargoes of grain for Corlett's flourmill, Bernard felt that a suitable ship was needed. The appropriately named **Ben Veg**, or "Little Girl" reintroduced the name of the original ship of 1914, and was 143' 8" x 26' 3" and drew 10' 3". She was launched by Clelands Shipbuilding Co of Wallsend on 16 December 1964 and commenced duties in March 1965. The story may be apocryphal, but Bernie assured me with due gravity that he had visited Laxey with a tape measure, and if the **Ben Veg** had been 143' 9" long she would have been too large to use the port! Visits to Laxey were rare but views appear in "100 Years of Mann 1860-1960" and in "A Century of Manx Transport in Colour", both published by The Manx Experience. Bernie had let us know she would be visiting Port St Mary, so I have decided to include this pretty port that has seen little commercial use for decades. Yacht owners in Laxey deeply resented the outrageous inconvenience of their sojourn in a commercial port being interrupted by the arrival of a cargo boat, and with considerable political clout, were able to get the port closed to commercial traffic in 1973, so that grain cargoes had to be delivered to Ramsey and hauled the ten miles to Laxey to the inconvenience of residents and road users. With her main purpose ended, her small size meant she was less economic to operate than the bigger boats so she was laid up in 1978 and subsequently sold.

After the **Ben Veg**, Bernie Swales reverted to second-hand tonnage, his last acquisition prior to retirement in 1983 being the **Ben Ain** in 1976. At exactly 500 grt, she was the biggest vessel yet to enter the fleet. She had been launched by Boele's Scheepswerven & Machinefabriek NV, Bolnes, in 1966 as the **Deben**. Once again the company had opted for the proven excellence of the Dutch motor coaster, but she was to herald the end of an era, as acquisitions for the rest of the twentieth century were to be from West German, Danish or British yards. She is depicted at the Ramsey Shipyard berth in February 1987. She was sold out of service in 1991, moving to Cyprus and then the Lebanon. Bernard Swales was a kindly man, who did not discard his Christianity after church on a Sunday morning, but wore it throughout his life. He had been born during the First World War, his father being an artillery-man, who was tragically killed in action shortly before he arrived. Bernie was a regular member of the congregation of the Catholic church of "Our Lady, Star of the Sea and St Maughold" on the promenade in Ramsey. Although the name **Ben Ain** had appeared on an earlier RSSCo boat, I have often wondered what role Bernie played in the selection of name, as **Ben Ain** can be translated as "My Girl" or as "Our Lady". It is a subtle ambiguity that could well have appealed to Bernie, but sadly I never thought to ask him.